OH YES, OH YES, WE ARE THE PPS

WILLIAM ROUTLEDGE

OH YES, OH YES, WE ARE THE PPS

FULL-ON TRUE STORIES OF PRESTON NORTH END'S MOST FANATICAL FOLLOWERS

JOHN BLAKE

Published by John Blake Publishing Ltd,
3 Bramber Court, 2 Bramber Road,
London W14 9PB, England

www.johnblakepublishing.co.uk

First published in paperback in 2010

ISBN: 978 1 84454 994 8

British Library Cataloguing-in-Publication Data:

A catalogue record for this book is available from the British Library.

Design by www.envydesign.co.uk

Printed in Great Britain by CPI Bookmarque, Croydon CR0 4TD

1 3 5 7 9 10 8 6 4 2

Papers used by John Blake Publishing are natural, recyclable products made from wood grown in sustainable forests. The manufacturing processes conform to the environmental regulations of the country of origin.

Crookie: top boy – gone but not forgotten
& Rob K
both fighters in different ways

P.N.E.
WE ARE SUPERIOR

ACKNOWLEDGEMENTS

RIP:
To lads, friends and family who have departed this world far too early. They are sadly missed, leaving many an aching heart – they shall be remembered for ever in our thoughts

Anyone and everyone who contributed in any way to the book with stories, photos and research – especially Nobby, Big Dave, Cuey, MP, Perc, Coxy and Jess – BIG THANKS

Thanks particularly to the lads too numerous to mention with whom I've stood side-by-side, on the terraces, in the streets and over land and sea, and also had a pint or two with in many a drinking establishment over the years

Thanks also to PNE and England, for draining me of a shedload of cash, shattered dreams and endless fun – without these two teams the book wouldn't have been possible

Special thanks to:
Vince, for typing, typing, and re-typing, and for putting up with me; Dee, for letting me take up a couple's precious time; Mum and Dad, for bringing me into the world and all their love and affection. They devoted their lives to each other and their family. If there is an afterlife, I hope they're reunited and at peace; Lucan, my son – I'll always be there, I love you, mate, even though I don't tell you;I should do – it's a man thing;

And, last but not least, Jackie – the Missus – who I've put through HELL over the years. You have stood by me in times of despair and hurt, no matter 'what' I've done – X

CONTENTS

[illegible]

Part [illegible]

[illegible] make sure [illegible]

[illegible]

Part [illegible]

[illegible]

Part [illegible]

[illegible]

[illegible] ve already b[illegible]

[illegible]

PREFACE

I'm sitting here in the Lane Ends pub on the outskirts of Burnley in an area called Rose Grove, hopefully not long before this book becomes a bestseller – I don't think so!

I'm reading big Dave's piece, 'The Good Old Days', laughing quietly to myself while peering round to make sure I'm not getting any strange looks as my body moves in the same manner as Frank Bruno's would. There are two lads in the vault directly in front of me sat side-by-side, both smoking – just before the ban – each with a pint of lager on the table, not even passing the time of day. An old man to my left is wrapped up like he's about to set off to the North Pole. He's sipping a pint of mild out of a barrelled glass and puffing on his pipe for all it's worth. I can only imagine the bloke must be rolling thoughts round his mind from times gone by. I do truly hope he's happy in his retirement. The barmaid is polishing glasses just like you see in the old gangster movies – waiting for her next customer to ogle her thre'penny bits or for the jukebox to kick in for a singalong with the latest tacky chart tune. I'd noticed on the up-and-coming events board on my way in that 'The Face Melters' would be here 'live on Sunday'. Fucking hell, what do they drink in here – Molotov cocktails? So you can see now why I'm a bit wary.

Back to the good old days: I'm trying to remember which parts I was or was not involved in. It's not even one o'clock on a Friday afternoon, only I'm here for a Sky evening kick-off at the Turf. Yes, I'm here eight hours before the match, having a few beers and planning to make my way towards the town centre. It would be rude not to sample the local establishments en route. I've already been out every night this week meeting the old lads with their grey, receding hairlines and wrinkles –

portraying a less youthful look. Many have expanding waistlines and now wear an XL as opposed to a medium or large in their heyday – but who cares? I bet they do.

Researching for this book, I've visited that many different pubs in and around Preston that I'll be writing for the Real Ale Cry next. Faces I haven't seen in years, hands shaken, 'How's the family? Where you working?' The usual spiel. Others I see week in, week out at the match or have a bevy with regularly. Even some that I wish I'd never see again – you know who you are! Only kidding, lads. Really, they are great lads and mates, the norm!

We've been reminiscing about naughty little habits we used to have and things we got up to. It is strange finding out that their offspring might be involved. Can it be possible we pass it on to future generations in our genes, elite DNA? Our semen must come out fighting, with only the strongest surviving. They go on to defend what's theirs, what's close to them and to their hearts. It's been going on for centuries, tribal warfare right up to today's governments making decisions for nations and declaring war. Violence is all around, whether right or wrong... but I'd better stop there on that subject!

The players in the hooligan game had or have a desire to be involved. Each individual has their own agenda – why do they do it? Ask them or ask yourself!

I've moved on now to a different pub ordering my third pint, looking at the nuts and mints on the bar in sort of clean ash trays for the customers – nice touch. There's no one in except me, Billy-no-mates.

Seven hours to go... I've finished my reading, folded it up and placed it into my inside coat pocket. I down the dregs of my pint of Guinness, a quick 'Thanks' to the landlord and out into the bleak surroundings.

Burnley isn't exactly a picture postcard town. Rows of boarded-up, terraced houses with polluted, stained, stone-and-cobbled streets, which were once working-class homes.

A public house sign is swinging in the wind ahead and the rain has stopped – now things are looking up. I push the door open and rub my hands to warm up a bit. There's a few in; I might even strike up a conversation with a local. 'Pint of bitter please, mate,' to the gadgie behind the bar as I nod to the bloke with the scruffy-looking dog tied to the brass bar rail. I survey my surroundings. Fucking hell, I've only gone and walked into a wake – not mine. 'See you later,' dog man says, and leaves. Left are about 20 people in black sat round a couple of tables with a few butties and pork pies, talking quietly. I pick up my pint and retreat into a corner to collect my thoughts, getting my pen back out.

You're going to read about a group of friends who have shedloads of mates and acquaintances, with respect given out and hopefully returned along the way. Friendships made up and down the country in different corners of Britain and beyond. But yes, I'm on my own.

As for the rest of the lads... where are they? Some are on banning orders, others have letters warning them not to attend, watching it in the pub – weak excuse; some have given up on PNE altogether. I've no doubt a few will show, the phone will ring... won't it?

Six hours, and counting. I gave 'it' up years ago but still get the buzz. I keep reminding myself that I'm here for the game. Down the hatch... two's enough in here; I could do with a change of scenery and atmosphere. I remember noticing a blackboard in the bogs when I went for a piss. I might go back in and write: 'I need help – I'm not to blame!'

I really need to sort my head out. I don't want to get involved again. Why fuck up my England away trips, or lose a big game when everyone does turn out for a good drink and the craic? Blinding days with the lads, and even the football's a pleasure to watch at most games.

Pot on the bar, zip up, there's a nip in the air and a good brisk walk before the next jar. I'd better slow down as I don't want to get too pissed; I won't be able to watch the derby game properly through bleary, double-vision eyes. I pass a bloke walking his whippet – not the first I've seen today, along with greyhounds, staffs and even racing pigeons circling above me. You can tell you're 'up norf' as it says on Chelsea Malcolm's flag who we meet up with at England games. 'For fuck's sake,' I shout out loud; I've stood in a turd. I'm now scraping my trainers on a few blades of grass on a small patch of wasteland adjoining the pavement trying to avoid broken bottles and more dog shit.

Moving on, I've got my act together and a smile back on my face. Town is approaching and the devil once more pops up next to my right ear: 'Go on... go in their pub... have a look... just a little one... what harm can it do?'

'No, don't, just have one in here,' the sensible voice is saying.

Into the Ministry of Ales – heaven. 'What do you recommend, mate?' I ask the portly landlord. It must be good, looking at the belly on him. A smooth, creamy pint of his best is flowing out of the hand pump – sorted. Nice fella, great beer, we start chatting and he informs me that he brews it on the premises himself. He tells me that he once had a pub near Preston, The Bridge Inn.

Karma is restored; I've finished with all that shit... but...

Part I

ONCE UPON A TIME

1

RIGHT TO WRITE

My name is William Routledge and, in the summer of 2006, I was away on duty with my beloved England football team for the World Cup Finals in the wonderful country of Germany. In a friendly atmosphere there were fan zones with welcoming arms for fans of every country – how nice – when my mobile started to go berserk with calls and texts. Why? People back home in Preston had purchased the *Lancashire Evening Post*, a local evening paper, which ran a feature on a book that had just been published.

The book in question was *Hooligans 2*, the 'M-Z' of Britain's football hooligan gangs, a follow-up to *Hooligans A-L*, by authors Nick Lowles and Andy Nicholls. In the book was a chapter about Preston North End:

Ground: Deepdale
Firms: Spotty Dog Crew, Town End Mob, Preston Para Soccer, Preston Foot Patrol
Rivals: Blackpool, Wigan and Stoke City

So why was my phone going mad? It was because, in the extract about Preston, a lad called Billy had told his stories following North End through the years, early Seventies right up until the modern day. Not the score, attendance or colour of kit PNE were wearing, but the drinking, trouble and disorder that went on while following them. If the clowns who'd got in touch with me had actually thought about it for more than one nanosecond, they'd have worked out the stories he was describing were ten years before my time. Maths wasn't one of the lad's strongest subjects when leaving boarding school.

You can understand my shock with little old me getting accused of something I'd not done. Not for the first time or no doubt the last. Innocent until proven guilty – isn't that the rule in our great British judicial system? God Save the Queen.

The funny thing is that the bloke in question was also in Germany, sat having a nice, cold Steiner in the same bar as me. Coincidence or what?

I've known him by sight for years, the odd 'All right?' exchanged but that was about it. I didn't know he was going to be over for the footy. Truthfully, I didn't know his past or didn't exactly know what he was about.

I got chatting to him while over there about this and that. He was a well-educated man and had climbed the ladder in his field of work to be one of the top men. He only actually mentioned football aggro once in the time I was speaking to him – talking about his last trip away with England. He had been to Italy in the early Eighties, which put him off going abroad to watch football for a long time. Not only had the locals had a go, but so had the Italian police and there was even trouble with inter-feuding England fans. There was no inkling that he'd put anything in a book so there was no reason to think it was him.

So, when the phone had gone red-hot like there was a problem in Gotham City, I honestly hadn't a clue that he was the lad in question. How many Bills, Billys, Wills, Williams and whoever's are out there? Goodbyes were said when we touched back down in Blighty.

I found out a few weeks later on home soil it was him. You live and learn, don't you?

By now, you must have comprehended or even guessed that I've done a few naughty things in my time. Nothing too serious – in my eyes. The reason I've decided to put pen to paper – I then asked a good mate Vince to type it up – is not to glorify what I, we or the lads did, but to put the record straight on a few points. Then bury it once and for all in a final resting place. That might be in Bamber Bridge which is near Preston. In this small town, there is an age-old tradition that involves my beloved football club and burying!

A coffin with a North End kit inside is buried in the cellar of the Trades Hall Club every time Preston get relegated. You can imagine many a Preston fan had a season ticket for the occasion.

So, before the words 'ashes to ashes, dust to dust' are spoken, the skeletons are out of the closets once and for all, and I'm getting the word 'bullshit' laid to rest.

Here it is then, the spooks, ghouls and ghosts... all of them! Who you gonna call? Not the Old Bill, I hope.

2

DON'T BLAME US

PRESTON NORTH END, CO-FOUNDERS OF THE FOOTBALL LEAGUE, FOUNDERS OF FOOTBALL VIOLENCE!

Yes, that's correct, you can't just blame us lot who are chronicled in this book. So who else is to blame for crowd trouble, disorder and hooliganism at Preston North End or England games? Well, over 150 years ago Preston supporters were top of the 'hoolie league':

- A match against Sunderland at Preston needed a large army and police presence to prevent any fisticuffs. The year – 1843!
- Railway officials knocked unconscious at Wigan Station by Preston fans en route to Newton Heath v Man United
- Preston spectators inflict violence on Bolton players and fans after a match
- A near riot was caused when a Preston player took out a

Queen Park opponent at a game in Glasgow. Fans spilled on to the pitch and later tried to attack the team at the train station
- An Aston Villa team was attacked by a mob with anything they could lay their hands on
- A friendly match at Notts County saw one fan get knocked out by a Preston player for voicing his views
- The same player got a Preston team run out of town when he gave the home Aston Villa fans a mouthful of verbal. Who? A certain Geordie Drummond was to blame
- Trouble again against Villa – fighting on the pitch ended up with the first half lasting 80 minutes

And all this was before the Football League was formed. Over a hundred years ago, there was reported trouble with Sheffield Wednesday, the match ending in a mass brawl involving both teams and the fans. And I would have liked to have seen the local news when a 70-year-old grandmother was arrested at a Preston match for being drunk and disorderly. I wonder if we're related somewhere down the line? After all, you can't teach your granny to suck eggs, can you, lads?

Crowd trouble gained momentum in the late Fifties and early Sixties due to different music cultures being brought to the match. National Service was abolished and Mods and Rockers ruled the roost. They were followed by the Boot-Boy Skinheads in the late Sixties and into the Seventies.

Flared-pant-wearing, long-haired fighters were to be found during the mid-Seventies, when skinheads returned again. There were Casual, sports kit-wearing lads in the Eighties, with everything skin-tight and didn't leave much room for puppy fat! Designer-wearing boys into the Nineties, spending fortunes on the latest gear. And so we come right up to the present day, when computer wizards and mobile phones arrange meets.

If the finger is being pointed, don't point it at us. It's part of history, tradition and modern-day life. As Brian Clough growled once: 'Football hooligans? Well, there are 92 club chairmen for a start.'

I make no excuses for my behaviour, but, if I was a drug user, alcoholic, gambler or even a sex addict, I would have been offered help in some way or form. Football hooligans could expect a fine, ban or to be banged up.

Can't risk it, won't risk it – that's not to say that I still don't get the buzz, a rush, adrenalin pump when I hear the roar. Well, kind of, I'm too old now... I'll need Viagra next. I picture myself soon being pushed into Deepdale with a tartan blanket over my lap, sneaking a hip-flask in. My wheelchair parked up in the disabled section – lads say I am already – and rabbiting on about the good old days, recalling stories of what me and the lads got up to, with everyone in earshot ignoring me, thinking 'Silly old sod'.

Before the inevitable happens, I want to let you into our secrets... or not-so secrets. What went on going to the match, and finally arriving home from our many trips – the life of a football lad? Through mine, Scotty's and the lads' eyes.

Mad, bad, sad or just plain thuggish, make your own mind up. We did what we did and still reminisce about the events over a pint or two, wishing we could change a few of our actions. But shit happens, and it did. We were involved, but most are not any more.

So let's get down to business then.

3

WHO AM I? WHO AM I? WHO AM I?

Coming into the world in the mid-Swinging Sixties, I was the last of three children to a loving, working-class couple – Mum and Dad, RIP.

The first football match I can remember watching was the 1966 World Cup Final, sat in a highchair, rattle in one hand, baby drinking cup in the other – screaming loudly when 'Some people are on the pitch...' As if! And the last time Preston were in an FA Cup Final (1964), I was swimming around in my dad's sack waiting to escape.

With help off the lads due to memory loss, drunken hazes, substance abuse and Alzheimer's setting in, I will tell mine and their stories in the most honest way I can.

In the words of my favourite band, Slaughter & the Dogs, 'Where have all the boot boys gone?' Football mates come, they go, some come back, some don't, new ones appear and old ones disappear. One of the things that the majority had inside of them, though, was the love of naughtiness at the match at some stage of their lives. No expert in 'cuntology' will ever be able to fully understand, nor do judges. Shirt-wearing football fans and Joe Public also have their own opinions on it.

Whether you're repulsed by us or simply dislike us, we've been around since the game started. And who are we? The football hooligan. They existed decades ago and still do. Every club has them, trust me, I know. Nearly every football fan abuses the opposition and their supporters in some way, either verbally, by singing, chanting or swearing with hand signals to boot. But what we did due to our passionate tribal instincts was dish out something else; right or wrong, it went on and still does. Our victims were/are other teams' lads, with most hoolies adhering to the unwritten codes of combat. These rules should be known and upheld. Every match day, people from different walks of life were involved, from the unemployed right up to professional businessmen and even teachers. Yes, I know them all personally and they have written pieces further on in the book. Who tried to stop these antics? Our friends, the police – and they also became the enemy in the hooligan game.

This is my story from beginning to end. I saw myself as one who played by certain rules and would have a word with others who stepped out of line. I'm not a man of many words so I hope you find it interesting reading.

I grew up on a council estate, Gamull Lane/Brookfield in Preston, and it was a decent one at the time of my childhood. I was as normal as a normal kid could have been... I think. The youngest of three by over 20 years, I must have been a mistake the mates say – 'a fucking big one, your dad should have had a wank...' Blah, blah, yawn.

Early school life at St Maria Goretti's was nothing out of the ordinary apart from bits of mischief, a few windows smashed, knock-a-door-run with plenty of leg slapping off the teachers and Mum to be had. Other times standing in the corner, outside the classroom or on a box in the school hall. We all did it – mess about – didn't we? On the whole, I was the shy, blushing type, the one in the background, pretty much like I am today – watch out for the quite ones at the back. A few scrapes here and there and I'd usually do OK until their big brothers joined in to help out. No such luck for me, mine having flown the nest before I could remember. 'Go hit 'em back,' I'd be told off by my mum and dad. I would, win or lose.

Nearing double figures, I was getting more of a daredevil, climbing trees and once throwing myself off the first-floor balcony of some retirement flats when an old dear came out chasing us with her broom. I landed on my back not being able to move or feel my legs with my mates having to carry me home after egging me on in my naughtiness. No wonder I have a bad back nowadays.

In my day, there were no computers or games consoles; our time was spent playing out and entertaining ourselves. Bird egging became a common boyhood misdemeanour. On one occasion, I was on my way home for Sunday dinner when three teenage lads confronted me and a mate, and dragged us back down to the woods. Both of us were made to stand on a wall overlooking a stream a good 30 foot up. It was nearly tea-time and the cunts kept whacking our legs with sticks. This would make us wobble and nearly fall off into the water below. A passing car's occupants came to the rescue, much to our relief, and took us home. That's why I hate bullies and this incident made me more determined to stand up for myself.

Another time I was knocked down by a car. I saw a group of kids, a similar age to me, who I'd had trouble with individually; one-on-one was no problem. However, eight is a different matter; I would stand no chance. So I bolted out from behind a stone wall before I got noticed and ran right into the path of an oncoming car – BANG! I ended up sliding along the tarmac using my face as a brake. As I lay there motionless, not really knowing what had happened, the driver's silhouette appeared above me.

'Are you all right, son?'

I nodded my head. He then picked me up carefully, and laid me down on the back seat of his motor. I just about got my address out and he took me home. The bloke had been on his way to a local jumble sale to sell pea soup and parched peas. He'd now to change his plans as both pans of the stuff were all over the car with me laid in the majority of it, like a ham shank. What a sight and smell! He had to wipe the windscreen inside with a cloth to see where he was going.

On arriving home, I still wasn't speaking, just minimal actions – a nod or a shake of the head. After a hot bath and into my jim-jams, Mum sat me on the settee and I suddenly burst into tears; I'd come out of my trauma and gone into shock. Crying was a rare thing for me to do, even as a kid.

Mum and Dad were from a different era, dressing me, as they thought, 'smart' – suede shoes, shorts, shirt and tie, cord jacket with side-parted hair and sometimes a trilby hat on my bonce. Yes, a trilby hat! But I got on with it, stick and all. I'd not been taken to a live football game yet. My old man was more into his horses and dogs, preferring to go to Preston greyhounds – a licensed flapping track – rather than Deepdale. He would take me in my early years on Saturday nights dressed as his 'mini me'. I'd have a drink of Rola Cola, and a cone of chips with plenty of salt and vinegar and smothered in tomato sauce. I was easily pleased then! Was that going to change over the years?

I would lean over the barrier chewing the lad's ear off who'd catch the hare – Bugsy.

I also had to accompany my father to church every Sunday until I was 15. This is when I informed him I was a non-believer of certain elements of the Bible and they repeated the same storylines every year. He would also have been sick of having to wake me up during the sermon, as I would be recovering from Saturday-night sessions.

The first football matches I attended – besides school games – were Saturday-afternoon pub matches. I don't really remember much apart from blokes with 'tashes and big sideburns in tight-fitting kits. The smell of wintergreen and Number 10 fags being smoked in the dressing room before the match, a smell I will never forget. The fag smell continued at half-time and after the game had finished, plus the smell of stale ale. The parks were like mud baths with an all-pile-in mentality. I would be kicking a ball about, jumpers for goalposts, pretending to be the player of the time.

My playing days started when I joined the local cub scouts, who were a top team for years, winning many league and cup doubles. Left-back was my position, the same as for the school team later on, even though I was right-footed. This was probably because I wasn't all that sparkling and no other lad had a left peg. I started getting better every game, never shirking a tackle or challenge, no matter their size. Some lads in the teams went on to play pro and semi-pro, the rest Saturday and Sunday park football usually, still half-cut.

I also joined a Saturday team with boys from different areas and schools, one whom I'm still big mates with today, who joined me on a round-the-world trip. We won a few medals along the way and the main highlight was getting them presented by Mike Elwiss and Roy Tunks – North End's top players at that time. I nearly creamed my shorts!

During this period, my sister's boyfriend had started taking me to Deepdale. The Spion Kop was the end, with its white wall in the middle, asbestos roof and panels with a gap at the top where kiddies would gob on fans queuing waiting to come in. Yes, they were home fans! A big, sweeping end full of lads and boys with scarves around their necks, wrists, heads, tucked in their flared jeans or Sta-Prest pants. Scarves were even sometimes also used as belts. These must-have items ranged from silk, wool or even home-made, knitted scarves by granny. Jam-jar lid badges, sewn-on patches, 'PNE RULE OK' or the two-fingered-style ones on Wrangler or Levi denim jackets.

This was the age where the scarf was the football fan's main accessory, the equivalent of today's replica shirt, as in those days shirts weren't produced on the scale of today's 'sell, sell, sell' approach to mass marketing.

One Christmas, I'd asked my mum for a PNE kit, so off she trotted down to Willie Cunningham's Sports Shop. Christmas Day arrived and I ripped open my pressies after Santa had emptied his sack at ours. What the... I feasted my eyes on a blue top, white shorts and blue socks. To this day, I don't know who had ballsed up – me, Mum or Willie. I sat there all day in an Everton kit with a big sulky face on. So you can see I'm not from a big football background, although my parents gave me plenty of encouragement and support when playing.

I played in some of the best-looking kits around at the time with Mitre or Gola boots from Tommy Ball's, a local, cheap shoe shop where they hung on racks with a piece of string holding the pair together. Some said that I'd forgotten to cut it, judging by the way I played.

Getting back to Deepdale, I'd listen inquisitively to chants like:

'Blackpool Tower's falling down, falling down, falling down
Blackpool Tower's falling down – Poor old Blackpool.
Build it up with Blue and White, Blue and White, Blue and White,
Build it up with Blue and White – Poor old Blackpool.'

'You're going home in a St John's Ambulance...' (Clap, clap, clap)

'Who's that jumping off the pier?
Who's that drowning in the sea?
It's [Blackpool's manager of the time] and his boys,
Making all the fucking noise,
'Cause they can't beat the famous PNE.'

'We had joy, we had fun, we had Blackpool on the run.
But the joy didn't last, 'cause the bastards ran too fast.'

'You're gonna get your fuckin' heads kicked in.' (Clap, clap, clap)

One day my sister's boyfriend picked me up in his Ford Capri Ghia, and parked it up near Skeffington Road. Walking down Lowthorpe Road and round to the Kop, it seemed a bit busier than normal with larger queues forming at turnstiles, and it took a good few minutes to gain entry – probably sporting a big greeny on the top of my head. We finally entered and went up to our usual position just before the curve, where there was a lot more to'ing, fro'ing and singing going on. Songs at full pelt, fans belting 'em out full of vigour. A group of lads to our left, the Spotty Dogs, were giving it plenty of vocal and finger-pointing to the opposite end of the ground, the Town End. It was a mass of tangerine-and-white singing back.

'Who are Preston playing today?' I asked.

'Blackpool,' was the reply.

I now had a team to put all the songs to that had been chanted at previous games. The score that day... I can't remember! What I do remember is my first sight of football violence. The events that unravelled, and were seen, are not too vivid; I never did do diaries about my early days. But if I'd looked up the dates, spoke to the Gentry or the Spotty Dogs – Preston's first firms – they would probably get the full story bang on. I'd rather tell it how it was to me through a small boy's wide, blue eyes.

A few Blackpool fans spilled on to the pitch while the match was in progress, followed by another 50, then 100 or so. A big, marauding mob in the eyes of a kid was making its way towards Preston's penalty box beckoning on the Kopites. Preston piled over the hoardings, running towards them, windmilling. Blackpool were now on the back foot, to the halfway line – a stand-off. Blackpool then started moving Preston back on to the Kop.

How long it lasted I've no idea; I didn't bother checking my Timex. I'd been standing behind my sister's boyfriend after being told to keep out of the way. My head was bobbing side to side, transfixed with the goings on – a kaleidoscopic cascade of events. I'd witnessed my first blood experience. Involved? No. Got the bug? No. I didn't really understand yet. A few years later, yes, seeing in an apprenticeship with plenty of experiences, some laughable, some nasty, some not even worth a mention.

Secondary school arrived, St John Southworth, which brought new challenges, new mates and new fights. Some people might not believe it, but I was in most of the top sets; I actually used my brain back then. Friendships were struck up with new lads who'd come from other schools, each having a top boy. Pecking orders sorted out over the first few months. One lad I became big mates with, a lad touching 6ft at the age of 11, was Bob. I started knocking around with him after school, going up to his local youth club at Moor Nook, and making more mates in an ever-growing circle.

We'd hit it off in one of our first music lessons, each pupil having to sing a scale for entry into the school choir. Five of us failed after a couple of attempts, wondering why we couldn't do it, later realising it was because our 'nads had dropped and we couldn't hit the high notes. Lads who got in thought they were the dog's bollocks, but really they were the no-balls brigade.

I got my head down in class and was still doing pretty well when the dreaded teens kicked in big time. Rebel without a cause, I became, and my clowning about was getting more and more serious. I was now level with most of the teachers' eyes, giving them grief and generally messing about, and it also affected my schoolwork.

I'd stepped up watching Preston with my new-found friends, still not a regular due to money and my other loves – skateboarding and music. I was travelling to a few skate parks around the North-West – Colne, Southport and Bolton, funded by Preston Borough Council.

Bolton was where I witnessed my first real football mob street fight. A few of us were hanging round the skateboard shop, when two groups of lads 100-strong went right at it opposite. We scrambled to get inside, out of the way. One set had come out of a boozer – Man City. The others were steaming down the road, Bolton Wanderers, with a roar going up. They'd been at it for a couple of minutes when the police turned up, blue flashing lights and sirens blaring. Bolton did one and City returned to the pub. When the Old Bill left, I noticed one lad standing outside with a cut to his forehead and another moaning to his mates to help him out. Two other Mancs managed to get his Wrangler jacket off exposing his bright-blue arm, and I could now understand why he was moaning. No, he wasn't wearing his team's colours, his arm had popped out of its socket in the mêlée. One grabbed him by the waist from behind; the other took hold of his arm which was going a darker shade of blue by the second. A few good tugs, screams and choice words, it popped back in. Hugs and back-slapping all round as they walked back into the boozer – drinking session back on!

I was going to the matches with my school chums and singing along with everyone on the Kop, and I suppose we were also gobbing on the fans queuing up to get in. Flashes of violence and fighting were probably going on around us but we still didn't take a lot of notice.

The last game of the 1977/78 season, the mates and me went on to the pitch after the final whistle, chanting, dancing and jumping up and down on the home dugout. We wanted the players to come back out into the Pavilion Stand for a standing ovation after a top season. The home dugout was the best view for a youngster, but not the best idea – we went right through the roof of it. It was made of plastic corrugated shite, cheap and nasty stuff. Nothing changes; it's just like our new stands today – cheap and nasty. Nobby Stiles, World Cup winner and our manager, had given me my best season in the few short years following PNE. Promotion was guaranteed when Wrexham held Peterborough to a goalless draw a few days later. I found out the Gentry, and Spotty Dogs, had gone to the Racecourse Ground at Wrexham to attend the match. After the game they kicked off. One older lad said, 'We couldn't resist twatting the Taffs!'

Next season started with a cracking home fixture, Blackburn Rovers, with scuffles in and around the ground. My away trips became more frequent – Oldham, Notts County, Burnley, Blackburn and further afield. I would usually travel on supporters' coaches or football special trains – everyone on board having a jolly old singsong.

By this time, I'd parked my skateboard up in the bin store at home, and moved on to my second love – punk rock music.

And it's still with me today. In fact, just at the time I was beginning to write this book, I purchased a ticket to go and see Wasted at Blackpool's Winter Gardens, a weekend-long festival with several bands on – old and new. Once more, I'll see Charlie Harper of the UK Subs trying to bounce around the stage to 'Strangle Hold'. He'll soon be off down the Post Office with pension book in hand – God bless him. There is something inside each of us that makes a person tick; Charlie's is his love of his music. Whether it's football, music, fighting or baking cakes, all of us have passion and feelings for things we love and love to do. How we express them is each to their own. (While in Blackpool I will be meeting a top bloke who used to run with a small army in football circles.) With a couple of paper rounds and a part-time job on the go, money was going into one hand and out of the other.

But back to the punk-loving kid that I was – I started to buy records, dress the part and go to concerts and school played second fiddle to my other passions. And, as a result, I started getting into more trouble; consequently, I ended up spending more time at home as school had suspended me. This happened on a regular basis. I once got suspended for pogo'ing like mad at a school disco, smashing into the trimmed-up Christmas tree, knocking it over and then being sick on it – dancing has never been a strong point of mine.

I fed my music fix by attending the Preston nightclub The Warehouse. Every Thursday, they had a punk night. Either a DJ would be spinning the decks or a band would be on. You are probably wondering how old I was. Well, I was 14, spotty, pizza-faced and 10st wet through, measuring just under 6ft tall. God only knows how I got in, but I did. Fun was to be had downing plenty of cider, lager, bitter, Newcastle Brown or any drink really.

I usually ducked my paper round on a Friday, and usually turned up for school half-pissed, put my head down on a desk and fell into a coma.

One night, a few of us were staggering home at about half-two in the morning, munching on a Real McCoy burger. They tasted beautiful after a skinful and, as we walked along, one lad, Shane, who I don't think was a full picnic, tried to start putting shop windows through with his head. With alarm bells going off, the boys in blue soon showed up and he turned his attention to the two police officers, nutting them both. While they were wrestling with him on the ground, police back-up appeared. The rest of the night was spent in the cells as we all got lifted.

They released us in the morning and they had to give Ray K and me a lift home because we were still minors. It wasn't my first time in a cell, but it was my first bed and breakfast.

The mates and I started travelling to other towns and cities to watch bands – King George's Hall, Blackburn, was a venue, and concert, that involved plenty of rucking. Slaughter and the Dogs had a gig with the support band being The Exploited, who until that night I'd never heard of, but afterwards would never forget. The security on the door searched everyone, taking anything that could be used as a weapon, including studded belts and wristbands. With us was a well-known black lad on the punk scene called Pete. Following the band that night was the Exploited Barmy Army – two coachloads of mad Jocks on tour.

Enter on stage Wattie, the lead singer. There must have been over 500 squashed in the place and he proceeded to unzip his biker's leather jacket, exposing half-a-dozen spikey studded belts around his torso. He then unloaded the belts into the waiting hands in the audience. There were also other strategically placed instruments on stage, and I don't mean ones you could play! The Barmy Army hadn't only been on the piss; they were whizzing off their heads and passing round bags of glue.

Within seconds of the first song, it went off. And the first one to get special attention was our mate Pete. Every song of Exploited's set triggered fighting with different mobs. The doormen were running in and pulling people out for fun. I think Pete did one and others disappeared. I stayed with a few to watch Slaughter and the Dogs' set: 'Cranked Up Really High', 'I'm Mad' and 'Where Have All the Boot Boys Gone?'... all sung and performed brilliantly. The ones who braved it out returned to Preston with lumps and bruises everywhere.

Another time we had it at the Warehouse with Lancaster and Morecambe punks when a band never turned up. It got a bit nasty that night with tables and chairs, and bottles and glasses being used as weapons. A lad I knew, Tony C, got knocked out with a cast-iron table in the free-for-all. It went on for a good 15 minutes before the police and an ambulance arrived. The police somehow managed to split up the two warring factions, and the ambulance crew carried Tony out on a stretcher – while the Lancaster and Morecambe punks punched Tony while he lay on it. This resulted in more fighting. Preston lads that night were not too happy about events, and it caused a feud with Lancaster and Morecambe for years. The lads who spring to mind that were present that night in the Warehouse, including Tony, were Grezz, Swamm, Mickey P – with a Crombie overcoat and fingerless gloves – and even big Bob, who went on to join the CID.

By now I was getting involved at the match, the first being Birmingham at home, who weren't yet known as the famous Zulu Army. Three weeks earlier, I'd been to Oldham, a couple of games into a new season. Preston tried taking Oldham's end that day – three times. If they'd gone in as one unit, they probably would have succeeded. Oldham and the police managed to move them out, one mob being a group of black lads who used to follow PNE. Each group was clapped and cheered by Preston's faithful while being led around the pitch – the older lads in the book remember it well. On entering the away end, each was given a hero's welcome, back slapping, knowing winks and handshakes all round. One, a small lad from school, Kelly, must have thought he'd grown 2ft taller with all the attention being lavished on him. Tales to tell on Monday back at school! I'm thinking, 'I want some of that.' The seed was well and truly planted, and I'd decided that Birmingham was going to be a big, big game.

The Brummies were coming to town! I met up with Bob from school at the bus station and we made tracks over to Morrison's which adjoined it. Two extra-large bottles of cider was our order of the day. Bob could have passed for 18 since the day I met him. We didn't want to get a pull off the Old Bill if they came into a pub, so that's why we purchased our apple juice. We then plonked ourselves down on a bench at the top of Meadow Street, an area on the way to Deepdale with over 15 pubs in and around it.

We'd not been parked up long when a set of lads came round the corner saying 'O'rite?' to Bob – they drank with his older brother. This group consisted of the Ribbleton Barmy Army and the Lion Lads, who drank in the Old England and the Lion. Their entertainment at weekends was to have mass brawls with the regulars and, when the dibble turned up, full attention was turned towards them. Both pubs have been shut down – I wonder why? The Old England is boarded up, waiting for some brave person to reopen it, and The Lion was burned out and knocked down.

We followed the hardened drinkers from pub to pub waiting outside, swigging our cider, until it was time to make tracks up to the ground.

On arrival, the said lads decided to go in the West Paddock instead of the Kop. Unusual, we thought, but it was easy for us two to jump over the turnstiles – an age-old tradition. (A classic was when a lad called Burkie tried it. He twatted his head while jumping over on a low board that knocked him back into a dirty, black puddle for his troubles.) We were now in and stood with some 'top boys' of the time. Preston's other boot boys were on the Kop in case it needed defending. By the late Seventies, both home and away ends had 10ft-high security fences erected facing the playing surface to stop pitch invasions.

The referee's whistle finally blew, and shrieks of 'Come on, Preston' echoed around the ground with the roar that signifies the start of play. The lads were full of Lion and Bodd's bitter and one came out with: 'Are we right for a singsong?'

A slurred 'Yeah' came from the rest.

'THE NORTH END...' clap, clap, clap. 'THE NORTH END...' clap, clap, clap.

A few minutes into the singing, I noticed to our left, about ten yards away, several large blokes started grouping up. One had a big sheepy coat on, drawing parallel with us. Then a roar went up from the rough-looking geezers: 'BIR-MING-HAM...' clap, clap, clap. 'BIR-MING-HAM...' clap, clap, clap.

This was followed by, 'COME ON THEN!'

Both sets of lads started fighting, 25 a side, punching, kicking and butting – a proper, full-blown scrap. I got my wish; I was thick in the action, I was involved. The Brummies to our right were starting to come over the fence in their droves with Preston's spectators not wanting to get involved in the situation, fleeing along the terracing. The 25 Preston were on the back foot due to the increasing number of Blues, and police pushing everyone away. The coppers were struggling to restore order. You could distinctly hear the chant going up of 'Get into 'em'. My first hands-on football fight, my adrenalin pumping that hard my heart felt like it might burst out of my rib cage. This while shitting myself with the situation that I'm in. If you could buy adrenalin, it would be the most addictive drug known to man, believe me. It seems to get weaker in later life, but now and then you can still get a bit of a buzz.

The score that day was a 0–0 thriller – I checked a book. Only that day a new thug was spawned. I'd begun a new way of life, with plenty of ups and downs. Some would go on to call me 'a nasty piece of work' who'd been released out into the big, wide world!

No doubt, though – I was hooked, big time!

School seemed to take a back seat, put on the back burner 'til I left. My social life stepped up a pace. Even though I hadn't finished school, I was out drinking and knocking round with the footy lads who were years older than me.

Every other week, we'd a big team home or away and I'd be at it, on the streets or in the ground. I remember once Preston played West Ham with us waiting on the Kop for them. We weren't let down, but only a token gesture of a mob appeared on the Kop. The rest of the ICF had gone into the seats, this being a new, upmarket tactic – Preston were still light years behind. We ploughed straight into the Hammers, doing them good style. They escaped by climbing the hoardings and scrambling on to the pitch.

As I turned round, and strutted back up to the stand, my technical drawing teacher clocked me and started shaking his head. Next lesson he was slagging me off in front of all the class.

I was now also a full-time regular outside the headmaster's office, the only way they would let me stay at school. This involved standing outside the office every break and dinnertime. The head once said to me, 'If there's one lad in this school I'd love to hit, it would be you.' I'd become a non-conformer; I'd rejected their system, having my own opinions, an anti-authoritarian with a mind of my own. They couldn't suppress me, not even the shrink they'd sent me to see, who'd tried to get into my head. That was another condition; I had to go and see a psychiatrist! My mates say I should still be under one to this day.

I gained good grades and passes in certain subjects, but fucked up big time in others before I left school.

4

BOY ABOUT TOWN

PRESTON

It's grim up North! Preston is an old cotton mill and working docks town; both industries are completely non-existent in today's working environment. The last of the cotton mills are now yuppie-type flats. One of the largest, on New Hall Lane, the gateway into our lovely city, is in a 'redevelopment' area. You're able to nip out at any time of day or night for a takeaway or a local working girl within a minute's walk – nice area or what?

There is also a memorial statue – the wrong way round – outside the Corn Exchange (now the Assembly pub) commemorating a march for better workers' rights and levels of pay. This ended in a riot with several shot and killed. Apart from Arkwright House – Arkwright was the inventor of the spinning frame – these are the only reminders today of a once-thriving cotton industry, which was one of the reasons the Asian community was attracted to this part of the world.

The Albert Edward Dock was promised to be redeveloped into an area for leisure and a wonderful day out. Really? Upmarket, over-priced housing and flats are on one side; offices, a cinema, fast-food restaurants, DIY stores and Sunday shops are on the other. There was even talk of building a new football stadium in this area. You might see the odd jogger or somebody walking their dog as you drive by, trying to get away.

When both industries were booming, Preston was second to only Southampton for public houses with its square mileage and population. No wonder the town's full of piss-heads! Surprisingly, though, the term 'teetotal' was coined in Preston after the first Temperance Society formed many moons ago. You would never guess!

Apart from our major claim to fame – Preston North End Football Club winning the first league and Cup double – Preston has the Preston bypass. The M6 bypass was the first motorway constructed in the country. The first Kentucky Fried Chicken shop in the UK was opened in Preston in 1965. Also, Preston has the biggest cemetery in England – to die for! Preston has always been a rough town and we can also claim to have one of the greatest outlaws in history as a former citizen. Butch Cassidy – immortalised in *Butch Cassidy and the Sundance Kid* – came from Preston, and it's said that he spoke with a 'Lanky' twang when barking orders in a hold-up!

Bemusingly, we are now meant to be the Third City of the North-West. Really? Town folk have been constantly told, and read about, the Tithebarn project, which will bring trade and jobs for the town. This is going to be a multi-million-pound regeneration evolution. It would change the face and heart of Preston forever, re-establishing the new city on the map. 'Towards a Prouder Preston', this was the last time planning documents were submitted on such a grand scale in 1946. This would have seen many a historical old building demolished. Thank God the project never got off the ground. These new proposals would make Preston the place to spend serious dosh in designer-label shops and chic boutiques. Dine out in Michelin-star restaurants and sample international cuisine while watching the world go by. You would be able to sit outside, al fresco, in elegant cafés and brasseries, drinking continental coffee or sparkling spring water. Sip a 'Long Hard Screw' cocktail or Moët champagne in exclusive VIP establishments. Dance the night away in the 'place-to-be-seen' clubs while top DJs spin the decks. Also, bands such as the Rolling Stones and U2 would be jumping at the chance of playing Preston. Just living in the town would make you feel like you owned a pad in Beverly Hills or a part of The World Island in Dubai.

Delay upon delay, knock-back after knock-back... revise, amend and modify. Will the ball ever start rolling and the first foundation stone ever be laid? I doubt it will be me who lays it. Will it start by the 2012 Preston Guild? Maybe by the next Guild, in 2032? I'm not holding my breath. Third city? Bollocks!

THE MOBS

The lads I knocked around with were from different parts of Preston, Leyland and other districts. A bit unusual because most other Preston mobs seemed to come from set areas. The Avenham lads for example –duckers and divers, bobbers and weavers. And partial to emptying the odd fag and fruit machine on their travels.

The Holme Slack boys, who one night gave me a severe beating outside their local disco with the help of the Blackpool

Road boys. I had bad feelings towards them for years but time's a great healer.

Another prominent group were the Black lads who held rank in two town-centre pubs, the Bull & Royal and, facing it, the Red Lion. These were the hubs in which they conducted their wheeling and dealing, and some were prone to carrying a bit of Sheffield steel.

The Moor Nook boys were sound and would turn out for the big games, and The Lane Ends, and Ashton lads, were always active.

There were also plenty of small mobs of lads from estates on the outskirts of town; Bamber Bridge, Lostock Hall, Leyland, Longridge and little towns and villages from the surrounding area were well represented. Sorry if you didn't get a mention; the old grey matter isn't what it was.

The drinkers: the Ribbleton Barmy Army, the Old England lads, the Broadgate boys and the Spotty Dogs were now taking a back seat, or bar stool, to sink more ale. One such lad, a small geezer touching 50, still appears now and again – false teeth in his top pocket and into the row he goes, a lovely bloke who drinks with his diamond of a missus. Even a few Asian lads who were game joined the ranks; one now owns an Indian restaurant in the city centre – nice plates in the gaff as well.

I reckon we would have been a bigger force if in-house feuding could have been sorted. This meant that on many occasions Preston would be roaming around in small mobs, not one big unit.

And last, but not least, the Lancaster and Morecambe Whites, who we've done many towns, cities and countries with over the years – recently on plenty of 40th birthday bashes!

AWAY DAYS

I started travelling with Preston around the country to the grounds of bigger clubs but usually only in small numbers. A couple that spring to mind are Chelsea, the one that appeared on *Minder*. Arthur had gone looking for Terry at Stamford Bridge with the camera panning on the away end. 'I'm there, I'm there...' I shouted to my mum while pointing at the TV screen – fame for one whole second.

Another that stands out is Wrexham on Boxing Day, coppers taking the laces out of our Dr Martens cherry reds, and removing steel-toe-capped boots off others, with lads having to stand on scarves in freezing conditions. Games came thick and fast and, with reality kicking in, I got myself a job.

I gained an apprenticeship in the building trade, money in my pocket, bring it on! More nights out, more football, more fighting, and I started waking up in unusual places after being on the ale. I once woke up on a bench outside Preston's Deepdale ground. I seemed to be drawn to my Mecca when completely out of it, miles from where I lived. Trouble began coming my way without even having to look for it. A fight outside the Painted Wagon pub resulted in me losing a shoe – actually, they weren't even mine, I'd borrowed them. I then had to limp home in a sodden, socked foot.

Chipped teeth, stitches in the head and multiple cuts and bruises became commonplace from fighting doormen at Snooty's nightclub and the Coconut Grove pub. Week in, week out, it seemed to become a full-time occupation. At this stage of my life, I also got 'loved up' to someone who would eventually go on to become the missus – and still is. Why, I haven't a clue! She must pray for forgiveness every day.

'Oi! Oi! Oi!' I'd changed from a punk to a skinhead, with

obligatory MA 1 green flying jacket, Lonsdale sweatshirt and bleached jeans – 'don't fuck with the baldies'. Then I was shedding another layer and became a young Casual. Pringle and Lyle & Scott, acquiring a good few from Gibson's Sports Shop, were the must-haves. Roll-necks from a ski shop, 20-inch Spanish belcher chain hanging out and pale-blue Lois jeans, cut up an inch at the sides. Adidas trainers or any 'in' makes that you could get your greasy mitts on! Side-parted or wedged-up hair, the look of a new army.

I travelled to Manchester, Liverpool, Leeds and London looking up towards ceilings for the latest brands. Security tags not yet attached so everything was out of arm's reach. Lacoste, Ellesse, Fila, Cerruti, Tacchini and Burberry became my uniform. I loved my clothes, and still do. I would take many a train trip after selling precious vinyl to fund my vanity obsession, seeking out and finding an 'it' brand first. Then strut round like a peacock, the look made you feel the dog's bollocks. I once got called a 'Manc cunt' when following an escort of Bolton up Deepdale Road. I was wearing a pink Fila T-shirt, yellow Tacchini bottoms and Nike Wimbledon trainers. I'd got the whole lot the weekend before from, yes... Manchester.

If I felt comfortable in something, even if it looked outrageous, I bought it. This would attract attention, both good and bad. You'd get noticed when it had gone off by either the Old Bill or lads pointing you out more for what you were wearing than for what you had done. Man United's 'Men in Black' got it right years later, blending in as a unit so as not to get sussed. I not only wasted some serious dosh on buying dodgy clothes, but getting them ripped, torn and full of claret or slashed ended up a pastime of mine. 'Not another top ruined?' her indoors would say.

'I fell... I tripped... I had a nose bleed... I got it caught on a door... There was a stampede... A tornado hit Deepdale... etc, etc.' This was the usual spiel and I was never to blame. Same with the police. 'It was them... They attacked us... They're our mates and we were just messing about... I've got busted ribs, I can't fight.' Some excuses worked, most didn't, and into the back of the van you'd go.

The broken ribs worked a treat once after getting lifted against Telford – yeah, Telford – in the car park outside the ground after an FA Cup match. I'd been telling a copper near the end of the game that I needed to stand to one side because I was off work with damaged ribs. And on the pitch that day, Preston got beat at home 4–1, that's how shit we were in the Eighties. Only I'd noticed a small mob of boys in the away section and arrangements were made through the segregation fencing for a meet near their van which was parked across from Deepdale. Things had just started when my collar got felt: 'You're nicked, son.'

I was sitting in a cell under our wonderful West Stand with another lad, Tommo – RIP – when a copper opened the cell door, and two PCs walked in, one saying, 'Right, you're off to Preston nick.'

The other one piped up, 'He can't have been fighting, he's got broken ribs, and there's no way any charges will stand up in court.'

I was kicked out into the fresh air with the words ringing in my ears: 'I'll get you another time, you little runt.'

I didn't even break 'em scrapping. They were broken by my mate, Rambie, who'd pushed me over on to a fireplace, messing about at a party. One rib just missed puncturing my lung by millimetres. Who needs enemies with friends like mine!

Around this time, I'd been to a wedding all day with PC Jock, a dog handler, also in attendance. After the speeches, he'd sunk a good few malts and when I was stood next to him, ordering myself a pint, he whispered into my ear, 'We know what you and all your mates are up to at the match!'

'Yeah?' I replied.

'Yeah, so be warned!'

'OK, thanks for the advice.'

Later on in the night, I had a chat with the bloke; he wasn't such a bad sort after all. What worried me most was that he seemed to be more in love with his German Shepherd than his wife!

After many weekend events, I'd get the Monday-morning blues, not looking forward to the weekly grind, but even the day job had its surprises. A lad labouring with me got arrested on-site and convicted of murdering an old, gay bloke. Another got nicked and put on trial with the charge of rape. Never mind the loonies I was knocking around with on Saturday, I was working with a killer and a rapist during the week. Not by choice, though.

THE WIFE

Why has she stayed with me? Well, I suppose that only she can answer that. But if I hadn't been in my relationship with the missus being by my side in times of need, I would have definitely done a stint in jail.

I finished with all my nonsense in the late Nineties after numerous fines, community service and looming prison sentences hanging over my head. I wholeheartedly apologise for all the worry and stress that I put the family through – sorry. I've always tried to provide for them, working seven days a week, 24 hours a day if necessary, and we've got a nice house and go on good holidays.

The following is her side of the story.

The Missus:

We married at a very early age and are still together so I ask myself: why? I didn't know, or want to know, any of the goings on while Bill was out for the day with his mates – which was most weekends during the football season. The phone would start ringing the day before, sometimes off people I'd never even seen or heard of, and they were making arrangements with him. He was up and out early the morning of the game. I always asked myself: why? Even I knew that kick-off was 3pm or 7.30pm, but he would always return home late or even the day after.

He'd trot off in his designer gear with me and the son having as normal day as could be. The son was always dressed in the up-to-date football kit, PNE or England. We sometimes went out and did a bit of shopping or something similar. It was later on in the day when I'd start to get a sickly feeling in my stomach. A ringing phone or a knock on the door would really worry me. On answering the phone, the police would sometimes ask if I was his next of kin. Or opening the front door, I'd often find the local constabulary stood on the doorstep. Another weekend ruined and I'd guarantee untold excuses would follow when he was released – wrong time, wrong place.

I'd think to myself that it was his release from all his responsibilities and pressures. Who knows? Five or six days a week, he was the most loving, caring person you could ever meet. He had a good head on his shoulders and you could honestly not meet a nicer person. The last game of the season would come along and I'd feel ecstatic – no more football for three months.

Take this for another instance. I was painting a wall in the bedroom at home once when the phone went late on.

'Hello, it's PC Smith... your husband will be with us 'til Monday, pending a court appearance.'

This would be followed by all the details of what he'd been up to, tears would start forming, knowing this time he might be sent to jail. You can guess that it wasn't his first, second or even third time. I pulled myself together and set off the next day to see him along with my sister for support. It sounds silly but many a time I'd take a clean set of clothes and a fresh set of underwear.

A train journey later and a taxi to the police station, I asked to see Bill. The officer laughed but allowed me to go in a small interview room. The look on Bill's face when he saw me was well worth the journey. And after a good verbal bashing from me, he was taken back to the cell like a scolded schoolboy.

'What now?' my sister asked. We found a B&B, and out on the town we went; club, curry, the works – all courteous of my loving hubby.

The next day we nearly missed his court appearance as we both were feeling really hungover! He got another fine. Why he never got a ban in all that time, I never could understand. I felt like begging the judge that day for one. It was probably due to his baby-face looks that he didn't receive the right penalty for the crime.

Another time, and the same old, same old. He didn't come home after the match – another night out cancelled.

Eventually, the phone rang about 10.45pm; he was on the end of it, hardly able to speak.

'If you're not home on the last bus, you can forget it,' I said. I knew that not only was he worried about us, he would also be worried about his precious clothes, so it was mind games.

An hour later, there was a knock on the door. I opened the door swiftly ready to give him what for, only it was the police once again and I'm thinking, 'What's he been up to now?'

'Your husband has been in an accident… could you accompany us to the hospital please?' the officer said.

All sorts were flashing through my mind as we made our way to the hospital, tears once more streaming down my cheeks.

On arrival at A&E, I couldn't believe what greeted me: he was sat in a wheelchair, with his jeans leg rolled up and a slight trickle of blood running down his shin. And a stupid grin on his face. He's also saying 'sorry' to anyone who'd listen.

What had happened was he was running for the last bus and he'd run out from behind another stationary bus right into the path of a taxi driving by. Because he was that drunk, the doctors thought that he'd run into a parked car. His injuries consisted of three stitches to a shin wound and two sprained wrists. He even had the audacity to blame me for telling him to get home or else.

The next day, the taxi driver came round for damages to his cab – what a cheek!

I can now just start to see the funny side of his antics. I'm married to a fanatical football fan and all that goes with it – warts and all. He's not into any of that mischief nowadays; he's even taken me to a few England tournaments abroad and I've seen how trouble can start. And I can tell you it's not always the way it is portrayed on TV or in the press over the years.

Bill is not such a bad lad, is he?

Part II

WHATEVER PEOPLE SAY WE ARE, THAT'S WHAT WE'RE NOT!

5

WE'RE THE ONE AND ONLY

In '69, when we went down into Division 3,
The Blackpool fans, they cried aloud,
'That's the end of PNE.'
Alan Ball he came, we played the game,
We went to Fulham too.
We won one-nil, and now we're back,
Into Division 2.
We'll win the league,
We'll win the Cup,
We'll go to Europe too.
And when we win the league this year,
We'll sing this song to you!
The North End... (clap, clap, clap)
The North End... (clap, clap, clap)
The North End... (clap, clap, clap)

Preston North End is one of the most famous football clubs in the world. They became founder members of the Football

League in 1888. In their first season of the newly formed football league, they not only won the league without losing a game, they also won the FA Cup without conceding a goal. (Surely that makes us European Champions, or even World Champions?) To this day, Preston hold the record of beating Hyde United in the FA Cup competition 26–0. So it's always going to be downhill after that, isn't it?

Being a Preston fan, I've had plenty of lows, lows and more lows. And only recently have I had a few highs. What does Robbie Williams sing in one of his songs? 'You've got to get high before you taste the lows...' Well, take it from me, that's bullshit! No sooner had I brass in my pocket to follow my beloved PNE, they started to freefall into a big, black hole.

In 1986, Preston finished 91st in the league and had to apply for re-election to secure their league status. A hundred years previous, the famous club were – allegedly – granted a royal status, as the first double-winners, meaning they never had to change strips – home or away. Less than a century later, they were on the verge of going bust. They didn't even own their own ground and were struggling so badly on the pitch that, one afternoon, a local lad called Mel Tottoh was summoned from his workplace at BAe, and called upon to pull on the white shirt for the once-famous Preston North End.

During this time, collection tins were a common sight, shaken by volunteers outside the ground. The stands were also given a lick of paint by the fans. And Preston were that skint matches kicked off at one o'clock because they couldn't afford the lecky to run the floodlights!

So anyone reading this who doesn't know what long-suffering PNE fans have gone through over the years might start to get an idea. Lots of Preston folk stopped coming to matches, many followed other teams, and some, classed as mentally insane, carried on watching. Good job guns weren't readily available – legally!

I remember a bloke I was working with while serving my time asking, 'What do you get up to at weekends, lad?'

'Follow Preston.'

'Fuck me, son. I'd draw the curtains if they were playing in the back garden.'

Cheeky cunt! What else is there to do on a Saturday afternoon other than watch your hometown team?

Nowadays, it is a completely different story. So wipe away your tears and blow your nose; Preston pulled out of their despair, and all looks relatively rosy for Preston North End, the family club.

The club was saved by the council who bought the ground and installed a multi-use plastic pitch, and helped to fund new floodlights. Preston have a modern, new-look stadium, and the ground is almost complete. Players have been bought and sold scrupulously but, on the other hand, the club has made good money on selling players.

I've watched play-off semis, finals, lengthy Cup runs, a league title, Wembley and even witnessed North End knocking on the door of the Premiership, although two defeats at Cardiff's Millennium Stadium have once more provided much sadness and despair. Once again, so near, yet so far.

Supporters are still slightly in the dark with what the new consortium – naming no names – allegedly contribute and actually do for the club. We seem to be losing money here, and losing money there. How much do we get from sponsors and catering deals? Why do we pay rent for the club shop and training ground? These are questions asked among fans on a regular basis on forums and radio phone-ins, in Internet chat rooms and public houses that are in and around Preston. I haven't got the answers, nor will I be judge or jury.

Fans are returning to Deepdale, even the part-time Rovers ones: 'We only go over to Blackburn to watch Premiership Football.' Die-hard fans are bringing their sons up the right way to watch their hometown team. Young kids dragging their mums and dads on after many a lost generation – North End operate a successful free initiative for under-8s. These kids are entertained by the Deepdale Duck, who has a wide variety of party tricks. I could do another chapter on his antics alone! Shirts are being seen worn out in Preston town centre and in surrounding areas – the shame has gone. We're back on the footballing map, competing with the big boys. Fans are desperate to savour the Prem, have Cup glory or even a European trip. But do we really want the plastic-wrapped prawn-sandwich brigade filling our seats? I personally don't.

There you are. I've had my little rant and rave now and I'll get off my soap box. It's only a game... or is it?

It's a whole new ball game at Deepdale nowadays. And while the basic game stays the same, the faces change – on and off the pitch. There's a lot more lads coming to the games now; old and new, only most being too young to remember the 'good old days'. Stone Island, Paul & Shark and the new Burberry Chav United look are the uniform of choice. Some of the clothes are OK, some I wouldn't be seen dead in – and that's saying something with what I've worn over the years. Still, clothes don't make you 'one of the lads', you've got to prove that on the battlefield.

The new accessories of warfare, mobile phones and computers, are tailor made for arranging a meet miles away from the ground. The Old Bill also have their own new gadget to even things up – CCTV – their modern weapon to try to combat trouble in stadiums, surrounding streets and town centres. And there's plenty of evidence that is plain to see on the Internet and hooligan websites of football firms still getting it on. Gone are the days of a chance meet on the streets or in a boozer smack in the middle of town and getting away with it. The police mostly have it sorted, bans seemingly handed out for such minor offences as farting. Or have they?

Me? I gave 'it' up a long time ago. My accessories these days are an easy chair, smoking jacket with corduroy carpet slippers and a mug of Horlicks – that's my main vice.

6

NEAREST AND DEAREST

The lads I fitted in, and ran, with were a crew from different areas in and around Preston. We'd firm up nearly every Saturday, come what may, usually about 25–30 of us, swelling for big games and teaming up with other Preston mobs on an even keel. Our lot, the usual suspects, were doing it week in, week out – hard graft! So let's meet a few of the lads who feature heavily in the stories.

One of the best was Scotty. He's a great bloke, friend and family man. He was always the one with 'balls of steel'. I know he wouldn't want me to harp on but the lad hasn't been too well over recent years. The man never let it show, though, still being daft as a brush and up to his old tricks, like throwing buckets full of water on passers-by from fifth-floor hotel windows. Never seen without a smile on his face, always cracking jokes and ever the jester while acting the goat – that's Scotty. But don't just take it from me:

Scott R, Maidstone:

The first time I met Scotty was in a pub called The Rose in Maidstone. He was a new – ugly – face about town, loud and brazen, but full of Lancashire wit. It was a good friend of mine who'd been working on-site with him who introduced us and we hit it off straight away – bonding. Next thing I knew I was drinking, rowing and going to football with him. We would go to Brighton, Preston and England games. He's straight as they come, taking shit from no one.

The first time I went to a game with him was a Gillingham – (Scum) – versus Preston match. Scotty met up with the Preston lads in Gillingham's boozer and Preston had come down in their droves. A fight broke out when Gillingham dared to come in the pub, but with Preston steaming them out. Outside, the Preston lads were going the wrong way when I shouted, 'No, this way.' I'm now surrounded with lads gunning for me, I suppose because of my southern accent and them not knowing me. I was thinking, 'I'm going to get ironed out any sec.'

'Leave it out, he's with me,' Scotty says, with everything calming down.

There are so many incidents and stories to tell with him being such a character, so here's one where he had to eat humble pie. We'd gone to the legendary Germany–England game, the 1–5 one (even Heskey scored!) and we were on a train going up to the match when Scotty thought it would be a laugh to shake a can of beer up and squirt it all over me, which he duly did. I wasn't too happy with him laughing, but Hector, the ticket collector, was behind me and he also got splashed and started going mad. Payback time; I grassed him up to Hector and he made him go to the toilet for some paper towels to clean up the mess off the floor. Who was laughing now?

Away from football he's worked wonders for the local youth round our way; he helped set up a youth club, and even mentored one young lad. He knows the score and talks to them on the level.

Even when he was ill, he never let it show; it never fazed him and he showed true strength, which I admire.

Scotty is well respected, a top lad and is a true pal.

I seemed to hit it off straight away with 'C' when I first met the Leyland lads. A great lad with a lasting friendship made, having done many a cell together over the years.

While researching with him I found out he'd a phenomenal memory of the weather conditions at nearly every game. Loves his clothes and can remember what he, and an opponent, was wearing when in the thick of it, even getting his trainers wet.

C:

Early Eighties, it could've been a pre-season friendly or shitty Cup game – I'm not sure. However, it's raining and we've come out of Blackpool's Bloomfield Road – bombsite – ground. We threw a sharp turn, trying to lose the police attention. It worked, and a couple of minutes into the walk up went the roar – the Bisons are steaming towards us, a hundred yards up ahead. In between both mobs was a giant puddle, due to the sudden downpour. They arrived at the mini-lake first not fancying it, only Preston were at full pelt, and there was no stopping, right through it we went! We're straight into Blackpool putting them on the back foot, only I was more bothered about my new trainers than getting a slap!

Rambie was the granddad of the bunch. His dress sense and haircuts over the years, well – he once had it dyed claret-and-blue! He has a memory like a sieve and it was hard work getting him to remember anything at all – that's probably due to his age!

I also found out, back in the day, he use to stand on the Kop, the Fulwood End, in his early teens behind girls. And if PNE scored he'd celebrate intensively with the girls in the excitement that followed!

Rambie:

No one would really admit it but we'd all like to see ourselves on TV at some stage in our lives – wouldn't we? Well, at least three times I wish I hadn't. The first was at Burnden Park being escorted off a Bolton section shown on Match of the Day. Then another two times on Granada Reports with Tony Wilson – RIP – reporting in disgust. As if he never did anything wrong!

The first Granada appearance was beamed from Wigan's Springfield Park and I was being thrown out with my arm up my back. The second was at Ewood Park. It was an FA Cup tie between Preston and a local non-league side, Chorley. The match was played at Ewood Park because of the great local interest in the game. I got serious grief off both teams' benches while being escorted to the away end.

The next day I was at home when the events unfolded on TV as I sank into the settee hoping no one had spotted me.

Our van man was usually Elli. He'd be the one who'd hire the transport for the majority of our jaunts away, putting his balls on the line for the van to come back in one piece, or to return at all!

Elli:

We'd drawn Shepshed Charter House in the FA Cup at Deepdale, and word was that some Leicester were making the trip with them. We didn't spot any before the game so a few of us paid to get into the Town End, the away section at the time. Not long into the game, Preston scored and up we went. A brawl ensued and I got nicked, getting charged later on. Not only was I charged with threatening behaviour but knocking an old dear over – which, I hasten to add, I never did, nor ever would. I didn't half get stick off the lads for the granny-bashing charge.

With nicknames ranging from 'Screaming-Skull' and 'Shaggy' to 'Oscar', the Muppet who lives in the bin, Pia always went in but had trouble staying upright. Also, his car never let us down on many occasions while on our travels – even though it was dropping to bits.

Pia:

'Wigan are here!' Up goes the shout, and it's not even our game, but we'll sort 'em out!

We'd gone to a Burnley v Wigan fixture at Turf Moor and I'm bouncing around in the entrance tunnel when – BANG – down I go. The lads helped me up and sorted Wigan out for Burnley. It didn't finish there. Two weeks later, Preston have got Wigan at home and I fly into them on

Church Street, when – BANG – again, back down I go. Not only have I been done twice off Wigan, but twice off the same lad!

Micky was a mountain of a man who we'd put to the front every time – not that he needed asking. If they moved him, it was time to go.

Micky:

We'd turned up at a Burnley v Man United game, for a laugh. After the game, we fronted a dozen or so Burnley bullies who were picking on two Manc lads. There was five of us, when one Burnley lad goes, 'You're not Mancs, you're Preston!' They turned sharpish to do one, when one lad smashes right into a lamp-post, slides down like a cartoon character, bounces up and he's off in a flash with the rest of his mates. We couldn't be bothered to chase them – we were all too busy pissing ourselves laughing holding our stomachs!

Ste was a quality lad who did the graft a million times!

Ste:

'Oh shit, I'm going to be nicked.' A copper on a horse wants me badly and I'm not giving in so I head towards a group of trees to take the piss. Backwards, forwards, round and round I go with the Old Bill getting madder and madder. I could hear the lads in the background cheering, egging me on. Finally, after a good few minutes, the inevitable happened – I got nicked. At least I had my fun!

Dave was the quiet one!

Dave:

We'd been chasing Wrexham at theirs after abandoning our cars near a roundabout; they'd done one down a grass banking – the front line didn't want to know. On arriving back at the cars, the Old Bill had turned up giving them the once-over for any weapons. The only things they found were a big pile of filthy porno mags.

'Right, whose are these?' asked a copper. Nobody was forthcoming. After half-a-dozen times of asking, and still no one owning up, the OB walked off with the evidence saying, 'Right then, we'll have them!' We thought they were going to nick someone for indecent material. There were blokes even interfering with pigs in them!

Wolfie was the scout, our spotter, the man in the know. Out early for the game with nearly always something to report back by the time we'd plotted up.

Wolfie:

'Who, me, officer?' I seemed to have a habit of getting lifted every time the missus was in hospital having one of our little ones. I even once got lifted in the hospital grounds, so I can remember certain games by the kids' birthdays. Good job my second name isn't Walton.

If you're looking for a one-man army, Bami's your man – no questions asked!

Bami:

We'd gone to Bolton one Friday night on a stag do, mainly the lads from the match. Bolton's lads clocked us in a nightclub, and it went off. This carried on outside in the streets – a mass brawl ensued. Lads from both sides were going down left, right and centre, when I get a blow to the head – claret was everywhere. Another lad and me were taken to the hospital in an ambulance; he'd been stabbed through his cheek. And while he's being stitched up, I'm X-rayed and the doctor informed me I'd been stabbed in the top of the head. Luckily the blade had snapped off in my skull.

Was I glad to have a thick head that night!

Vic is living proof that all good things come in small packages... sort of!

Vic:

Apart from a Grimsby trip, the only other time I drove to a game was to Rotherham. I took the car because certain lads had important engagements that night so it would be a safer bet to get straight home after the game. But no, I got nicked, charged and kept in 'til 3am.

My crime? The charge was for punching a police horse in the snout – but what would you do if it had just snotted all over your new Marc O'Polo sweatshirt?

I've known H Butt since school, and he's always loved to throw the forehead in.

H Butt:

I was walking back to the car after a game in Mansfield behind about 15 of their lads and I overheard them saying, 'There's Preston up the road... let's get into them!'

I decided to overtake, turning sharpish to face them. I picked out the biggest one and stuck a cracking head right on the button. His legs went like Bambi's and down he dropped. The rest had it on their toes. Next thing, a Maria pulls up alongside me. 'Oh shit, I'm going to be nicked,' I thought.

No, they just drove past and had a look. Phew!

D Ladd was a great lad who seemed to attract wood and weapons in all various shapes and forms. You'd think he was Woody Woodpecker.

D Ladd:

The first time I met Bill was when waiting at Preston Station before setting off for a game at Wrexham. After buying a ticket, a roar went up and a good 100 lads came running off the station up the concourse towards us – it was Wigan's firm. There were only 30 Preston, and just a few stood with us having to go on the back foot. On turning to get off, I got tripped up, going down with fist and kicks raining in on me. Then the Wigan bastards tried to pull my leather jacket off over my head. It was a Christmas present off my mum and dad, and they would have killed me if I'd lost it, that's if Wigan didn't first. The next second I was being picked up – Bill and the lads had turned up – they'd arrived on the scene, entering the fray.

I still owe him a pint for that. And now, over 20 years later, we're still close mates.

The Big Fella is a big, sloppy bear – who likes cuddling you after a few too many beers.

The Big Fella:

We'd been informed that Paul Heaton, the BBC main face, and ten other Blades had been in the Deepdale pub before an FA Cup game at Preston. So after the match we went for a nosey and their minibus was parked up behind the away end. Eye contact was made and, before anything could happen, the police's attention was drawn towards the bus.

'Oi, Heaton!' I shouted.

'What?'

'You know your problem?'

He looks over.

'You keep it all in!'

The old ones are always the best, aren't they?

A late arrival on the scene was J1. And I wish he'd come with a volume control because he never shuts the fuck up!

J1:

Four of us were walking down Deepdale Road before a game against Cardiff, when up pulls four black cabs. Each taxi contained five Grant Mitchell lookalikes who proceeded to get out, one saying, 'The Bluebirds are here! The Bluebirds are here!'

'What the fuck are you going to do about it?'

Well, one loon who's there zips up his cardigan and smashes the bloke all over the place while the back-pedalling Taffy calls for back-up from his mates. The one who backs him up gets a boot in the nuts. And, as this is happening, a copper on a motorcycle pulls up. On seeing their ages, he tells them, 'Behave yourselves, and get on your way!'

Will the nutter ever learn?

7

OUR NICKNAMES

The Lilywhites, North End, a.k.a. Sheep-Shaggers... take your pick. The lads, the boys, the crew, the firm, the mob, drinking buddies, beer monsters...does it matter what we're known as? At the end of the day, it's just us. However, every group has to go under an umbrella, don't they? And we've had several names that have been tagged to us – so here they are.

THE GENTRY

Alan Ball, the manager at Preston in the early Seventies came up with the name, after an away match at Halifax. A mass following of fans sang throughout the full 90 minutes of the game. It's unknown if he was referring to a historian's quote or his appreciation of them. Preston fans soon after took to wearing bowler hats and carrying brollies – later used as weapons. This was also reflected in a classic film in the early Seventies, Stanley Kubrick's *A Clockwork Orange*.

SPOTTY DOG CREW

'Spotty Dogs... raise your paws!'

I was bombarded with 101 reasons as to how the name came about. Sourcing its origins was a task on its own.

One report I had was that a mob of Preston in the Seventies kicked to death a Dalmatian dog! Bit hard to swallow and far-fetched, I think.

Preston town in general during the Fifties and Sixties had an influx of Afro-Caribbeans swelling its ever-growing population. They left their idyllic islands with the promise of a better way of life and job prospects! The younger element, mainly teenagers, started moon stomping together with white youths at local discos to mod and blues sounds. Then leading into the late Sixties' skinhead culture, their smart, natty dress was soon cottoned on to by the in-crowd. This progressed to both black and white standing side by side on the terraces in the Seventies. Birmingham may claim to have had the first multi-racial crew, but Preston lads' black, white and Asian mobs have been witnessed in battle against other firms through the years. The black lads from the Seventies, and my era, were feared everywhere Preston went. Three of whom I've personally witnessed move mobs on their own. They have since moved on in life, one turning to God! Also three Asian lads, who were around in the early Eighties, would mix it with the best. One who ran with us was wholly accepted, with race, colour or religion not once being a problem.

Getting back to the Seventies, Preston had some handy lads whether they were blue, red or green! The name Spotty Dogs may have sprouted from a mixture of colour within the firm.

Another possibility comes from a set of lads from Leyland who mainly worked at Leyland Motors truck factory. The said lads started turning up for away matches in white paper overalls which made them stand out on a dark winter's day when trying to take the opponents' end.

The group of lads who I remember as being the Spotty Dogs would mob up on the Spion Kop, in the left-hand corner, singing unusual songs – which were way above me at the time. The blokes I know personally are now in their fifties, being classed as Preston boys back then, and they'd stopped being involved well before my time. This was largely due to two deaths in the late Seventies. Both fatalities were away from football. One was on a night out, ending in a street-brawl stabbing. The other was at Preston Polytechnic – UCLAN – during a punk concert. The gig erupted into a mass free-for-all after chants of 'Preston are magic' and 'Seaside aggro'. A 22-year-old from Preston died after being hit over the head with a chair. Even though a Preston man was charged with murder and later acquitted, it was classed as football related. Suspicion then turned towards Blackpool followers who allegedly might have caused his death.

These incidents put a spotlight on the Spotty Dogs and Preston's footy lads. They started to receive special attention off the police whether at the match, out drinking – the Barmy Army – or generally going about their daily business. An accumulation of football-related incidents, jibbing people with sharpened metal afro combs, throwing the opposition through shop windows and generally kicking the crap out of other teams' lads with steel-toe-capped boots didn't help matters! This led to many of them packing in following PNE, and never bothering with football, or aggro, ever again. Others went on to watch, and follow, other teams – shame on you.

Some North Enders have said that the name originates from the localities of the smaller groups. Different groups of lads from different estates, districts and surrounding villages. On match days, they would join up into one big mob and on one such day a lad came out with, 'We're from 101 different areas, just like that film about them spotty dogs!'

Finally, last but not least, and after extensive research into its roots, a well-respected old lad gave me a starter for ten. The birth of the Spotty Dog crew was after a fascination about a cartoon character by some of the PNE lads when growing up – and certain mind-bending substances. This character was a wooden spotty dog, out of the Wooden Tops, in the programme *Watch with Mother*. One lad who was heavily into scooters, and still is, insisted on an initiation ceremony. This initiation to most outside the circle of mates seemed very weird. To join the Spotty Dog family, the lad had to... bite you! Weird fuckers!

The actual reason as to how the name came about will perhaps remain in Preston folklore forever, but, however they got their name, the foundations were formed, and let mayhem begin, week in, week out.

So, if you ever heard howling at a Preston match in the mid- to late Seventies under a full moon, it was probably because one of the lads had contracted rabies. The Spotty Dog crew's bite was definitely worse than its bark!

Other names that came about at the time were taken from modern culture. Many lads, skinheads and teenagers went under the names Black Cat Mob and the Schooner Boys. Both names were taken from coffee bars that they hung round in as most were too young to enter public houses.

NO-NAMES

The lads and little firms that were about in the early to mid-Eighties which I mentioned earlier, what collective name did they or we have? In the M-Z of *Hooligans*, we were given the name Town End Mob – new to me! The Trendies was another name bandied about, mainly by the older beer monsters and non-dressers, a few of whom we distanced ourselves from, just because of clobber. Being young and brash, we probably weren't giving out respect where respect was due.

So, our name, well... err... we never had one! How strange is that in modern-day football-firm culture? How useless and uninventive we were! Here's two that nearly came to be.

SECTION 4/5

This came about because every lad in our circle at some stage had upon his person a charge sheet, usually from their last nicking at the match. Lads would be asking what they should plead or what they might get, showing the sheet off like a first-prize certificate. Preston's younger element of the time that would be hanging around constantly heard us go on and on about 'section this' and 'section that'. They labelled us with the nickname, only to realise a few years down the line that they'd started to receive the exact same documents!

THE SS/SUICIDE SQUAD

I know exactly what you are thinking! You're thinking that's Burnley's nickname. Another time, another place and we could've been labelled with it. Here's a couple of stories as to why it was nearly ours.

It was about the time when videos were starting to flood every household, making all the banned films readily available. *Monty Python's Life of Brian* had never been shown in Preston due to our righteous council not letting us have the pleasure of viewing the masterpiece. Not that we were old enough when the classic came out. Then the good old Betamax kicked in and the tape did the rounds, having being copied more times than the Burberry check. Today, the DVD takes pride of place in my collection. Lads would be at each other with lines out of the film – 'Oi, big nose – move!'... 'It's a sign he's bought a round,' and whistling 'Always Look on the Bright Side of Life' when moving from pub to pub.

So, one wet and windy day, we had Burnley at home. A great lad of ours at the time, CP, had lived with one of Burnley's lads nicknamed Chukkie – and, no, they weren't gay. He'd been out and about drinking in CP's manor a few times and knew quite a lot of the Leyland lads. Anyway, 20 of us had managed to get on Moor Park Avenue, pretending to be trees – well, hiding behind them, as this used to be the way that they took the escorts back to Preston Station.

At the top of the park, near the Moor Park gates, about 15–20 lads started jogging down the avenue, while the main escort surrounded by police were coming across Deepdale Road. We peeled off from our hiding places like John Rambo to take the advancing Burnley by surprise. About ten yards from us, these lads started shouting, 'We're from Leyland... Burnley are after us.'

Our guard dropped for a split second, plus we'd also seen that Burnley had broken the escort heading our way. Thinking now we'd got 40, we'd give it a go with the Clarets. Then someone shouted, 'They're not Leyland... they're Burnley.' Game on!

It was Chukkie and the top Burnley boys; both sets went into toe-to-toe action. We had them on the back foot 'til another 40 Burnley arrived, as well as the police with a couple on horseback. Exit us, doing mini Grand Nationals over hedges and fences. One Preston lad was getting chased round the trees in the park by a copper on a horse, ducking and diving, bobbing and weaving around tree trunks and bushes. He finally got caught, to cheers and roars of laughter off the Burnley escort.

Later on, we met up in our local – stories were bandied about on the day's events. The banter had *Life of Brian* quotes thrown in as usual, when someone piped up, 'That was suicidal today with the numbers we had... yeah, just like the suicide squad in the *Life of Brian...*' to side-splitting laughter from the lads. Now, I don't know if anyone came out with any quotes while we were practising *Come Dancing* with Burnley on the park, but the name was toyed with for the next few weeks.

Also two of the lads, C and Rambie, had a long conversation after a few shandies one night when walking to an engagement do about adopting the name Suicide Squad. Then one day someone said, 'Don't be so fucking stupid... they all did themselves in!' The name was then dropped like a ton of bricks!

A year later, we'd played Burnley at the Turf, and we were escorted back to our cars and vans that were parked down a dark road near a bridge after the game. Just as we were ready to get into the transport, on police advice, a roar went up in the surrounding gloom. A copper shouted, 'The Suicide Squad is here... watch out!' We burst into fits of laughter. It then started raining bricks to the sound of 'Su-Su-Su-i-cide'. They'd nicked our name. Well, not really, because we never bothered using it.

So who had it first? I've no idea, but it's still a good nickname, so every credit.

PRESTON PARA SOCCER (PPS)

Most of the lads who went on to become the PPS had been travelling away together from around 1983/84, only they'd never had a name, or reputation, to speak of until 1986/87. Preston were doing well under John McGrath – RIP. This was also the season the famous bread van appeared like a TARDIS. Preston started taking larger numbers everywhere, while at the same time we were having a good few results on and off the pitch.

'Oh yes, oh yes, we are the PPS!'

'P... P... PPS!'

The name didn't come along until sometime during the following season. It was coined by a Penwortham lad, and initially it was a bit of a joke after being basically ripped from two other mobs, Leeds and Wolves, with similar names. Calling cards were printed, and on the back of the Town End – away end – 'PPS' graffiti was scrawled. The rest, as they say, is history.

A few of the lads involved started wearing NBC (Nuclear, Biological and Chemical) jackets in honour of the Para bit, with lads on leave from the Army bringing home other presents for them too. At one point, a Grimsby newspaper ran an article on the name Preston Riot Squad, and apparent motives:

> *And in Preston the supporters tended to be split into rival groups – the CDN and Preston Riot Squad. Most of the members aged between 14 and 18 in each group adhere to the IRA or the UDA.*

PYF – PRESTON YOUTH FIRM; PFP – PRESTON FOOT PATROL

Two new kids on the block, with other numerous little youth firms' names being bandied about. Both are still allegedly involved today. But being young, and naive, they foolishly post messages on the Internet which are easily accessible to the Old Bill.

The lads I hung around with years ago are still having their doors knocked on, and bells rang off the Old Bill. Not for what they've done, but for what their offspring are up to! So, whatever the names, the top boys nowadays are still managing to put on a show.

8

DOES SIZE MATTER?

Not your knob – your mob! Big, small, 100-plus, 1000s, threes and fours, or on your own. As the saying goes, 'It's not what you've got, it's how you use it!' I've never had that problem myself! Seen them all – big, ugly-looking beer monsters, down to little baby-faced assassins with Uncle Stanley in hands. Pluses and minuses never seem to add up, so don't think you're invincible or you might come unstuck and forever regret it. A few can sometimes move mobs if they stay tight, are pumped up and committed.

Three of us – well, two, actually – thought we could take on the Burnley Suicide Squad at Deepdale once. One lad, a history teacher, thought better, knowing our chances after studying different conflicts over the years. I think he based his decision on the big army facing a small army theory – I don't blame him! Just us two superheroes, then. Er, no we weren't.

We were holding our own against 2... 4... 8... 16... yes, we can do this... 32... 64... no, we fucking can't! I took a few slaps in the mêlée after putting a couple down and my mate was holding his own when the rest of the Suicide Squad set about us. I managed to wriggle out, nearly losing my Paul & Shark coat hood, and my mate appeared a couple of minutes later at the junction of St George's Road, near the ground. It was pouring with rain and he'd gone down, taking a good kicking against a pie-shop front, putting his arms up to protect himself. 'Fucking arm's killing me,' he said.

'Shut up, you soft cunt... you've got another to lift your pint up with,' I replied as we both walked off to the boozer, laughing at our escapade.

When I phoned him the next day, he was just leaving Casualty with a double fracture of the arm in plaster. He knew the score but he was feeling a bit down with time off work looming. Now I was feeling bad; he had kids, a mortgage and bills on his doormat. Brainwave! It didn't work out too bad in the end!

Size, though, wasn't everything. The look of your mob was also a major factor as to what sort of reception you'd get. When you'd see a big firm pile off a train or come round the corner, it could sometimes put the fear of God into you: 'I'm a footy thug, get the fuck out of here, now.' You want to be invisible and vaporise. Then, on closer observation, are they really the business? And you'd try to work out whether they were or not, after casting a hoolie-eye over them. Numbers are impressive, as well as smartly dressed lads. Credit goes out to their organisation, with phone calls made and hours in the mirror choosing which frock to wear. However, it can all end in tears when a smaller, quality, pristine mob takes it to them. Ripped, torn, scuffed, slashed or even 'that will fit me nicely'. Job done! Bodies laid out, claret everywhere. Lads scattering off in different directions, some having to beg for mercy, others trying to mingle in with shoppers or standing at a bus stop to avoid a leathering. 'What time is it, mate?' The old ones are always the best. I've done it, and been done off other teams' lads in alike encounters. No one is invincible, are they? You wouldn't think so when you read some of the books out there.

It can become messy when two large mobs go to war, like with us against Bolton or Carlisle, not knowing who's who. Similar accents, similar dress. You might get split up, trapped and serious damage done to your personal self – very edgy stuff. Enjoying the moment but also shitting yourself. Then a quick check of the underwear when there's a quiet moment!

When you were on the move with the mob, you could be strutting, fast walking, jogging and sometimes full steam ahead... although that wasn't often over the years with the size of some of our lot's guts. Running past windows, taking a quick glance, adjusting your tie! It looks awesome, your reflection on the move, all togged up. No solid sounds on the pavement, just squeaking, sweaty trainers on feet. The distinctive sound of nylon cagoules brushing each other and rubbing your torso as your arms go to and fro. No, we're not window shopping, we're here for a row. The pavements are dampened with rain – especially 'ooop Norf'! Dodging the dog shit and around puddles in which, if you're lucky, you can catch a glimpse of your newly purchased strides. You don't want to ruin your top-of-the-range trainers. Looks do matter! Especially when you're marching round a foreign town or city, shoppers stop and gawp. Commuters on buses twisting their necks *Exorcist* style to see what's going on and who you are. At this point in time, you're the bollocks, the bee's knees, you're untouchable; it's your time and they'd better know it!

We've had some big turnouts without a punch even thrown

in anger. I've no need to lie. I tell it 99 per cent as it was, maybe 1 per cent rose-tinted, perhaps? But not complete nonsense like some of the stories I've had the pleasure of reading during my research: 'never been run, never been done'! Why do firms, especially local rivals, never admit to a bad day at the office? Come on, we've all had them; us probably more than most.

A nice 20 v 20, or 10 on 10 was about right. Going for it big time, and later on, over a pint, you'd listen to everyone's angle on how we'd performed and gone on. Shaking heads, comparing bruises and scars, while taking the piss out of each other. No serious injuries, trips to the hospital or anyone nicked was a result. Win or lose, we would always have some booze.

Even a one on one, two against one – most having been there. Black eyes, cut lip, busted nose, split knuckle, battle scars for everyone to see – a prized asset. My pet hate was shiners – black eyes – slowly coming up, taking days, even weeks, to go.

Like I say, it's not always about numbers; it's who would stand at the critical moment. Reputations can get ruined by a golden opportunity or a chance meet but one big motherfucker can put the wind up superior numbers, scattering lads in the streets. Odds stacked against you, lads leaving the scene rapido – excuses made later!

And there were women involved as well – P.M.T.-raging geezer girls. I've seen a few not to get on the wrong side of. Once at an away game at Wycombe Wanderers we'd turned up late with no tickets and paid on the home end. No, we weren't trying to take it, just watch the match. I'd had a curry the night before and was letting off big time with the mates moving along the terracing, complaining like mad about the pungent smell. After a good dozen or so farts in the first 30 minutes, a girl behind me says, 'If that fackin' caant don't stop fartin', I'll chin him.' Not fancying my chances, I moved along the terracing to join the mates and pollute another part of the home end.

That weekend had its fun. We stopped in London after the last match of the season and kept constantly bumping into Southampton's lads! We were knocked back from endless pubs and kept getting told by the Old Bill to 'Go home'.

Next day, with a spot of sightseeing done, and a few beers inside us, I'd nipped into a phone booth, grabbed a couple of calling cards, then slipped them into my mate Rambie's bag, duly forgetting about them.

On Monday after work, as I entered the house, my better half says sternly, 'I want a word with you!' She'd had Rambie's other half on the phone and she'd found a blonde hair on one of his T-shirts along with Wendy Whiplash's card in his Head bag. On closer inspection, the over-educated Wendy apparently had O- and A-levels to her name! Rambie – the cold biscuit – wasn't quite as educated, and had to work hard to explain his weekend's exploits. He'd had to take his top off, with the wife looking for welt marks. 'You dirty bastard, I know what you've been up to this weekend.' My missus didn't go down that route – instead, she rang several brothel numbers asking if a couple of Northern lads with 'MADE IN ENGLAND' tattooed on their bums had visited their establishments that weekend. I had to smooth things over on both fronts; after all, it was only a wind-up.

The methods we used for our planned operations would range from flying out of side streets in and around Deepdale attacking our prey; moving down back alleys; or creeping up on our targets, fingers on lips... 'Ssssh'. Then along St George's Road – keep me English 'til my dying day – with the smell of spices wafting through the air. Hiding behind hedges, walls or in bus shelters like a game of hide and seek.

Another favourite in the early Eighties was to whistle 'Tom Hark' covered by the Piranhas. Lads would mingle in with other fans or in an escort letting each other know they were there. There was another favourite sung on the terraces: 'The Blackpool sing, I don't know why, 'cause after the match, they're gonna die... na, na, na-na...'

Another classic tactic was to deploy spotters – we'd send lads to have a look at what was going on, who was where, bobbing in and out of pubs. They're here, they're there, they're every fucking where... reports would come back. We had lads who didn't touch a drop of alcohol who'd do a bit of detective work on a recce. One stood outside the boozer we were in and one up the road sorting a route out for a surprise attack. Everyone had a role to play.

We'd use tactics like looking at tax discs for areas, car stickers or number plates which would give their transport away. A fatal mistake was to hire a van with the company's logo embossed down the side. Tyres would be let down, slashed or punctured. I remember a tyre was done on a van with a sharp instrument, the pressure blowing the perpetrator backwards like he'd been shot by a 12-bore shotgun!

A couple of motors from Oxford had been done once in the car park outside Deepdale. And on seeing their flat tyres, they opened their boots for the spares. Preston came out of hiding ready for a ruck when this black lad pulled out what looked like a sawn-off. 'It's a gun, it's a gun!' someone shouted. Lads scattered in shock, alerting the Old Bill to the situation. Looking over, from a distance, it was a wheel brace that he'd been holding like a shooter. Nice one, it worked.

Quite a few times if it panned out, the majority of the away following were travelling by coach or transport other than the train; then we'd try plan B. If the Old Bill were on top around the ground or the car park, a favourite that worked half-a-dozen times was to get on to Blackpool Road. This was a road which the police would direct away supporters on to and away. The cover of darkness was preferred but sometimes you just had to make do. Lads would hide in gardens and bushes waiting 'til numerous traffic lights would turn to red, then steam out like banshees launching milk bottles and any household waste they could lay their hands on.

One classic was a night game against Sheffield Wednesday. Knowing their lads had come on coaches, we left early, heading to a haven of bushes that Alan Titchmarsh would've been proud of. As we positioned ourselves commando-style in shrubs, one lad rubbed mud into his face – very weird – he must have been watching too many American movies. An innocent-looking lad was left patrolling the main road waiting for the expected – the coaches.

When the enemy was clocked, his arm went up as a signal and lads started to come out of the undergrowth. His hand movement quickly changed to a halt motion. Two coppers had arrived with a dog; luckily, the lads had remained in the shadows. The spotter couldn't wait any longer and did his job pushing the zebra-crossing button. Brakes were now heard being slammed on, and by this time the lads just couldn't resist it. 'Come on,' the cry went up. The two boys in blue didn't have a clue what was going on, and, on seeing endless huge, dark figures running towards them, they did one with their German Shepherd leading the way. This left a few minutes' free time until the reinforcements arrived. Motorbikes and Black Marias could be heard, with the blue lights lighting up the dark skies – damage limitation.

This was the last big one. From then on, a tight escort of bikes used to take the coaches down to the motorway with others parked up on every set of lights and crossings.

9

OPPONENTS

Other teams... love them, hate them, like, dislike, fear or laugh at. Historically, and locally, our long-term rivals are Blackpool: The Lashers, the Donkeys – Donkey Lashers – the Scum, Tangerine B... call 'em what you like! Preston lies 18 miles to the east of Blackpool, and they have to travel through God's country if they want to get out of the hell-hole. Here's a list of my injuries sustained against Blackpool, not mentioning bust noses, cut lips or black eyes, in the Donkey derbies.

ROUND 1

The first occurred when we'd arrived outside Yates's unexpectedly and Preston charged over the road as quick as a flash to collect a prize, no back-pedalling. I was full at it, when I felt my right arm being dragged at an unusual angle by a dead weight. Glancing to the side, I noticed a German Shepherd dangling off the end of my arm, cashing in on its own jackpot. A big shout went up behind me and Preston steamed back into

Blackpool. The dog and his handler seemed to have more pressing business and let me go – cheers, lads.

Later, back in Preston, I had to go to the hospital for a tetanus jab not knowing who else the rabid dog had had its mouth round. You know what Blackpool is the capital of England for, don't you?

ROUND 2

We'd been down to Wembley for an England game, and on the way back, travelling by train, a mate struck up a bit of banter with a few Blackpool – five young 'uns and one lad around our age. 'You're going nowhere in football with a shit team, laughable ground and an alleged sex case for a chairman.' They were giving us similar nonsense back.

We arrived at Preston Station, and exited the train, and they also got off to change for Blackpool. The rest of the lads headed into town for a few beers; me and the said mate decided we'd had enough and went looking for a taxi home. Walking up the ramp towards the exit, the older Blackpool lad and my mate were squabbling again. The next thing, they started fighting, with me diving in to break it up and get a dig off a mucker for my troubles. Things sorted, hands shook, they turned left over the footbridge to their platform, while we left the station and looked outside for a taxi. There were none parked up, or in sight, so the mate went in search of one and I waited just in case one did appear. Suddenly, I got a tap on the shoulder and, as I start to turn round, I heard the words 'Our train is delayed, and we've got some unfinished business...'

Blows started raining in on my half-turned head and survival instincts kicked in. God loves a trier, but six against one just wasn't working, and they were slowly pulling me down to put the boot in, as I caught a glimpse of my mate entering the fray. One lad dragged me backwards by my jumper and I ended up sitting on my arse on the wet pavement, struggling to get back up.

'FUCK OFF!' A nice, top-of-the-range trainer slammed right into my face, quickly followed by a second one for good measure, smashing my skull into the kerb. Not content with only busting my nose, they gave me a nice parting in my hairline when my head made contact with the concrete moulding.

I was now struggling to lift my head up with the *Magic Roundabout* theme tune going on inside it. Dazed, but not out, I looked around to find my new friends were on their toes. Within minutes, I was in the back of a free, white taxi complete with blue flashing lights, taking me for a ride to the A&E. A few X-rays showed nothing too serious – surprise, surprise. I just needed stitches to the back of the head, and a good night's sleep in crisp, white, linen sheets in the A&E ward.

Next morning, I was up early and dressed. And just as I was heading for the exit door, a nurse caught up with me, saying, 'You can't go until the doctor has done his rounds.'

'I've seen enough blokes in white coats in my life,' I replied. 'Plus the wife's arranged a barbecue and will kill me if I don't get home to give her a hand.' I'm gone, door swinging.

It's a bit cuntish, six on one or six on two. Only a few months later a cheque dropped on my doormat that more than made up for my troubles!

ROUND 3

I'd found myself mingled in with Blackpool, in the dark, after a game at Bloomfield Road, as Preston were being escorted on the opposite side of the street. Blackpool were giving it 'Preston wankers... Preston twats!' and like a dick I piped up, 'I'm Preston...'

Before I could finish my sentence – BANG! – from the side of me. My nose ended up 90 degrees from its normal position; it was now resting on the side of my cheek. I staggered backwards into the middle of the road like someone had put an electric cattle prod up it.

I eventually made my way to some toilets near the Castle pub to try to straighten my nose while cleaning myself up – that hurt more than having it smashed. I had panda eyes for the next two weeks; a consequence of my own stupid fault. Not the first or last time.

FOURTH AND FINAL ROUND

This was sustained on Deepdale Road after a home match, a broken wrist. Let's just say some people have hard heads!

For donkey's years, when I was just a fresh-faced whipper-snapper, they might have edged it. Preston definitely moved forward. Yesterday's news is tomorrow's chip-shop wrappers and there are plenty of chippies selling battered Mars Bars in Blackpool! It's the favourite food for their lads, who, I've heard, run the show there nowadays.

But what about some of the other firms we've come up against? Well, Burnley slagged us off a bit in their book *Suicide Squad*. I'm not a great buyer of hoolie books – until recently, for research purposes – the exception being *Steaming In*, which is a classic. I personally think it's been 50/50 over the years, although they seem to see it differently, forgetting times when they've arrived late or stopped off for a drink in Bamber Bridge, plus other times at theirs. A certain Rocky Mills seems to typify their colony, I think!

We've had great times with Bolton in years gone by, with a lot of respect given out. Always on their game, home and away, but there has been no trouble recently in the leagues, or at the play-off final in Cardiff – not that I'm involved any more. A few words were exchanged in Zurich before an England match in Liechtenstein. Mistaken facts, places and identities... it got sorted.

I remember once going to a game at Burnden Park in my teens with a few Chelsea fans from Preston. Preston had no game that day. And I received a lump of concrete to the head while stood on the away terracing for my troubles. 'I'll get the bastards back in a few weeks when I come here with Preston.' Blood trickling down my brow and splitting headache kicking in, my Chelsea mates just cracked up; I'd gone big time.

Then at half-time, both Chelsea and Bolton fans tried to kick the gates down under the stand, wanting to polish their boots on each other's faces. Preston also tried this trick on several visits but they never did give way. You've even got to watch out for their midgets! Just ask Paddy and Max out of *Phoenix Nights*.

As for Wigan, Preston have always seen them as second rate, coming out on top in the majority of run-ins. It could be a different ball game with big numbers of the younger element turning out over recent years.

What about Blackburn? Now come on, and correct me if I'm wrong, but I can't remember anything apart from a token (jester) turnout over the years. Preston have been there that many times, wandering round like headless chickens, game after game. I even got my first football charge there for attacking a fence! We played them on many occasions up until the early Eighties, then a big gap until we played them once again in a 1997 League Cup fixture. It was an 'everywhere we go, we take over' day. Lads got lifted for being naughty and bored.

Sorry, I did bump into Blackburn once – well, one lad – while sitting in a cell for something I didn't do. It was at an England friendly v Italy at Elland Road.

A good drink was had by a minibus-load of us that day round Leeds city centre, and then we drove up to the ground for the match. Two of us had tickets for the upper section in the Gelderd End, away from the rest of the lads. We park our arses up in front of the wall just after kick-off and a bloke touching 7ft comes and sits next to us in a spare seat. He starts giving it all small talk, his knees touching his nose – what a sight. Something should have clicked earlier, but we'd had a good day. The one-sided conversation shortly moves on to football violence. I can't exactly get his angle but I'm thinking, is he trying to suck me into something?

'Not being funny, mate, are you... you know, or what's your problem?'

No answer.

'Well, are you or what?'

No reply. Then for the next 20 minutes I volley a load of abuse into him before he ups and disappears. The half-time whistle goes and we grab a pie, piss and Bovril – no alcohol available.

When we return to our seats for the second half, two uniformed police approach in our direction, one curling his finger towards himself and says, 'Can you come with me, sir?' I'm looking round thinking he means someone else. 'No... you!' he says, as he looks me up and down.

I make my way over, none the wiser. 'Can I help you, officers?' I ask.

'We're arresting you for being intoxicated in a sporting arena.'

They then grab my arm and take me down to the custody suite under the stand. My mind's working overtime; I've missed my lift home, a day off work looming, a morning court appearance, with a poxy little fine, I guess, and, worst of all, a possible ban. What for? The cell door clangs shut.

'O'rite, mate, what you in for?' a lad with a northern accent asks.

'Allegedly being pissed... you?'

'Swearing!'

I find out chatting away that he's from Blackburn; at least we can share a taxi home later or tomorrow. Then the copper comes to tell us the final score while asking if we'd mind if the Japanese and the Korean press just take a look and a few photos? I presumed for a pre-World Cup article.

Enter the press. I quickly pull my red Paul & Shark duffel over my head trying to avoid all the flashing camera lenses. Aaaah, that's why they've arrested me – they must think I have robbed Paddington Bear's coat! The Blackburn lad is sat bold as brass pointing at his Stone Island badge saying, 'A week's wage this cost me, you peasants – loads of money!' He must have wanted his face in every paper from here to Timbuktu; all for a bit of verbal.

The snappers go, and he's sat there with a big smile across his face like he'd just won first prize in a Mr Knob Head UK competition.

The next thing, the cell door opened. 'Right, go to the desk and get your gear – you can go,' said the desk sergeant.

Bit of a mystery, that one. I suppose it might have been too much paperwork or because I wasn't really drunk or they may have felt sorry for me having been padded up with a plant-pot from Blackburn, that being my punishment. Anyway, I was out, just making last orders and the minibus home – result. I still wonder who that 7ft geezer was.

We played Middlesbrough away in the FA Cup in 1987. We were huddled around the radio in my local boozer, The Fulwood & Railway, listening to the games dropping to the 'big freeze'. We'd booked a coach and were listening closely to the 11am pitch inspection.

'Middlesbrough v Preston is definitely on...' we hear. Quick as a flash, the boys board the coach, foot on the gas, we're running late but we'll make it just in time for kick-off. Two carloads join us on route, following us into Middlesbrough.

On arrival in 'Boro, we went under a footbridge and bricks started bouncing off the bus's roof. 'Stop!' nearly everyone on board shouted. Surprisingly, the driver did. The emergency-exit door opened and the locals didn't wait around, only heels to be seen. By now, the coach had attracted the attention of a police motorbike, which then escorted us to Ayresome Park, which isn't the most inviting of places at the best of times, and it is minging in winter! The lads were a little wary of what was in store. The bus pulled up outside the away end and we were pushed into the turnstiles by the police – definitely no chance of a drink before the match.

'Boro were perched at the top of the old Third Division, and we were second in the Fourth. Obviously, they were hot favourites to win, but enter little Ronnie Hildersley. He hit a screaming shot from just beyond the halfway line, and the ball ended up nestled in the back of the net, putting Preston 1–0 up. 'Boro never looked like getting back into the match after that.

To our left, the natives were getting restless and, nearing the end of the game, around 500 boys thought fence-climbing was part of the entrance fee – Neanderthal cavemen, big growlers and lads all wanting a piece of us. The police and stewards then started using water hoses to calm them down. That was the first and last time I've seen them used at a match. Coppers were whacking 'Boro on their sausage-like fingers through the meshing with their clothes and donkey jackets now dripping wet. A few looked like they could do with a wash as if they'd just come from the steelworks or the docks. They are known locally as the Smoggies and I'm sure that chemical fumes in the atmosphere in and around Teesside from all the oversized chimneys and water coolers has made them disfigured and crazy. Good job they did have the water cannons out or we would have had them that day.

The final whistle blew and we were out on to the street, the coaches having been parked behind the stand again. Looking to our right, the same 500-strong, marauding pack were trying to get to us once again. A little safety fence had been erected with half-a-dozen coppers on horseback, a dozen dog handlers and their dogs, and 30 PCs with their batons drawn holding the front line in front of it. For 20 minutes, wave after wave of 'Boro tried to break the holding line. Finally, they got moved on somehow, or did they just get pissed off and bored? 'I hope to fuck they don't do a pincer move on us,' I'm thinking.

'Boro body count – there must have been a good ten out cold and more with wounds staggering about on the streets. The boys in blue then started pushing us on to our buses, telling the drivers to get out of town quickly.

Foot down, once again, and out of town we went – the lads didn't fancy a drink anyway.

A few undies and even socks got thrown away that day, I bet. Some other Preston lads in a car got stripped naked; everything taken apart from their soiled, stained Y-fronts. They were the most violent mob I've ever seen, wanting to dish out some punishment. It could have been a massacre!

We met some 'Boro lads at Italia '90, and they were mad as brushes, but we'd a good laugh with them. They would get cuffed together every night at last orders by the local police for being a bit rowdy and led back to their hotel – what a sight.

A downside to 'Boro was that a few mouthy ones came out of the ground after an FA Cup game at Preston. They were told to come round the corner away from the cameras and the Old Bill – but they didn't. Well, every team has a few rotten apples, don't they?

And last but not least, Crystal Palace. This encounter took place while in Amsterdam before an England game against Holland. Good old easyJet getting us there for less than a ton. We checked into yet another 5-star pad – jacuzzi, the works! Phone calls were exchanged with different groups of Preston that were over to meet ASAP in the bar in our hotel.

Tick, tock... tick, tock... only a few of the lads made it. The rest were sampling the delights of our host city: drinking, smoking and whatever else goes on behind closed doors.

Fifteen of us started to make a move when ten more staggered in stoned out of their heads. We then set off walking round the red-light district window shopping, and looking for a bar.

A few bars and drinks later, we went into a themed Hawaiian beach bar decked out with bamboo tables and chairs. Why they want us to feel like we're on Waikiki Beach is beyond me! Then one of the lads fancied a bit of a sing-song, lager taking its toll when, is it a bird... is it a plane? No, it's him flying past us, shortly followed by all the lovely furniture!

Some Preston lads were struggling to stand up, Mr Spliffy having done his job.

Twenty-five-a-side were fronting each other, when one lad shouted, 'Come on then, Norwich!' just as the Beach Boys music was switched off.

'We're not Norwich... what's your problem?' I said, as a lad with short black hair stepped forward.

'Sorry, we thought you were Norwich.'

Before any more reasoning went on, sirens were audible... exit stage right! We split up, heads down, walking off, and then regrouped five minutes later outside a pizza shop, now just seven of us. In the seven was my son, who was in his mid-teens, and also another lad's son of the same age – so five, really. The 25 came out of nowhere, right in our faces: 'We're Palace, who the fuck are you?'

'Preston... not fucking Norwich!' I bark back.

You could tell most of them were beaked off their boxes – ready for it.

'We thought you were Canary twats.'

Now I don't know what's gone on with them and Norwich previously, but we were in the frame. Then one very clever cunt stepped forward. 'We don't give a flying fuck who you are!' He was bigging it up to his mates looking round for approval, smiles on their faces. It's one face I save to the memory bank, a ringer for Sean Bean.

'You either come for a drink with us right now, or you'll get it.'

Breaking point; explosions in my head with the red mist coming down. Just before I lost it, I somehow remembered the two young 'uns with us. I'll take a kicking, plus the others would be right behind me and willing and steam in. But not the kids with us – no way, I couldn't forgive myself if they got hurt. I don't know how I held it together.

'OK then... the young lads are just getting a slice of pizza, we'll see you in there.'

A good majority of them broke out laughing as they strutted over to the pub like peacocks. Only a couple of them hung back. 'Why?' I said to the voice of reason.

'Too much sniff for some of them... no worries, mate.'

I made small-talk with him. 'We're off to Millwall next Saturday... do you know of a nice quiet boozer?' Blah, blah, blah.

He seemed all right, more or less apologising for the rest.

We eventually entered the pub together with more silly grins thrown our way. Beers bought, we moved to the back of the pub; it was quite full, and we tried to drum up a bit of back-up off some Geordies. But they were having their own problems with some Mackems. So much for chilling out in 'Dam; everyone's at each other's throats. Nothing went off that night and we made our way back to the hotel bar late on – not before the kids had filled their boots. One twice!

The next day, 50 of us were on a prowl like a pack of wolves, with no Palace to be found. Our meal of choice that day was chocolate bombs to calm and relax us later on.

We returned home the day after and I found 'something' in my Stone Island coat hood – you can probably guess what. Nice one, son! I didn't even know it was there.

A few years later, we stayed in Prague on our way to a game in Bratislava against Slovakia. That night, 20 of us were in a nightclub, where the drinks were marked down on a chitty. A few drinks in, watching the entertainment, a row started. An English lad had lost his piece of paper and it was over £50 in

English money to get out and he was having none of it. It went pear-shaped – glasses, bottles, ashtrays, tables and chairs started being used as payment. Only it didn't take a genius to realise that there was one way in – down the stairs – so there could only have been one way out – up the same stairs. Blocking the way were 15 mean-looking doormen tooled up.

Then the local dibble turned up – a signal for the bouncers to use pepper spray, right in my fucking eyes, game over.

In the mêlée that followed, we managed to get out, notes checked and bills paid. With me being Stevie Wondered, they could have stitched me up, good and proper, for any amount, but a mate, Kel, sorted it. I was helped upstairs into the cold night air, and I could hear from different accents off lads that were milling around, 'Don't rub, don't rub.' Water was also being splashed into my eyes and they slowly opened, and guess what sight greeted me? Mr Smiley, fucking Crystal Palace... Sean Bean lookalike!

I launched forward at him.

'I thought we'd sorted it,' he screamed.

'I'll tell you when it's sorted.' CLOG! (Seeing as we're in Holland!) I stuck one right on him. Beanie and his mate then legged it like Linford Christie; I bet he wasn't grinning when he stopped for breath.

The next day, while on the train to Bratislava, Beanie and his mate were spotted. They had designer black eyes to match their togs and were pretending to be asleep!

I have no hatred towards Crystal Palace, but to the clever fuckers that night in the 'Dam, they needed a lesson in equity and manners! Humiliation is the biggest ever revenge.

THE CHALLENGERS

The next three stories are by lads who I know personally; good mates that I have a drink with now and then. Let's call them Mr A, Mr B and Mr C. They don't live in Preston and want to remain anonymous – I respect that. I asked for a truthful opinion on what they really thought about Preston's firms.

Mr A:

'Yeah, smack that cunt Routledge!'

Central Drive, Blackpool, near the Mecca Club, in the early Eighties as we steamed into Nobenders. That was the first time I had heard Bill's name mentioned. One of Blackpool's lads did just that, straight over the road and gave him a whack.

In the early Seventies, but more so into the early Eighties, we – Blackpool – always had the better mob than Preston. We were named on the BBC as one of the top six in Britain. My mates and I come from Carny – Carnforth – and we had our own mob. We all supported different teams – Blackpool, PNE, Bolton and Burnley – that didn't matter! When we played each other, we'd meet up for a drink. A few times on Preston Station other teams have wondered what the fuck's happening when a mix of 10–15 lads supporting different teams steamed into them.

I have had good times, and I've had bad times involving PNE and Blackpool. Early Eighties, we took two cars and parked on Moor Park. After the game we took the piss, chasing Preston all over the park. Our problems started when we walked back and eight of us stood against fifteen. If you have ever been kicked in the head by someone wearing Docs, you know what I mean when I say my head was sore and scarred like a grass burn for fucking days.

Again in the Eighties, we played Preston in the FA Cup.

Ten of us went down on the train and the first thing we saw was a mob of Bennys and a bigger mob of Rammys – everywhere you looked there was Blackpool. I have talked to Nobenders since who still say Blackpool took the piss that day. There wasn't much fighting, just chasing shadows all day.

The worst I have been whacked at Preston was the Night of Shame game when, shouting abuse to my Preston mates from the Kop, 'someone' whacked me with his stick. I asked why he'd done it but he just did it again! After the third time of asking I grabbed the stick, but the Old Bill came over waving truncheons. I dropped the stick but only after getting a slap off them. They were well on top all night.

One time at Preston Station, ten of us had come back from Blackpool, having avoided relegation. The same day as Everton had also, by beating Wimbledon. Twenty to twenty-five PPS came off a train and thought we were Everton. We were pissed up and singing and they soon realised we were Blackpool as we gave it to them. A good few whacks put them on their toes but they soon realised they outnumbered us and came back for another go. We got on our train and set fire extinguishers off at them as they ran alongside shouting, 'Get off!'

Nowadays, everyone would have been on CCTV and collars would be felt, but not one lad was nicked.

One Preston fan from Carnforth, a good mate of mine, started going round with Bill and his mates and at the odd England game we'd meet up with them. We wouldn't really talk after a bit of trouble between one of our Blackpool lads and some Preston at an England v Scotland game. But a full day on the drink and funny fags in 'Dam broke the ice, and got us all chatting.

Even though I still hate PNE, we all go to England games together, with me, Bill and a few others from Preston going to punk festivals together too. On such occasions, I have introduced him to a few of my Blackpool mates – most hoolies, ex- or still active. We're exactly the same; it's just that we support different teams.

Friendships aside, you need to remember that Blackpool were and still are number one, especially now, with the Muckers taking the piss everywhere they go! The future is bright... the future is tangerine.

Mr B:

During the late Seventies, and up until the mid-Eighties, there can be no doubt that Bolton were the most active and organised of any of the Lancastrian towns' football mobs. If Bolton were in town, disorder and violence took place on a large and violent scale. Everton away in 1977 is still remembered by Everton's lads with genuine respect and disbelief.

Bolton had some unusual names for its mobs: Mongy's Cuckoo Boys; Billy Whizz Fan Club; Tonge Moor Slashers; and the Horwich Casuals. Many of these were heavily influenced by the Casual movement that was prevalent at the time. Clobber would be purchased or acquired from the various shops around town, and also Manchester which was just a number-8 bus-ride away.

Most crews fell apart at the end of the Eighties due to a number of police raids, a successful anti-hooligan policy by the club and more destructively scag [heroin] which wrecked many lives, and is still a major blight on our proud town.

The boys still put on a show when the old faces turn out with some of the young 'uns trying to make a name for themselves – most recently Blackburn away 2006, Wigan home and away in the Premiership and all the Euro trips.

Preston was always a trip that the boys looked forward to as it was less than 25 miles away by bus, train or car. Bolton usually took a sizeable crew and like-minded lads would be there to greet them. Preston knew how to guard their town and their famous old Deepdale Stadium. The Seventies brought quite a few meetings, with outbreaks of trouble before, during and after the games.

My first memory of travelling to Preston is as a 13-year-old – I was taken to Deepdale in 1981 for a mate's birthday treat. It was a crucial relegation match and, upon sitting in the old Pavilion Stand, we watched animatedly as trouble broke out during the match – witnessed by a crowd of 8,505. Bolton won 2–1 and the natives were restless. Trouble broke out on the road and car park outside the stadium with us having to take refuge in a chippy near the ground, then duck under seats on a bus to hide from the battling hordes. My mate's dad was struggling to look after himself, never mind two scarfed-up, petrified teenagers. The last bit of the treat, before setting off home, was KFC; I don't think Bolton had one at the time. Bloody hell, it tasted fantastic in the back of the car and at last we felt safe.

Bolton and North End, in the Eighties, slipped through the leagues and meetings would be in front of some pitiful crowds of some 6,000–8,000. A sad sight for the famous old clubs but both had an active hooligan element and trouble was a regular distraction from pretty crap football.

On Boxing Day 1988, Bolton brought a huge following to Deepdale, with the police and stewards caught on the hop. Police intelligence should have known better as by now Bolton were causing mayhem every week. Boxing Day also always saw a big turnout. Lads had been down to Preston the week before, dropping calling cards in a few pubs to let Preston know that we meant business. As usual, North End didn't let the town down with a tasty crew of their own. Trouble broke out before the match outside the ground with Bolton shepherded into the Town End. The stewards struggled to control the mass hordes and didn't open further sections until we eventually spilled on to the pitch.

During the game, a crew of North End in the corner of the old stand traded blows and missiles with us and certainly stood their corner well. The game was given further spice by Nigel Jemson turning out for Bolton and giving his former employers gestures every time he ran past them – he was crap for Bolton as well. North End gained respect, but it was Bolton's day. On the pitch, PNE won 3–1.

Another game well remembered is from the 1992/93 season; Bolton up, North End down, an encounter witnessed by 21,270 at Burnden with many more locked out, mostly PNE. A large amount of these were encamped in Yates's Wine Lodge during the game, unable to get in due to another ticketing cock-up. Bolton won the game 1–0 thanks to a John McGinlay penalty given away by a certain Simon Burton – a Bolton fan. Cheers, mate. Bolton have never really looked back – North End have come so close, so often, but never made the Prem.

After the match, Bolton's mob made their way back into town and the North End lads really dug in, putting on a top show holding on to Yates's and another pub. In the end, it was only heavy-handed policing that shifted Preston. North End held their ground that day and I would say got the best result at Bolton. They gained much respect, which lasts to this day.

Games recently, and Cardiff 2000, were relatively trouble-free. On England duty, relationships are cordial with both teams laughing at Blackburn and Burnley; well, they are in-bred and have no brains.

The Seventies and Eighties were unpredictable and spontaneous, not 50 lads with plenty of phone calls – we were 500 boys and pure bedlam.

Mr C:

As a true-blue Carlisle United fan, and a peripheral associate of the Border City Firm – now retired – it was with some trepidation that I agreed to pen a few lines for the author in relation to my personal thoughts about the Preston North End boys. The reason being that there has always been history between Carlisle and Preston, in that we see any game with a team who are less than 100 miles from the border city as a derby. As a result of this, I can recall a number of clashes between the two clubs – both on and off the pitch.

Although now a thing of the past, some of my early recollections of travelling on Football Special trains were to matches in Preston, at Deepdale. Exiting the train station in numbers, up to 1,000, we'd all be in full voice to alert the locals to the fact that we'd arrived – it always used to make the hairs on the back of the neck stand up.

I remember one occasion in the early Eighties when we disembarked from the train at Preston; we were to be met by half-a-dozen or so of the old heads who'd travelled on an earlier train. They were eager to show their battle scars and talk of the skirmishes that they'd already had.

Incidents like these have occurred on a regular basis, or at least when we were in the same division over the years. That's why there is a history between the two clubs. As a result of this, I was faced with the dilemma of whether or not I should contribute to a book compiled by those who follow Preston North End, as my loyalty is, and will always remain, 100 per cent behind Carlisle United. However, given the relationship that I personally have developed with some of Preston's main boys over the years, I felt compelled to assist in what little way I could. And rest assured, those who were involved will know what I'm referring to.

During the early Nineties, there were a couple of memorable games at Brunton Park, one of which lead to an 'off', which boys of both clubs still reminisce about. Following one game, the police didn't keep back Preston, who'd come up in good numbers and they were allowed to leave the ground. They came behind the main stand, which is where the bulk of the Carlisle boys had been during the game. Inevitably, a face-off occurred with sizeable numbers of the main boys from both Carlisle and Preston, who were separated only by a line of nervous police. Nobody is able to recall who threw the first punch, but the toe-to-toe fighting carried on for a good 8–10 minutes without either side giving ground. As previously stated, this game is remembered by those of both sides as a proper do, and led to mutual respect.

This respect has been tested on a number of occasions as I know that some of Carlisle boys feel that they were wronged when attacked on a train travelling home from an away match. They feel they were far outnumbered by PNE. However, it is not all one-way traffic as I am aware that a number of Preston lads have been done when attending matches at Carlisle. One of their main lads – you know who you are – seems never to tire of regaling me with the story of the time that he left his teeth in Carlisle, having had them knocked out.

Given this history, it may seem strange that a Carlisle fan is willing to speak of the Preston boys in a positive light. This developed as a result of the fact that I moved away from Carlisle and, following a bit of a nomadic lifestyle, finally landed in Lancashire where I have remained for many years. The vast majority of the boys in this area, excluding the trophy-hunting Mancs and Scousers, are either PNE supporters or those of their archrivals Blackpool – Donkey Lashers. Given that I have always played football, as well as watching it, it was inevitable that when I started playing in my new-found area I would come into contact with those who supported PNE. This then developed so that their circle of friends also became my circle of friends and it wasn't too long before we were meeting each other on England trips.

My first real insight into the Preston boys was when I travelled to Bulgaria to watch England. It was a qualifying game for Euro 2000. Five or six of us travelled to the seaside resort of Sunny Beach where it would seem that the majority of the England supporters were based. Preston had a mob of 40–50, but, despite the fact that they outnumbered many of the supposed high-profile firms, they didn't intimidate or bully anyone else. It became obvious to me from then on that they take the same view as I do that when you're away with England you all stick together as England and put club rivalries to one side. As the trip lasted for a week, I built up friendships with many of the Preston boys who were there, which have continued to develop over the years.

Initially, however, they thought we were a strange lot as we all bought the tiniest pairs of Speedos – 'Peedo' – the 'S' had fallen off – to parade along the beach, obviously breathing in every time a fit bird walked by. We're all relatively big lads, or certainly big around the waist, and these trunks all had a 28in waist. They left little to the imagination and I'm sure they thought that we were bandits.

Some years later, I was told that they thought that we were good lads, but they were sure that we were either gay or paedophiles. Clearly, Preston boys are not renowned for their sense of humour, although I accept it wasn't perhaps the funniest of jokes.

When the Euro 2000 finals actually took place, I spent the first week or so based in Brussels. However, the lads that I'd travelled with had to return to England and were scheduled to fly back out for the final if England got that far. Yet again, we were to be disappointed by our team.

When the lads had left, I decided to travel up to Amsterdam and stay there for a short while – contacting a few of Carlisle's boys so I could stay with them. I'd arranged to meet them at the Grasshopper pub but when I got there they were nowhere to be seen. However, there was a mob of perhaps 30–40 Everton who were sat outside and, to illustrate the other side of England not sticking together when abroad, they gave me a hard time. They knew I was on my own and looking for my mates, but being typical Scousers they threatened to steal my watch, passport and wallet. Without too much persuasion, I quickly made my excuses and left.

I was then extremely relieved to walk round the corner towards the red-light district and come across half-a-dozen or so of Preston's Under-5s. Given that we'd met previously, they contacted some of the older boys and, after a brief discussion, which I was not privy to, they agreed to take me to their hotel and put me up for the next four or five days. Although I only vaguely knew these younger lads, they really looked after me – and they again know who they are.

Since those initial meetings with both the main firm and the main Under-5s, I have maintained strong links with the PNE boys to such an extent that I'm pleased to be able to call a number of them mates. We have jovial banter about the fact that we follow rival teams but not one of them has ever been aggressive towards me and, likewise, neither have I been aggressive towards them. I am aware that some of their older boys will be up for anything and I've seen how game they can be. I've seen this with both England and when they've been following Preston.

I know quite a few of Bolton's boys, who, for some – or at least it seems to me – inexplicable reason, also follow Hibs. Hibs had a pre-season friendly a few years ago at Deepdale. Apparently, they'd not played a friendly in England for over ten years, and, given the fact that there is no love lost between our two great nations, their firm saw this as an opportunity to maraud south of Hadrian's Wall. I met the Bolton boys, who subsequently introduced me to the main lads of Hibs in a Preston pub and they must have numbered 150–200. I was unaware that they had the ability to turn out such numbers but it would seem that this was a one-off given that it had been so long since they had played in England. There were some real mean lads among them, one of whom had only just been released from prison, having served life for a double murder, or so he said.

Given the calibre of the opposition, I decided that it would be wise to alert the Preston boys as to what they would be up against. In effect, I told them to stay well clear, but typically half-a-dozen of the main lads marched into the pub within minutes of me giving that warning call. Obviously, I had to acknowledge them and, given that I'd only just been introduced to the Hibs boys, I felt extremely awkward as they were looking at me as if I were some sort of enemy within the camp. Luckily, nothing went off as the Preston boys had a drink and left shortly afterwards, having sized up the opposition. This illustrates first how game they were to walk into the lion's den, but also that they were sensible enough to walk away and live to fight another day, given the imbalance in the numbers.

When I first began to consider what to put down in this little piece, I was initially concerned that I wouldn't be able to contribute anything that would be of value. However, I would like to say that I have a great deal of admiration for Preston and their boys and hope to continue my association with them long into the future.

Part III

WE'RE JUST A BUNCH OF NORTH END BASTARDS!

10

LEARNING CURVE

From the times in the late seventies of wearing an MA-1 Flight – battlin' – jacket, after jibbing in to old, decrepit football grounds and standing on crumbling, concrete terraces chanting songs; to the eighties and running through town centres on the rampage, causing chaos, while wrapped up snugly in a Ellesse Aspen – 'it' – ski jacket; to striking a pose on your bitterest rivals' away end with the hood of your mega buck, CP Company Mille Miglia – goggled-up – driving coat and hiding your identity from prying CCTV cameras in the nineties. And finally, taking my obsession of all things casual, to donning a Garbstore Woodland Slide Racer – 'in' – jacket to the match, and concentrating intensely on the field of play activities, sat in my regular seat, rather than scanning the away section for potential lads, as the noughties draw to a close..

I'm now going to take you on a trip down memory lane with anecdotes about following my club, Preston North End. Games and dates will be as close as I can get them, but not necessarily in chronological order. After reading – and hopefully belly-laughing – your way through the short stories, you can make your own mind up about just how foolish, or game, I, we or even yourself, were. And, contrary to many people's beliefs, I was – and still am – a football fan too!

The 1978/79 season was the first in which I became a fully fledged follower of PNE. Preston had gained promotion into Division 2 with the first home game against our local rivals Blackburn Rovers. Preston ran out that day 4–1 winners with Mick – Robbo – Robinson notching one of the four. I had hoped the rest of the season would live up to this, but alas no, as it took Preston 12 more league games to record a win. A 6–1 destruction of Charlton Athletic at home on 12 December was the only thing really worth shouting about.

The season petered out with too many draws and a bad Easter. Preston finished seventh in the league after doing the double over Blackburn. Robinson went on to sign for Manchester City with Preston receiving a club record fee of £756,000. Big Malcolm Allison was splashing the cash and, if the board had held out, Preston could have banked a million for him.

Off the pitch, I was more of an observer than a participator in events – fights, scuffles, chasing and being chased! Was this what going to the match was all about? It didn't put me off, as my main activity was still singing with my scarf aloft.

The 1979/80 season started with a 3–0 away win at Charlton. Then a lack of consistency saw 19 matches drawn, with North End finishing tenth in the league. Our local rivals that season were Burnley, with Preston winning at home and drawing away at Turf Moor.

Preston played some big teams at that time with substantial away followings coming to Deepdale – Birmingham, Chelsea, Newcastle, Sunderland and West Ham, to name but a few.

I was now involved off the pitch, as you have read earlier, with one of my main contributions being the Birmingham game at home. There was no turning back now, as I was hooked BIG TIME.

The FA Cup threw up a massive game for us – Preston drew the team of the moment, Ipswich Town, in an early round at Deepdale. The Mod scene had just kicked in for the second time with the two-tone suits and a lot of pork-pie hats being worn to the games. Me, I was in mid-transition from punk to skin.

Both sets of fans were crammed into Deepdale, with the biggest turnout and attendance of the season – 16,986. Verbal was being thrown between the fences along with other more substantial objects. Enter on the Ipswich end a 6ft-6in Sid Vicious lookalike – black, spiky hair, leather and a red swastika T-shirt – giving it the Vs. It was now like being at a concert with the Preston Mods covering him in phlegm. Sid's gone ape-shit trying to get at the Sta-Prest boys, with the coppers grabbing him and lobbing him out.

Five minutes later he returns, coming up the paddock tunnel behind us. The bloke sticks out like a nun in a brothel and the gangsters combine, ploughing into him, Brighton style. He soon looks like a tractor has run over him and he's thrown out again. What a long trip, when he could have lay down in a field and got the same treatment off a local farmer near his home. Poor sod, Sid.

Preston that day got turned over 3–0.

When we played QPR at home, Preston got hammered 3–0, shown later on *Match of the Day*. I'm one of five little urchins outside the ground fronting three big geezers. One was wearing a donkey jacket with a nasty scar across the side of his face – he never got that from a joke shop. We were soon learning to duck and dive, bobbing and weaving about against the big boys, a couple of powder-puff slugs thrown, with us backing off – young bull, old bull. We're not hanging around for a crack back, being still fledglings and not yet in full plume.

With only one win in Preston's first ten games in the 1980/81 season, the stall was set out for the coming season. The main highlight that season was a run in the League Cup only to go out to West Bromwich Albion after a second replay. Led by manager big Ron Atkinson, WBA were a team full of superstars with dodgy perms.

Relegation was more or less rubber-stamped when Swansea came to town with thousands of followers, and beat Preston 3–1. They gained promotion to the First Division for the first time in their history. Preston also sacked Nobby Stiles.

I remember my first ever trip to Pieland, and Preston's first ever competitive game against Wigan at Springfield Park. I took my uniform off, hung it up in the wardrobe – well, threw it in the corner, actually – and hot-footed it round to Parky's, then on to Nip's, with all three of us squeezing into his two-seater pick-up.

We'd played them the week before at home and I hadn't witnessed any trouble but a rumour was going round that they were up for it at theirs. Wigan lads were known to the older heads from going to Northern Soul all-nighters at Wigan Casino, plus a few used to come to Preston for big games. One we'd nicknamed Noddy, as, no matter what the weather, he always had a big woolly hat on.

The rave scene in the late Eighties nearly ended hooliganism but what about the all-nighters? In the Seventies and early Eighties, lads would turn up from all over Lancashire and surrounding areas to the likes of Wigan Casino, Blackpool

Mecca, Morecambe Pier and other venues. They were all mates while whizzing off their boxes on the dance floors on Friday nights, then they'd knock lumps out of each other on Saturday afternoons – just have a think about that one!

Preston met up outside the Bull & Royal with arrangements sorted, a quick flyer down the necks on a warm evening and off we went. We set off in various shapes and sizes of transport going via Leyland, picking more recruits up on the way. The troops were rallied and it was 'Wigan, here we come'.

Having parked up a good mile away from the ground, I helped seasoned warriors comb the terraced-lined streets of Wigan looking for prey. With no real takers found, a top boy decided to go on the Wigan end. We queued up giving it Wigan lingo so as not to get sussed – me through the juvenile turnstile. Inside, we mobbed up, making our way to the side where the pie-eaters were singing, 'Wigan... Wigan... Wigan.'

Our 50 moved slowly. 'Excuse me, can I just get past please?' Manners maketh the man. What panache was shown, moving in on our unaware target.

Springfield was nearly at capacity, the ground never having hosted a big team like Preston before. Wigan had only been in the league a few seasons, ironically after Preston had changed their re-election vote, with Southport going out – how times change.

We were locked in on our target. Thirty, twenty, ten yards, then someone started singing, 'The North End... clap, clap, clap,' followed by the roar. We either had an STD or stank of shit as a gap began to appear quickly round us in every direction. Preston had the ring of confidence. A lone Latic tried his luck, then others; they were outnumbered and outclassed by Preston. The ones who did get through received knuckle sandwiches off tattooed hands, left-right, love-hate, followed by a Timpson for good measure and down they went. I bypassed a young lad singing, 'Preston... Preston...' as fast as he could; I stuck one on an advancing face.

I was shaking my right hand which fucking hurt now. The lad I cracked was holding his mouth, blood trickling through his fingers. On pulling them away, he had 'all I want for Christmas is my two front teeth' in his hand. Lads were surging in for anyone who wanted it. I was moved sideways with all the to'ing and fro'ing away from my victim – I do hope the tooth fairy visited that night to help out with his dentist bill.

The coppers were arriving, trying to regain order with it taking well over five minutes before they did. Both Wigan and Preston lads were getting thrown off or arrested and the rest of us got pushed round to the away section.

Being new to the league, the ground had no proper fencing or segregation, with just a thin blue line keeping us apart. Preston's job was done. Actions speak louder than words and we took Wigan's end. I wanted to soak up, and milk, what I'd been waiting for for the last couple of years. I was pumped up to the max, feeling 10ft tall. Nice and slowly I take it, hands are already out to greet us. North Enders show their appreciation, chanting, 'Preston agro... Preston agro...' followed by 'Preston here, Preston there, Preston every fucking where...'

I was getting my back slapped, hand squeezed, hair rubbed and a knowing wink of approval. I want this moment to last as long as possible, looking round at my surrogate thug family, lapping it up. My first away end – taken – and it nearly beats one of my other exploits: the fumbled sex behind the bike shed!

Later, while watching the game, I overheard two lads, one with a big, black 'tash saying, 'Fuck me! Did you see that young 'un giving it out? He's well up for it.'

Hands in pockets, I was bouncing up and down on tip-toes. What a feeling, being recognised by fellow Preston hooligans for my role in proceedings. Does it get any better than this?

With minutes to go before the end and Preston 2–1 up, 3–1 on aggregate, I got a nudge in the side; it's Parky saying, 'We're off.'

The lads I was with made their way over to the still closed gates, although they weren't for long – a few good kicks in unison soon opened them. Someone had noticed Wigan's lads leaving and round two was on. I hadn't noticed, as I was still reliving the moment over and over again.

Preston were on the jog, singing a song: 'We had a chip butty, but the chips fell off... We had a chip butty but the chips fell off... We had a chip butty but the chips fell off... We had a chip butty but the chips fell off...'

I was thinking to myself, 'What the fuck are these lot on?' while on the move.

'We had a wheelbarrow, but the wheel fell off...' What a bunch of loonies!

No joy, no Wigan found, home we go.

That night in bed, I was tossing and turning over that night's events which kept running through my clouded mind. I didn't need the alarm clock for my morning paper-round; I was up before the dawn chorus. I read every different national newspaper while doing my round to see if we'd made it into any match reports or even managed a column of our own – we were big time, weren't we? None was found.

At the bus stop, on the back seat of the bus, in the schoolyard, I've got a captivated audience, giving them a running commentary about the previous night's events. One lad who had gone with his dad, so he could back up my every word, said, 'Any chance we can come with you next Saturday?'

'I'll let you know when I've seen the lads out on Friday night.'

I was right full of myself. I needed to calm down – although that's taken me over 20 years.

I did see the lads on Friday after I'd bunked off school at dinnertime and gone to the local tattoo parlour, Mick Fizzy's, the skin artist near Preston Station. I'd borrowed a lad's birth certificate, who was over 18, and it was a good job you didn't have to have your name tattooed, as his was Bob. Etched on to my arm that day was my beloved team's emblem, the first of many tattoos, most of which I regret, but not this one. The warm, pain sensation when the needle penetrates your skin was well worth it, as Mick witters on to me about once spelling 'ENGLAND' wrongly on a bloke's arm. I then watched him like a hawk as he inked 'PRESTON NORTH END' on the town's coat of arms. It was bang on, I was chuffed to bits, and I couldn't wait to show it off in the pub later. I was now 'Preston 'Til I Die'.

While I was writing up this story, I had visions and flashbacks of a Wigan fan throwing a pie in my direction. I found I had to correct myself; it was a figment of my imagination. There is no way they'd part with any of their staple diet in any shape, form or flavour. The only pie seen that day was humble, and we all know where Wigan's nickname really comes from, don't we, Wiganers? 'Tha knows, eh?'

After being broken in at the Wigan away match, I fancied some more. Preston disposed of Oxford at home 1–0 in the next round of the League Cup. WBA away was next. A 0–0 draw, back to ours, then a 1–1 draw, with Alex Bruce having a perfectly good goal disallowed. Then it was back to the Hawthorns again. This time we lost 2–1 after taking the lead. I had to bunk off school for both of the away fixtures. The Brummie coppers were well OTT every time someone didn't mind their Ps and Qs. It was arm up the back, and off they were marched. The song that got most thrown out was: 'Oh I do like to be beside the seaside, Oh I do like to be beside the sea, Oh I do like to stroll along the prom, prom, prom, where the brass band plays fuck off – come on – West Brom...'

There was loads of fronting each other going back to the coaches both home and away, mainly handbags, and my mate Bami has a good story to tell:

Bami:

One of the lads had agreed to hire a Luton removal van for the trip to West Brom. We met up at the Bull & Royal pub at four-ish to be informed that the hire company were dropping it off, which they did well after six o'clock. Nearly 40 of the boys piled in the van after the papers were signed to a look of astonishment on the face of the woman who had driven it there from the leasing company. We knew it would be a struggle to get there for kick-off but the driver put his foot down and we made good time until we got stuck in a traffic jam – it was horrendous. I was up front with a couple of lads when we made a decision to pull off the motorway and go to Stoke, who were at home to Manchester City.

We parked up in a side street, quite near to the ground and let the lads out of the back who then began to notice fans walking past wearing either red-and-white or light-blue-and-white scarves. 'Where are we?' one lad asks.

'Stoke... we weren't going to make it.'

Anyway, we went to the game and there wasn't any fun and games to be had during the 90 minutes. After the match, there was just a little skirmish outside, not knowing who was who, and the police were on top.

Finally, we got back to the van, loaded up the troops and started to head home after a reasonably quiet night for us.

Driving back, I was sat in the front and half-an-hour in I was dying for a piss so I asked the driver to pull off at Knutsford Services – he did. Lo and behold, it was only full of Man City, so I let the lads out of the back and we made our way to the toilets, when the roar went up. City started running up the stairs and over the concourse. Being nosey cunts, we followed.

Arriving on the other side of the services, City are bang at it in the canteen with who we found out to be Tottenham – they were coming back from Man United. While this was going on, the light-fingered ones among City's lads have yanked up the security covers of the services' shop and were exiting with arms full of goodies. Not wanting to look a gift horse in the mouth, Preston lads joined in with the supermarket sweep. We then headed back over to the van, jumped in, banged down the shutter and away we went.

We'd done about two miles when blue flashing lights appeared in the mirror and we were pulled over on to the hard shoulder. A copper walked up to the rolled-down window and said, 'We believe you have been involved in an incident at Knutsford Services and we're placing everyone in the van under arrest. And we need to take a look in the back.'

Well, when the shutter came back up once again, stacked in between the lads were box after box of chocolate bars, toffees, crisps – City had had all the good stuff – a few boxes of cigars and one of the lads was sat there with his arm around a green 3ft fluffy owl that he'd nicked for his girlfriend! Talk about being caught red-handed! The police took a note of what was in the van and locked the shutters with everyone and everything in the back with a pair of handcuffs. This was so no one could unload any of the contraband, with our driver placed in a panda car and a copper having to drive the van to the station.

The van was reversed into the station yard and we were made to stand behind it while the OB opened the shutter. They then turned on the yard's floodlight, which was pointing to the back of the van. And when it rolled up, it looked like a scene from a rap video. A big plume of blue smoke curled out, and, when it finally cleared, there were lads sat with chocolate all over their faces – one complaining of toothache. They'd tried to smoke and eat the evidence with the rest of the gear being stuffed down the plywood panels in the back – apart from the cuddly toy.

We were then taken into the nick, processed, put in cells and later questioned. While this was happening, they had to call out someone to remove the panels in the back of the van for the rest of the stashed goodies.

In the morning, we started to get released but the police wouldn't let us have the van back; it was held as evidence. So most of us had to make our way to the train station, with the others trying to thumb a lift home.

And, if I remember correctly, there were only three people charged, one of those being the lad who considerately obtained his girlfriend a present from the service station!

My first football trip to the city paved with gold woke me up to the risks of entering other teams' manors without a firm behind me. One of the mates had booked four of us on a local pub coach to London. Not many other buses or modes of transport made the trip, leading to a very poor turnout – I wonder why? One of our four was a Chelsea fan on his first visit to Stamford Bridge and off he trotted round to the Shed while we went to the big semi-circular North Stand, the away end.

As we entered the North Stand, leaning against a wall was a small group of lads, definitely not Preston. You could tell they were Southerners, very different in dress compared to us scruffy Northerners. Their attention was drawn towards us, breaking out of their cockney rhyming-slang conversation. I was still only 15, but oozing with confidence after recent exploits, along with two relatively seasoned campaigners who were both just under 21, and not knowing what was about to happen. One lad, who was now staring our way had a black eye, a cut to his face and an arm in a sling – I think they'd played West Ham the week before – said, 'What's it like to come to Chelsea?' His mates were nodding, but blank looks from us three. 'Well, you're not fackin' going home, are ya!' He had a 'who wants it?' expression on his boat-race, lurching forward, with a lion's growl kicking in.

Another lad said, 'Cam on, you norvan mankies.'

On our toes, we scarpered, not bothering to ask what their problem was. We had eight big fuckers right up our arses, and didn't fancy being lambs to the slaughter. Down on to the terracing we spilled and it was one of the only times we were glad to see the Old Bill. We hadn't bearded the lions in their den, so why?

Slumped on a barrier, catching our breath, we were looking at each other not saying a word but knowing what a lucky escape we'd just had. There was no steward's inquiry into this one; we were well out of our depth. The Chelsea boys were stood at the back of the stand, a good 50 yards away, gloating – psychological torture going on. If we wanted to go for a piss or a pie, we knew what fate awaited us. The stuffing was well and truly knocked out of us without a blow thrown.

Then the team ran out to 'The Liquidator', and Chelsea were in full voice. Our attention was then drawn to the pitch, and we also noticed a couple of lads being dragged out of the Shed, putting up a bit of a fight. There were also a couple of camera crews not pointing towards the game but into the stands. We found out later they were filming a scene for the series *Minder*. Terry, a Fulham fan, has gone to the game because Fulham are away, and Arthur has come looking for him. This was when my first, but not last, film part was recorded.

The game petered out in a 1–1 draw. In the heart of the defence that day for Chelsea was a certain Mickey Droy, beard and all. What a beast of a man and player he was. He could have led Chelsea's Headhunters into battle on his own, such was his presence – a man mountain.

On leaving the ground, our next mission was to get back on the coach in one piece. Knowing our destination, hopefully it would be damage limitation. Heads down, hands in pockets, confidence drained, we tried mingling in with the 13,500 Chelsea, with the majority heading towards Fulham Broadway Tube station. The three of us were superglued together like the blind leading the blind when 'Hey up, lads, the coach is this way...' a deep northern accent bellowed across the road.

It was the organiser of the transport pointing which way to go. 'Oh, for fuck's sake...' I wished the ground would open up and swallow us sharpish because the cockneys around were taking note. We can count our blessings that we never got a dig or a boot up the arse. Carrying on walking, we focused on the cracks in the pavement with the odd glance up checking our route back.

Yes, we made it, and we were climbing up the steps on to the coach. I felt like a captain ascending the steps at Wembley to lift the FA Cup – 'relieved' wasn't the word. I plonked myself down into a seat with a totally drained body.

We started to head off home – the North – and I began to reflect to myself that the fun I'd recently been experiencing at the match was missing today. Did I need this sort of shit... as I drifted off into a deep sleep for the next three hours with my mind racing.

On awaking, spirits were raised as there was always Shrewsbury next week or Newcastle in a fortnight's time for some action. I didn't fancy a swift return to the capital against Orient for Preston's next away fixture.

I did, though, return to London that season – to Loftus Road, home of QPR or the 'Rs'. I was getting older but not necessarily wiser, and was with the two other musketeers once again. This time there was an air of anxiety, not cocksure like the last.

We arrived early after making good time on the same pub coach. The scarfers and the flask brigade went straight on to the half-developed ground – two sides had had seats installed, elevated over the existing terracing, a really weird sight. Us three rascals fancied a bit of a shufti about, so we went walkies.

On our travels we walked past the famous White City Greyhound Track in a stage of being knocked down. I suppose more high-rise flats were needed for the ever-growing London population. The area surrounding the track was already saturated with cold, eerie, concrete tenant blocks. This was a perfect location for an ambush, a nightmare place when getting chased, losing your way and getting trapped in dead ends.

The season before, when pulling away from the ground, a coach had come under attack getting the majority of its windows put through. Lads had jumped through shattered glass windows and the emergency door, trying to catch the perpetrators who disappeared quicker than they had appeared. A cold trip home was had with lads cursing through chattering teeth.

We'd reached a mini-Spaghetti Junction with smog rising and noise bouncing off all the man-made structures. There was hardly a blade of grass to be seen. In front of us was a large public house which we entered – and we were seemingly transported, TARDIS-fashion, to a Jamaican beach bar without the beach. We'd only taken a couple of steps inside when the bloke behind the bar shouted over, 'You boys will get a drink in the other side.'

Fifty pairs of brown eyes focused on us, we about-turned, doing as we were told, turning left into the other side. This side of the pub was full of geezers wearing QPR tops and scarves. We ordered three lagers and sat ourselves down at a table near the dartboard. Two pubs in Preston, the Bull & Royal and Red Lion, had similar clientele, but not to this extent – a South African apartheid feel, very surreal. We supped our pints slowly until the Rangers fans made a move, with us following suit, not wanting to outstay our welcome.

We paid to get on to the open away end, and once more Preston had a sparse, thinly spread following. 'I never felt more like singing the blues...' was being played over the Tannoy system. In with North End were a few QPR lads dotted about. They were whistling away to their song, letting each other know they were in, willing and waiting.

Preston never took a mob, or a firm, and I started wondering why I bothered travelling – just where were the rest of us?

Heading home on the coach later, I was mulling over if it was worth all the mileage just to watch a game. Of course it was! I'm following Preston North End, the best team the world has ever seen. Who needs trouble for a good day out anyway?

Back at home, and it's a night game against Sheffield Wednesday. Twenty or so of the boys, including me, were hanging around on the car park outside the ground when a lad came running up shouting, 'Wednesday's 'ere.' He'd spotted them at the junction of St George's and Deepdale Road making their way up, about equal numbers. We set off jogging down, unexpectedly bumping into them when level with the TA barracks. I got a wallop in the face off an Owl wearing a blue Sheffield Wednesday cagoule. So I threw one back into his. A toe-to-toe started, lasting a good two minutes before the police arrived to break it up.

Our young firm was now starting to hold their own against men! We were getting wiser by the game.

A game against Bolton was called off after downpours during the week and rain on Saturday morning. It didn't stop Bolton turning up and we never thought that a bit of rain would. Preston lads had also heard rumours that Bolton were coming en masse and didn't want to let the Trotters down.

Both sets of lads were well monitored walking round town until the pubs opened at 11am – thank God for all-day drinking nowadays. Little skirmishes were occurring in between, and around, shoppers when possible.

At the time, I got one of my biggest trophies, namely a small bloke aged about 25–30 with long black hair and a 'tash. Thinking he was really cool, always at the back of their mob, he kept glancing over his shoulder giving it, 'Come on then, boy.' Well, I did, putting him on his arse with a sweet one – up there for thinking, down there for dancing.

I saw a picture of him a few years later on the back page of a daily newspaper sat on his arse at an England game. Not quite the big trophy then, eh!

One bad note that day, Crookie and a Bolton lad got nicked for having a chat trying to set a meet for a drink. This ended up with Crookie getting sent down for that and other additional offences.

Recruiting leaflets were handed out in Bolton that day urging Wanderers fans to go to Preston as warriors. There were 11 arrests, some police assaulted and several lads ended up in Casualty after being slashed – courtesy of good old Woolies' DIY department. And there wasn't even a ball kicked in anger!

We didn't always have it our own way on our own turf. Against Chelsea, Preston had been moved twice early on, off two decent-sized Blues mobs, a case of boys against men. Preston finally moved the third one, dispersing them all over town.

Later, near the Spindlemakers Arms pub, some big geezers started bowling out, tooled up with pool cues, pool balls and glasses. Preston's main lads fronted them while others tried to get in different entrances around the public house to get behind them. More Chelsea kept piling out and a few Blackpool faces were noticed mixed in their firm – why? The reinforced, wired glass doors and windows got obliterated, pinning other Chelsea back in. The pub was under siege with North End pinning them in as they tried coming back out with more weapons. It didn't take long for the police to arrive, as Lawson Street Police Station is about 500 yards away, their presence scattering everyone.

I began doing the old 'I'm just walking past on me own' walk, when a panda car pulled on to the grass verge behind me, hitting its brakes. Glancing round, I saw a bizzie slam the car door into the back of a Preston lad's legs and he fell down on to his knees. I bet he was praying he wasn't going to get nicked – wrong! The cuffs were slammed on his wrists and I was away, quick march.

Our mob had been split up into tens and twenties who were making tracks towards Deepdale, with numbers building back up en route and small skirmishes on the streets. Most of the Preston lads headed towards the Fulwood Spion Kop to defend what was theirs, as it was still the days of taking ends.

Elli:

That day we had a few run-ins with different Chelsea mobs; some we moved, some moving us. This ended with a good toe-to-toe outside the Spindlemakers Arms before blue flashing lights turned up to put an end to it.

After a few lads from both Chelsea and Preston had been lifted, we made our way to the ground still on the prowl. We know it's the era of end-taking, so we head towards the Kop half-an-hour before kick-off to see if any Headhunters fancy their chances.

On arrival, behind the Kop, there was a bigger than normal police presence. They, Chelsea, really do fancy their chances today and the Old Bill must be on to it. 'Can you come with me, sonny? I need to ask you a few questions.' A copper then grips my arm, leading me round the corner to an awaiting bus which is already rammed with Preston lads.

'What's going on?' I'm asking the copper.

'A serious incident has happened and we need to ask you and the others a few questions down at the station.'

They quickly fill the bus and off we go to the nick with everyone on board not knowing what's gone on. As we head towards Preston Police Station, you could hear the clink-clank of assorted weapons being dropped on to the floor and pool balls running past feet.

The Preston lads I was with got in the ground and waited behind the turnstiles to see how many of us were left.

With five minutes gone, and all the remaining lads in, you could hear Chelsea singing above in the higher part of the Kop. Coming out of the lower tunnel, anticipation escalated with what numbers we might be about to face. Chelsea had taken a high position, bang in the middle of the Kop. 'You'll never move the Chelsea... You'll never move the Chelsea' was being chanted again and again. A mixture of shapes and sizes, numbering about 80–100 Chelsea fans, were beckoning us on. I remember one tall, blond long-haired bloke, arms outstretched, with his mane swishing side-to-side as he bounced up and down – yay, trendy cockneys.

Preston made a quick dash up the concrete steps, stopping just as they turned to wood. Chelsea had the advantage with higher ground, swaying backwards, forwards and left to right, like starlings going to roost. We gave it our best shot, shouting, 'Come on,' as we charged into no-man's land, windmilling through what coppers were there, trying to restrain both baying mobs.

Chelsea kept tight, backing us off time after time – it's always better to hold the upper part of the stand. Old Bill reinforcements arrived to help their colleagues out, eventually managing to move Chelsea down the stands and on to the perimeter cinder path before walking them to the away end. This wasn't without Preston launching a few digs in, helping them on their way. Every credit to Chelsea; it took help from the police to do what should have been our job. Round the pitch they went, arms aloft, to rapturous applause and chanting from the Chelsea fans on the away end.

That day I was with, in my eyes, Preston's top boy – I was serving my apprenticeship. He was really mad, muttering, 'Wait 'til after, just wait 'til after... they'll see.' For the next two hours, he was simmering and stewing.

Game over, score irrelevant – it was 1–0 to the Lilywhites, courtesy of Super Bruce. Out of the big blue gates we flowed into a sea of Chelsea boys, running down Deepdale Road towards the Sumners pub. We ended up on Blackpool Road, at the junction with Deepdale Road. 'Right... who wants it first?' Crookie shouted, rolling up his sleeves.

Chelsea stopped in their tracks with one big bloke fronting him. BANG! The big bloke went down and another soon followed, with Preston steaming in, outnumbered but putting on a game show. Within 30 seconds the cavalry arrived, the law on horseback, closely followed by the foot-patrol officers. Good job, as it was getting on top and it was every man for himself. Our one-man army, Crookie, dived into some bushes but a Mountie had spotted him. Crookie had the same curly hairstyle as David Bellamy, only slightly shaved up at the sides, so he'd have felt quite comfortable in the deepest jungle looking for new species. The long arm of the law reached into his hiding place, and pulled him up with a mass of curls in hand. The horse and copper on its back then trotted off to an awaiting meat wagon, with Crookie jogging at his side, and he was bundled into the back.

Sheer numbers that day had us playing hide-and-seek tactics following Chelsea back to the train station, having a pop when faced with similar-sized groups.

The young lads I ran with couldn't yet handle vast numbers. Our favourite ploy for picking groups off was to hang round in a chip shop near the station, not ordering anything, until you saw the boys in blue staring through the steamed-up windows. Next, a head would pop round the door with the all-too-familiar words: 'Move on or you'll be nicked...'

My mate H Butt also remembers Chelsea as a significant moment, saying, 'My first memories of aggro are when I was a 14-year-old on the Kop against Chelsea, half-an-hour before kick- off. Over 80 of their boys came on trying to take it with the older lads, doing well 'til the police waded in. I was hooked.'

Like him, I was finding my feet and trying to find my wings, ready to throw caution to the winds.

There's an extra little story to be told about that day, and it's a sad one. We played Chelsea on 28 February 1981, a day on which a Chelsea fan, Gary Blissett-Lee, slipped and plunged nearly 20ft to his death as a group of his friends watched in horror. The 23-year-old's mother was told of the tragedy as she watched Chelsea play North End at Deepdale. Police believe he was taking a shortcut back into town before going to the match when he lost his footing and fell into a market services area. By Monday, police enquiries into the incident were finished and there were no suspicious circumstances. A very sad day. RIP, Gary Blissett-Lee.

For the match away at Derby, we'd met up at Preston bus station after vans had been booked for the last away game of the season, but if I remember rightly it was cancelled due to a waterlogged pitch. Anyway, like I say, the vans had been booked, so, to make the most of the transport, the daily newspapers came out over brekkie to look for a game of local interest – and we decided on Wigan v Wimbledon.

After a few beers, we set off, parked up and made an entrance on to the Wigan end on the stroke of kick-off. Fifty of us walked round, right into the middle of where the Wigan fans had congregated, unveiling a Union Jack with 'PNE' in big white letters painted on it. This was followed by a few North End songs, a round of applause, end taken again – it's like shelling peas, full stop.

A big cheer went up from the few Wombles who'd made the trip. This was the season they started to make their climb up to Division One – what a dream. The Old Bill were really pissed off and started to remove us from the terracing around the pitch and out. A quick few quid down the drain but well worth it, I thought.

We were then stood outside milling about deciding what to do next with the Dons trying to kick the gates open to let us back in. But back to the vans we went, and for us it was day over – or so we thought.

As we drove off under a railway bridge, a train must have dislodged about 30 bricks on to the van's roof and through the windscreen of a car behind us. The brakes slammed on, and there was a mass exodus to see where they had really come from. There was a little crew of pie-eaters releasing Volume II from the top of the bridge and then on their little toes they went. Half of our lot were after them, the other half got back into the transport trying to get further down the line via the warrens of roads in Wigan.

All of a sudden, we ground to another swift halt. This time it was the plod that were blocking our way in a Black Maria. There was a Luton van in front of us and the lads in the back of it were not able to see exactly what was going on. Plus, the roller shutter couldn't be pulled up from the inside so a couple of PCs helped it on its way. Up it rattled and a few lads had got presents ready for Wigan above their heads, and were about to release them. The would-be donors got a good whack across the shins for their troubles, with others hiding tools and blades between their arse-cheeks. What a scene! We were pissing ourselves sat in the van parked up behind.

When we were being escorted to the local nick, we could see Preston lads who'd been trying to find the pie-heads appearing, and disappearing, on street corners.

We were then banged up about ten to a cell and a sergeant entered ours with a face like thunder asking for our names, addresses and whether we had been in trouble before, jotting down all the given details. Some yes, some no, and then he got to a scooter lad called John, who had a terrible stammer. 'Have you been in trouble before, sonny?'

'Y-y-y-y-ye-ye-ye-ye-yes, s-s-sarge.'

'What for?' he barked.

'F-f-f-for assault on a P-P-PC.'

'You hit a bobby!'

'Y-y-y-yes.'

'You shit-house, you little shit-house, you good for nothing shit-house...'

We're trying to hold it together like the Biggus Dickus scene in *The Life of Brian.*

Sarge gone, we literally pissed ourselves laughing. It must have been his favourite word, 'shit-house', because if I'd a dollar for every time I heard it, as he went cell to cell, I would have been a rich man.

A couple of hours passed – they must have been checking us all out. Smelly farts, beer belches and last night's takeaways started making an appearance when the Sarge came back. 'Right, you shit-houses, get out of my town and don't come back shit-housing here ever again, now.'

Rapidly we left, jumped into the vans and off we went to Preston for the rest of the night with tales to tell for any listening ears.

Two games, one match seen for five minutes, banged up and the sound of 'shit-house' rattling round in our empty heads. Just another normal day out with the lads!

The 1981/82 season heralded Preston's worst era ever – we were in freefall. Tommy – The Doc – Docherty was one of three managers that year at the helm of the sinking ship, then Alan Kelly on a caretaker basis, before Gordon Lee was appointed.

Preston North End's centenary year saw them rock bottom at the turn of the year, before eventually finishing 14th with really no game that season worth a mention. But I did have the pleasure of meeting the 6:57 crew for the first time at Preston's first home game of season. I'd heard about their reputation and just how violent they were off the older lads – they'd had quite a few run-ins with them over the years.

Some of Preston's lads were up early, being out and about around ten-ish; these lads must have shit the bed. One of them had seen Portsmouth arrive early doors. We'd got a tight, committed 30 out but a bigger force was to be met.

After having a look round town, we made our way past Preston Prison, turning left on to Deepdale Road, then, at the time, past the boarded-up Robert Peel pub (now Finney's Sports Bar), and then a couple of lads came into view on the horizon. Then a few more. 30... 60... nearly 100 Pompey lads appeared on Meadow Street. They spotted our meagre 30 who gave it the usual, 'Don't run, stand!'

Now in full stride, the 6:57 were rolling towards us and, within striking distance, the arses of over half of Preston's 30 went – this left us with about a dozen to hold the line. The fastest sprinters among the Hampshire boys got the odd punch in, we retaliated, and then away we went, but there was far too big a number to handle. Preston had to back-pedal; with sheer numbers stacked against us, we were on our pinkies.

This went on, stopping and starting, all the way back into town.

We found ourselves opposite Fine Fare, a motorbike shop these days on some wasteland, now a car park, and bricks are launched into the baying Portsmouth mob, which consisted of different ages and various clothing styles, some still in shirts and ties from the night before. Preston held them for a good few minutes until the police arrived.

You know when you've met a firm that has got it organised. For us, it was a wake-up call and we'd definitely smelled the coffee. We had to get our act together as Portsmouth were an A1 class act. Come to think of it, they might have been stopping in Blackpool, so they might not have been that early to rise! We'd been well and truly rolled by the 6:57 – every credit.

In contrast with our encounter with the 6:57 crew, a night game at Huddersfield (which is just over an hour away from Preston) became one of our better nights on and off the pitch.

Wolfie, a mate, and me went for a scout about and noticed a pub on Leeds Road near the ground. On entering it, we got clocked straight away. The door had creaky hinges and a noisy latch that clicked when opened; heads turned and eyes were locked in on us – we all did it when anyone entered a boozer near a ground. Shit, it was full of big bruisers and we were halfway in. Autopilot had now kicked in as if we knew the layout of the pub and we moved towards the bar. 'It's o'rite, I know 'em,' a lad standing with the group said in a Yorkshire accent.

Exactly why he said that, I haven't a clue. Either he felt sorry for us two youths or needed a trip to Specsavers. Wolfie led the way heading towards the toilet sign. There was a short corridor and, noticing an emergency exit, we knew it was time to leave. We didn't want the aforesaid saviour to reach into the inside pocket of his donkey jacket and pull out his specs or outstay our welcome, so we booted the door open and leaped over a wall.

'Close shave there, mate!' I said.

'Yeah, let's get back to the lads,' Wolfie replied.

We found out that the lads had been herded on to the away end and we hurriedly joined them, not fancying a few right hooks and a pummelling on a cold, wet night.

Alex Bruce (2 goals) and Steve Elliott (1) gave North End a 3–2 win in an end-to-end game.

We came out into the shadows thrown down off the floodlights behind the Cow Shed Stand, and had a big toe-to-toe in the car park with rough-looking blokes. Other small mobs clashed until order was restored by the police, who sent us on our way back to Lancashire.

Come to think of it, why on earth I used the phrase 'close shave' to Wolfie is beyond me. By 15, he had a 'tash that a German biker would have been proud of. And in his late teens, his mush had more hair on it than Grizzly Adams and his bear put together and he also had a mop of hair like Brian May out of Queen. Just to let you know, he's now as bald as a coot.

Another encounter I remember was when I was coming off the bus station in Preston one day with some mates and there was a big mob of Carlisle outside the Moonraker pub. They were shortly met by an equal set of Preston that came up the street behind them and a good clash was had.

Later on, I was in some toilets which used to be in the middle of Church Street. After dodging traffic to enter them, you'd go down 30-odd steps into Victorian surroundings. I was just getting a load off my mind – having a shit – when it went off again above me. I heard the roar, wiped my arse, pulled up the strides while on the move and, by the time I'd hit the last step, it was all over with the police having showed.

We then followed the tight escort up to the ground, although with no chance of anything happening.

Entering the West Stand seating, we found a few Carlisle in, and soon dispatched them with a good kicking towards the sanctuary of the police.

We'd been sitting down watching the game for five minutes when another ten or so Carlisle came up the stairs, scanning round, not knowing the surroundings or if they were in the right section. They never did manage to take their seats as Preston steamed right into them, giving them a right slapping. Lads were diving over each other to get a dig in, hitting each other more than Carlisle. I remember two of them were thrown over the barrier down into the terracing below, followed by their mates like lemmings off a cliff.

Bami also remembers our brush with Carlisle:

Bami:

My brother decided to come with me one Saturday, as he'd never been to a PNE game or any match, come to think of it. He was more into his women, clothes and his looks, a 'wannabe' part-time model.

Anyway, we bumped into this mob of Carlisle outside

the Moonraker pub and it went off. I start battling and our kid is at the side of me when a lad whacks him. He's then leaning backwards throwing punches which aren't connecting, trying to keep the lad at bay. The Carlisle lad had slugged him right in the kipper, and our kid's shouting, 'Not the face... not the face!'

The police arrive, putting a stop to the fighting, and our kid heads home with a bruised mush, not even bothering going on the game.

That night, when I saw him out, he said, 'Never again.'

The opening game of the 1982/83 season against Millwall at home was watched by a crowd of 4,483, summing up what Preston fans felt about where their club was heading. A local sports writer mentioned something along the lines of: 'If the thousands of Preston fans watching TV or shopping had bothered to come, they would have been treated to an entertaining match with more goal-scoring chances than I have ever previously seen...' I wish I could remember the game.

Preston won the match 3–2; they then went on to win only 3 in the next 17 games. Preston's bit of glory this season was progressing to the third round of the FA Cup where they went out 3–0 against the mighty Leeds. Even Super Bruce moved on to pastures new – our near neighbours Wigan. North End's final league position was 16th.

But, although our future wasn't particularly sunny, the weather was fucking sweltering for the first game of the season. It was well into the nineties, and we'd been standing outside various pubs along Meadow Street, like the Army & Navy and the Royal Consort, soaking up the rays, drinking ice-cold lager. Could life get any better?

A few of us made a move up towards Deepdale, walking and chatting leisurely about the feared Millwall, while wiping our brows in the sweltering heat. What I didn't realise was that shortly I would get my first proper introduction to the Londoners.

We'd just drawn level with Preston bus depot, as a single-decker, blue-and-white corporation bus pulled slowly past us. 'Miiiiilll-waaaaaallllll... Up the Lions!' was shouted out of a pulled-back window in a cockney accent.

Glancing up, I noticed a lad, bizarrely with a sheepskin coat on, giving it plenty out of the window with other faces pressed up against the glass, growling at us. The traffic lights were 50 yards up ahead and turning to red. So, not wasting any time, we jogged up alongside the bus, beckoning the Millwall lads off. Sheepy had a girl with him – a geezer bird – and half-a-dozen mates, making it equal numbers, only we didn't have a girl in tow. They pressed the emergency button and bounced right off into us. I think a couple of Preston lads did one, but I was too preoccupied at the time to realise.

I was brawling away with one of the Millwall boys when – SLAM! – I've been hit round the back of the head with what felt like a sledgehammer. I was fumbling about in a dazed state when – BANG! – down I went, but not out. It's quite obvious Millwall must have been stopping over in Blackpool that weekend and were testing their skills out for the funfair's first prize later on.

Now looking up from my position on the pavement, I noticed a lad standing over me with an orange-and-white sand-filled traffic cone. Once more, he brought it down towards my face. I spun quickly to my left, his cone missing the target and bouncing free from his grip. Thank God for that, as it would have spoiled my boyish good looks! Weapon gone, he went to work, pogo'ing on my head. He must have been playing the Clash's 'White Riot' on his Walkman that day, as he really went to town enjoying himself at my expense. He had more moves than John Travolta. His contoured face had an evil grin etched on it as I caught a glance through my fingers, trying to protect myself. Bells began ringing both in my head and from an advancing cop car. The Millwall lads did one.

Parky, a mate who'd also been wrestling with a Lion, was picking me up with the widest grin I'd ever seen on his boat-race.

'What the fuck's so funny?' I asked, struggling to get to my feet.

'You've got an imprint on your forehead. And it looks like it'ssss...a size-nine Kicker boot.'

He let go of my arm and I fell back down on to the flagstones which you could fry an egg on, which caused Parky to nearly piss himself laughing.

I had a headache for days on end, to add to the strange looks I received at the match and around town that night. I love Kicker shoes, but every time I see the sole and tread of one, it brings back such bad memories.

I think these lyrics by Generation X sum up the day: 'So let's sink another drink, 'cause it'll give me time to think... I was dancing with myself!'

Pia:

We'd arrived at Leeds in vans, and parked up a walk away from Elland Road. Just after leaving our transport, we found out, round a corner, that we'd a welcoming committee on a grass verge waiting. It went off straight away with nearly 100 a side. In less than a minute, it was broken up by the police with us being escorted to the ground. We didn't even have time for a pint before the match in Leeds territory.

Now inside the ground, we're stood on a terrace, kicking our heels when the seats behind us start to fill up. Just before kick-off, Leeds lads start to jump down into the Preston enclosure – Leeds having the balls to do so. Preston were giving them a right whacking because they weren't doing it in decent numbers.

Just after the whistle for start of play, a big skinhead sky-dived in and I found myself one-on-one with him. Next thing I know, I hit the ground, not from a punch which makes a change, but two Old Bill who have dived on us to break up the fight. We're both nicked, cuffed and dragged on to the perimeter of the pitch. They'd a habit at Leeds that, when you were arrested on the game, they would take you off backwards. When I passed the Gelderd End, backwards, one of the two coppers linking arms with me says in a deep Yorkshire accent, 'Can you run, sonny?'

'Why?' I reply.

'You'll soon find out.'

The two dibble break into a jog with me struggling to keep on my feet. It was like being in the stocks with pies, bottles of pop and hot Bovril being thrown at the three of us. I later found out in the cells that Leeds hate the local coppers nearly as much as the away fans.

A little later, any lads that had been arrested were let out of their cells and lined up against a wall with a few words dished out by an inspector, before being put into an awaiting meat wagon. My Leeds skinhead mate gave the aforesaid inspector a piece of his mind and what he thought of him... he regretted it! We were taken to a police station a good five or six miles away, processed, details taken and released just after six in the evening following being charged.

I come out of the station to find the big, lumpy bonehead I'd been rolling about with stood at a bus stop. His hand comes out and shakes mine with respect given both ways. He tells me, 'You can catch the bus back into Leeds and I'm heading that way.'

On the journey back to the city centre, he informs me that his girlfriend will give him a load of grief later because he's meant to be back home in Bradford for six o'clock. The local skins had arranged to attack a mosque which she'd be missing out on. It takes all sorts.

Arriving in Leeds city centre, we both disembark the bus near the train station which still has a couple of hundred Leeds lads milling about. Surely the Preston who'd come on the train have gone home by now. The mine of information I'm with informs me that they're waiting for Chelsea after their game at Huddersfield earlier in the day.

Right on cue, Chelsea spill out of the train station even though there is a large police presence in attendance, and it goes off big time. Super skinhead flies in once more, not into a Chelsea fan but right on to the back of a copper trying to contain order, and starts hitting him like mad in the back of the head. I've had enough of my 'Made in Britain' mate, so I sidestep the trouble and do one for home sharpish.

Like Pia explained, it had gone badly wrong before the match with us ending up in the ground early. By kick-off time, I'd clocked a group of dressers of various ages in the middle of the away end. We'd soon sussed that they weren't Preston as you'd usually know a face, plus we could smell a rat. A few of us slowly squeezed our way through the packed terracing not wanting to raise suspicion, an element of surprise wanted. Just before arriving at our destination, Leeds scored and one lad who'd been sitting on a crush barrier, wearing a deer-stalker hat, leaped into the air. A big surge occurred with fists windmilling into the Leeds boys. Preston attacked, moving them down to the front fencing and out they went after a copper quickly opened a gate for them. Brave but not brave enough.

The other thing which pissed Preston fans off that day was a Union Jack flag with 'Leeds Whites of Preston', or words to that effect, hanging over the hoardings. The lads behind the flag goaded the travelling Preston fans with 'V' and 'wanker' signs throughout the match.

At a subsequent home match against Doncaster, four of us had decided to go on the Town End at Preston which was the away end at the time. We'd watched what type of Doncaster fans had arrived and, fancying our chances, if any dancing was to be had, we paid our money to take up the challenge, and in we went. Four young lads against fifty; what were we thinking? We split into pairs and mingled in between groups of Rovers fans waiting for the kick-off. The idea was that, if someone scored, a row would break out and, if the coppers waded in, you'd make out that you'd accidentally ended up in the wrong end!

Well, the referee had his whistle in his mouth, ready to blow for the start of play, and on to the wooden stand came another 50 Donny. These were the biggest miners you would ever see this side of the Pennines, complete with NCB donkey jackets from the local pit. Within minutes, we were sussed as young fresh-faced wannabe trendies. We did a Speedy Gonzales dash to the no-man's land section which split the Town End into two. A steward opened the gate, once we'd rapidly told him that we'd made a mistake – a massive one – about which end we'd come on. This time it was us who were not brave enough.

In the safety of the home section with pointed fingers and verbal being thrown our way, we were holding our stomachs, openly laughing at them, giving it large. The funny thing was, we'd made arrangements to meet a fifth lad there who'd gone for a hairdresser's appointment. We noticed him walking on behind the motley Yorkshire crew with his newly cut, mushroom flick-head. A few Donny gave him the same attention they'd given us. He got out by the skin of his teeth with an AirWair up his arse. 'I thought you were meeting me on the away end,' he said. We soon explained to him why we'd scarpered.

Through the fencing, arrangements were made for a meet after the game when we'd got the rest of the lads together who were sat in the seats to the left of the Doncaster mob. And, with ten minutes to go, the exit gates opened, supposedly for PNE fans to get out early to avoid the rush of the large crowds at the final whistle. Why I really think that they did that was for blokes to buy *The Pink Football Post*, have their tea and be out for six o'clock to drown their sorrows. The opening of the gates was also used by local Asians, boys who hadn't managed to nick on, lads meeting their mates and sometimes away fans charging on the opposite way. But there wouldn't be many sorrows drowned that day – North End had won 4–1.

We exited to go down the alleyway behind the stand, dodging dirty, black puddles in the divoted, cinder-ash path. You don't want to ruin your sparkling, white Adidas or Nike trainers, do you?

On the way down the ginnel, two pissed-up blokes tagged along wanting a ruck after receiving some bad news. I don't think they'd been to the match but were just out for a bit of trouble, us not knowing them from Adam.

I would have loved a mobile that day because coming our way, filling the opposite end, were the Doncaster boys, some the size of local coal slags. We knew that us boys just out of nappies in the hooligan stakes and tipping the scales just the other side of 10st really didn't stand a chance. Being outnumbered about 5:1, we gave the old 'Well, come on then' arms outstretched, making sure we kept at a safe distance, and then on our toes, now not bothering about the puddles.

We knew the score and we weren't going to move them, but our new-found friends, the drunks, didn't; we had decided that a longer trip around the ground to rally the troops was required. I think they'd have woken up the next day with more than a sore head from alcohol.

We were about to go back to help out when we noticed the Old Bill behind the Doncaster, coming to the Preston blokes' rescue. By now, having been noticed at the match on a regular basis by certain police officers, we weren't waiting round to get our collars felt.

We jogged round and up into the seats to get the lads out only to find the coppers pushing the Rovers on to their awaiting coaches. A few one-on-ones were in evidence, with Preston lads getting nicked. Valuable lessons were being learned by us upstarts for new challenges ahead.

I remember once going to a night match at Doncaster, arriving nearly into the second half after one of the cars in our party had broken down en route. After coming out at the end of the match, there was a bit of a stand-off between us and the

Donny lads. The Old Bill forced us Preston lads back to our transport by drawing their batons. A good mate of mine, Kirky ('I'm a lover, not a fighter'), received a right good slap around the face by a leather glove! I think he was giving them facts about what the miners were going through during the national strike. He'd a red hand-mark across his face that any Ulsterman would have been proud of, all the way home. We did, though, break down once more on a petrol station forecourt. Luckily, an AA man – what a very nice man – was also filling up and we'd a whip-round sorted. And I can still remember the ones who didn't chip in to this day. You know who you are!

Then we had a chance to face up to the 6:57 again. And just as I thought Preston were beginning to see daylight, it was more a case of, in the cold light of day, we need to wake up! We'd a few more out this time but, as usual, we weren't mobbed when we spotted Portsmouth in the Black-a-Moor Head boozer; they clocked us before we could get sorted. I would have given my right arm to have a firm like theirs and I nearly did. As they bowled out of the pub, we squared up. I threw a fist out, putting one's shoulder to the wheel, only for a Portsmouth lad to duck sideways, grabbing me by the arm. He was wildly trying to pull it out of its socket, and I just managed to break free before it got broken or ripped off.

The 6:57, having the numbers, started moving us back along Lancaster Road towards Preston's Guildhall, with them gaining the upper hand. On glancing back, the said lad was stood with his arms akimbo, having failed to wrench his caveman's meat feast breakfast from my torso.

We were trying to get our act together, catching a breather, with one lad jogging up to the Red Lion pub for reinforcements, believing more hands make light work. Although if we're talking about hands, then the saying about the left hand not knowing what the right hand is doing probably better describes Preston's firm. We had our hands full that day and we knew it.

The 6:57 were dab hands at coming to town early and taking the piss, with us just pissing in the wind. You have to hand it to Pompey as their firm was a right handful. What we needed to do was mobilise bigger numbers and have close hand-to-hand combat. That said, I've got to hold my hand up and say that Portsmouth were a top firm, with Preston on a wing and a prayer.

We turned up towards the bus station and more Preston were slowly joining us. It should have been pronto, with it being a race against the clock to get back round to the Black-a-Moor Head. We weren't throwing our hand in yet, but the arrival of the Old Bill meant that Preston had to split into small splinter-pockets to avoid being detected.

Now thinking Pompey were pinned in the alehouse, we started to make our way to Meadow Street. But they weren't pinned down, as some older Hampshire lads had managed to escape the police's clutches. Our half-a-dozen beckoned them over, going through the bus station, where we'd have been out of the sight of the Old Bill if Portsmouth were to follow. It worked and they played right into our hands – or so we thought. These huge grizzlies came through the glass sliding doors, not wanting to catch a number eight bus. 'Cam on, you norvern wankers!' These blokes definitely wanted some action.

I was with Bami, as I had been on many occasions. He steamed right in, fists flying, with the Pompey lads meaning business, slugging back. Into the fray we went – in for a penny, in for a pound.

Bami:

I'd run over and started scrapping with this big mush who'd black, curly hair, a chunky, mustard jumper on with a thick gold chain hanging out. I thought that I'd keep my eye on that; it might find its way into my hand during the action.

We're battling away as more Portsmouth arrive on the scene. Somehow, I've ended up behind the Pompey lad, trying to pull him backwards and down. I seem to be the first one that the new arrivals pay special attention to and I end up being punched silly while staggering about, as my mates try and help me. Eventually, the police sirens are heard – not by me – and everyone leaves the scene, pronto. My nose has well and truly been smashed all over my face with my light-blue cagoule that I was wearing now a deep red.

I can't remember what pub the lads took me to to get cleaned up, but it was day over and I didn't make the match.

After cleaning Bami up in the Red Lion, we made a move with the police being on top and we didn't see any 6:57 en route to the ground after a shufti about.

Having paid to get into the seats next to the away end, one lad said, 'Sounds noisy up there. There must be plenty of Preston on today.'

I was thinking, 'Where were they earlier to give us a hand?'

We skipped up the stairs to be greeted by two sections full of Pompey with a sparse spreading of Old Bill keeping them in check. What a nightmare! The only luck we'd had was that the stairs came up the middle of the two groups so we only had to run the gauntlet past one of them – phew. Turning left sharpish, we tried to get into no-man's land between Portsmouth and our Preston mates. It was a free-for-all with fists and sneakers raining down on to our ears, eyes, noses, mouths, jaws, cheeks, chests, guts, kidneys and livers! It was the longest ten seconds of my life, apart from the odd time against Millwall. The dozen of us never stood a chance, moving along making sure all and sundry could have a dig. We'd entered the tunnel of death which was scarier than the haunted house in Blackpool. Our arms and hands were used for protection rather than to inflict any sort of return attack. We finally got through what I can only describe as a conveyer belt in a hooligan factory, not yet the final package, miraculously with no lasting injuries. We'd been well and truly kicked from pillar to post. Right then, 'Come on!'

We had a go back, trying to launch into the nearest Pompey, only for both sets to be batoned back by the ever-growing police presence. Us going towards the 50 or so Preston lads, and Portsmouth, a good 150-plus, giving us a slow hand clap... or was it a round of applause?

Looking down at my Pringle jumper, it would now fit two heads through the V-neck and it felt like I'd two. Oh well, I'd still got my gold belcher chain intact which was some small compensation.

All through the game, both sets baited each other with two thin blue lines of coppers and two empty sections keeping us apart – they needed it. What was strange was that the Old Bill let three of us go to the back into no-man's land, and three 6:57 as well, during half-time. It was no good kicking off, it being a cert you'd get lifted. Just a chat was had, us giving out respect for their firm, them to our game little show. One lad told me my Pringle jumper was as hard to get as rocking-horse shit round Portsmouth. This led me to think, 'What about what you've just done to mine?'

I remember one Pompey lad who was dressed far differently

– big gold earrings, a brown suede jacket and Aquascutum shirt. Give us Northerners another year and we would catch up, apart from the gypsy earrings. We were trying to sort things out for later when an inspector pointed up towards us and sent a couple of coppers to break up our little rendezvous.

The game ended 0–0, with Portsmouth more intent on making their way over the wooden seats rather than the long trek home. The police were concentrating on holding them back, leaving only a couple to watch Preston.

So, left to their own devices, Preston began a bit of woodwork and dismantling. They weren't proper wooden seats, more like benches and, underneath, between what you sat on and the filthy floor, ran a piece of four-by-one with seat numbers painted on. Now I've been back-heeled a few times and so had a few ugly fuckers that I knocked round with, so they're thinking it's about time that they put theirs to use. The lads went to work smashing up lengths of timber, finding row 12, seats 30, 31, 32 and 33 between hands, and mounting a charge. It looked like a mixture of a re-enactment of *Braveheart*, Saint George going for the slay and Luke Skywalker with his light sabre all rolled into one. Various lengths of wood were held aloft between a foot and eight-foot long, then crashed down on heads, prodded into bodies like knights jousting or thrown Zulu spear-style. Portsmouth caught on quick and attention from the police soon turned towards Preston, with them showing off what a real piece of lathed hardwood looked and felt like. It took a few minutes for the law to regain order with both mobs being forced back along the stands and out of the ground.

The police were in complete control outside with dogs and horses taking Portsmouth, wrapped up tightly, to the train station and home.

Portsmouth went on to win the league that season, leading to the kick-start of their reign of terror on bigger and better mobs when they rolled into town. We never had the pleasure of playing Pompey for some considerable time but elephants never forget and, by the time we do, most of the lads are the size of elephants, or bigger.

And talking of elephants – or, at least, thinking about who ate all the pies – Wigan didn't show in any numbers on New Year's Day at Deepdale. If they did, they must have sneaked in or I was still hungover. Preston had a good turnout with loads of new tops and jumpers on show. Also it was North End's best result of the season on the pitch that day, a 4–1 home win. This sent everyone home happy for the forthcoming year and hopefully Preston were back to winning ways. Or not!

Survival complete, it was Wigan away in glorious sunshine for the last game of the season. We had an early drink in a mate's pub, setting off about ten-ish to avoid any unwanted attention. We stopped off en route in Leyland and Chorley, other lads' cars and vans joining, and we'd got ourselves a convoy – rubber duck. Elli, the van man, brought some surgical masks and a couple of gowns, with doctor and nurses games being played in the back of the van. Operation that day was: smash Wigan up... and it was Wigan, here we come, for the end-of-season knees-up.

Arriving undetected, we parked the white van up, our role-playing changing to unbalanced nutcases while falling out of the van's back doors. On the move, still larking about, it was party time and we stumbled across the White Heart, White Horse or White whatever, just opening right on cue for the boys. Mr Landlord greeted our 20 with: 'What can I get you, lads?' We were shortly followed by another 150 North End loonies.

His joyful facial expression quickly turned to one of an anxiety-riddled, slapped kipper. He'd only got one barmaid on, so he shouted up to the missus to give him a hand. The boozer was rammed to the rafters, swaying like a crowd at the match and lads were waving £5s, £10s and £20s in the air gagging for a bevy. We were eventually served, standing to one side, admiring Preston's turnout.

I'd noticed the till on the bar near the door with a bit of wrought iron round it. And every time the keys on the till were pressed after an order, a bulging wad came into view like a jack-in-the-box. It wasn't long before its contents were emptied and off someone went.

Outside, we were catching a few rays, having the end-of-season banter with Preston's numbers swelling to 200-plus. There's no way that Wigan would move Preston that day. Little packs of pie-heads were spotted taking a scout then vaporising into Saturday shoppers after seeing an unknown 200-plus, sun-soaked faces. A decision was then made to break up into splinter groups to go on walkabout into different pubs for a gander. There were only a couple of coppers keeping a distant eye on Preston's base and the singing also started: 'Wigan, where are you? Wigan, where are you?'

It was time to move on. Our mob left first, passing bewildered shoppers, gawping at the sight of 20 lads with face-masks on as though the black plague had broken out in Wigan. There must have been some Wigan out to defend their town and serious faces were soon put on with masks being put in bins – dropping them on the floor would result in an instant fine nowadays. It was a good walk to Springfield with plenty of alcohol outlets on the way and it was thirsty work in the heat, so plenty of alehouses were visited. There were a few little scuffles over the next two hours, but nothing major.

Finally, we made the game and paid to get on to a packed away end with Preston already rowing with the coppers. Groups of Preston were being taken off the Wigan end and smoke bombs started flying through the air, leading to mounted horses being deployed into the crowd. Lads galore were getting lifted and thrown out, with Rambie on *Look Northwest*, and *Granada Reports*, on Monday night. He was on the box that much he'd have to apply for his equity card next.

I found myself taking time out for a sweaty, greasy, excuse of a burger, because I'd been informed, 'Sorry, luv, there's no pies left!'

Leaning up against a wall, I surveyed the riotous scene going on all around Springfield Park and it was total chaos. Finishing up the vile thing, I wiped my face with a serviette, and the horrible excuse for a burger came back into the fray! It was the only solids I had had that day. Tell a lie, I went back for another one – I must have been a glutton for punishment. It was hungry work, this hoolie lark.

Alan Gowling scored the winner, signalling a final attack on the Old Bill and Wigan. And just before full-time, the gates were booted open and out we went. The lads were well up for it today.

C:

We make our way down towards a petrol station after leaving Springfield, and mob up with the rest of the lads before setting off into town. As we move off, a Wigan lad is grabbed hold of and asked politely, 'Where the fuck's your boys?'

'I don't know.'

'Well go and fuckin' get them, quickly.'

The pace is slowing down heading towards the town centre when a bizzie car slowly cruises past, and some idiot throws a brick at it. Day over. Within minutes, cop bikes, cars and vans have surrounded us and it's all gone pear-shaped. They take us all back towards our transport and escort us out of town. It's back to Preston on the piss with a good end to another shit season.

11

WHO YOU LAUGHING AT?

Rome wasn't built, nor did the walls of Jericho fall, in one day. The apprenticeship was over, and with no line of command – it was down to a simple question: who's gamer than game? – and it was full steam ahead. The night before a match would be spent tossing and turning, thinking about what encounters lay ahead. When they came, the adrenalin would pump and the hairs on the back of the neck stood to attention. My life was now summed up in the phrase: 'Come on, let's 'ave it!'

In the 1983/84 season, attendances were dire, averaging 4,571, and, with only 1 win in the first 15 games following 8 successive defeats, Gordon Lee was off. Alan Kelly was once more appointed caretaker, and we had a bit of a run in the League Cup, and bombed out of the FA Cup in the first round at the hands of Scunthorpe.

Preston's most memorable game that season was beating the same Scunthorpe team in the league away from home 5–1, with Ian – Beefy – Botham getting sliced to pieces.

And I remember that season the possibility of being on the

receiving end of a slicing myself when we met Tranmere. I was disembarking a council bus at our lovely lump of concrete, piss-smelling, sick-stained bus station. For once, I managed to dodge someone tapping you for ten pence 'for a cup of tea' – I don't think so.

It was about five-ish and I clocked a lad who I used to go to school with. He was outside the Bucky bingo hall but he wasn't waiting for eyes down. He was stood with a couple of others, so I made my way over, as I noticed a mob of about 30 lads walking towards them past a nightclub called the Piper. I vaulted over the fence and just managed to get to the eight or so Preston lads, two of them snapping 3ft aerials off parked cars. Up went the familiar 'Come on then, la'', in a Scouse accent. Before I could blink an eyelid, about 6ft away there were 30 lads and one had a blade out. The aerials were now used as whips and their numbers moved us, plus no one wanted to get cut up.

We headed towards the Red Lion pub as fast as our legs would take us, over a little park; one lad went down over a hump in the grass. Stumbling over, he went into a forward roll, and then sprang back up and was off – maximum tens on the score card. We passed the Guildhall and round the corner we went and more troops were rallied. It was about even numbers now, so we bounced back for a pop. Shit! They've been collared by the plod – fair play for catching us off guard, though.

The police moved them past the Parish Church on Church Street with Preston lads monitoring them on the other side of the road. One Tranmere lad was hanging back trying to communicate with Preston, giving it large. I darted across the road and started running tight to the church wall. He'd got a dodgy eye like Clarence the Lion, and hadn't noticed me. I was in full flight, just about to 'surprise, surprise' him as he had a bigger gob than his Merseyside counterpart Cilla Black, when he got a shout, 'Watch your back, Charlie!' This also prompted a copper to turn round, looking in my direction. He gave it quick feet back to his mates and into the escort. I had to do a sharp right down a cobbled ally that leads to the Warehouse nightclub, nearly breaking my ankles.

After the match, they got put in another tight escort, and were taken without any more action to the train station. No joy that night, but there was always the away leg two weeks later. And while I looked forward to meeting up with the Scousers again, I found out that actually I hadn't met the 'Scousers' at all! I was educated, while being thrown around in the back of the van, that Tranmere's lads weren't Scousers but 'Birkenheaders' from the Wirral, the other side of the river Mersey.

We were approaching Prenton Park, the adrenalin was kicking in and, for a change, we had clear heads, after only a couple of beers had been sunk before setting off. You've got to have your wits about you when you could end up looking like a patchwork quilt. I've read both Blue and Red lads' stories, saying that the majority of the lads didn't use blades – really? I can only believe their word on that. I was never one for carrying a blade but I knew one or two Preston lads might have. Maybe for self-defence?

Our mob were fresh-faced Casuals, no one older than their early twenties, so looks mattered if you wanted to find a nice lady. A pink or white scar across the boat-race – no thanks. It never entered our minds that broken noses, missing teeth or half an ear actually spoiled your looks; it seemed to be accepted among us, the norm. We were prepared for the worst!

Parking up, we decided to go for a little mooch around, keeping it tight, our 30 or so. A short walk was undertaken to the ground with no scallies found. We then rounded the corner behind the old

Everton Stand, and a good bunch of urchins were lying in wait; they were trying to mingle in with fans queuing up at turnstiles; Mr Inconspicuous they were not. The best form of defence is attack, and in one quick hit we steamed into them. 'Come on, you Scouse twats!' We'd forgotten already – what goldfish!

As the song goes: 'You can keep your cathedral, and your pier head, we are not Scousers, we're from Birkenhead!'

It worked though, and we moved them with a few slaps being dished out. We were now met with an assortment of blades with Tranmere on the back foot. There was more steel pulled out than in any knife-amnesty bin around the country. One Birkenheader even pulled out a sharpened-up paint scraper – he must have been well into his DIY. Needless to say, it stopped us in our tracks. The roar had also attracted the bizzies with Dixon of Dock Green leading the charge before any of their armoury could be tested out.

Once in the ground, we were in the lower part of the stand, and it was standing room only. Tranmere were in the seats behind us with threat after threat being thrown our way while the game was going on and how they were going to 'cut us up'.

After the final whistle, the police kindly escorted us back to our vans and sent us on our way – not that anyone was complaining as it was dark and great cover for any concealed weapon.

We'd only driven a couple of hundred yards when we hit a couple of traffic lights starting to turn red. At the junction, there were a good 100 or so heads with an assortment of hairstyles: wedgeheads – flicks; bobs – mushrooms grow well in shit; suedeheads – curly-haired lads who'd cut it short well before GHDs (styling accessories) were about; and mullets! And two teamed ski hats. Ages ranged from 10 to 25, and they were all waiting to cross the road with not a Z-car in sight. Shit! Not fancying stopping any longer in the Wirral, the driver put his foot down, hitting the accelerator with us all domino'ing into the back doors. Luckily, they remained shut and off we sped.

Driving back through Liverpool, we spotted a broken-down car from Preston with a couple of lads who we knew standing on the pavement – lucky spot. Our van pulled over to help them out in any way that we could. Three young scallywags were hanging about, aged ten if a day. What on earth they were doing out at this time of night with school in the morning, I don't know! One even had a Lacoste jumper on, which some in our party could barely afford. His dad must have been on a shopping spree in Europe recently.

'We'll get you a car, mister, if you've got a pair of scissors,' one chirps up, full of Scouse wit – and cheek. Why do all Scousers think they are great singers or comedians? They do, though, don't they?

The car finally gets up and running so we all piled back in the van, grabbing one of the young Liverpudlians for a joke. We were messing about like we were going to kidnap him when his mate pulled out a Stanley knife. 'I'll slash your tyres and cut you up if you don't let him go, mister.'

Calm down, calm down. The lads released him, not doubting for one minute that the kid wouldn't do as he'd said. Driving off into the distance, we laughed about what age they'd been given a blade as a present. I do wonder what those three grew up to be.

Of course, our travels took us to all sorts of places, and some not quite as local as we'd have liked. One such trek – or pilgrimage more like – was Plymouth.

C:

The regular Friday night around town was undertaken, heading to Louis Long Bar for last orders – this being the pick-up point for Plymouth. One lad, Trev, who wasn't coming, needed a lift home to Leyland. 'No worries, jump in and I'll drop you off,' Elli says. Then Trev fell asleep more or less as soon as he got in the back of the van. 'Sssssh.'

While travelling, the lads' bladders were well full and plenty of piss-stops were required. On one such stop, a mate, Queeny – who you could normally tell what he'd eaten that day because half of it was usually down the front of what he'd be wearing – decided that he needed a change. He obtained a cream Lyle & Scott jumper. Cuntish I know, but needs must with him.

Elli:

I – again – had the pleasure of driving – booked it, packed it and off we go. A van full of pissed-up lads to put up with once more. Trev, a mate, asked for a lift home to Leyland Junction just south of Preston, and I obliged. He couldn't make the trip, as he was the key holder, and branch manager, of an electrics store in Preston. So I'd to endure the usual for the next five hours: 'Pull over for a piss...'; 'Stop, I'm going to be sick...'; 'Are we nearly there yet?'

By the time I reached Exeter, I decided a bit of shut-eye was needed for the long day ahead.

Early morning, after an hour's kip, I shake the cramp and stiffness out of my limbs then set off to Plymouth.

Wolfie:

We'd arrived about seven in the morning, well and truly shattered with our growling bellies needing a fill. A greasy spoon café was found, big brekkies ordered and soon walloped down. You never know when you get to dine again and the grub you usually get in the nick is never up to much!

Wandering down the Hoe, we bumped into a coachload of lads that had arrived from Preston and a 30-odd-a-side footy match is our only entertainment, due to it being early doors. Wiggie, who travelled down on the coach, didn't have much coin, so a challenge was set up for him to dive off a springboard on the pier into the sea to raise funds for his ale.

C:

Wiggie then strips off bollock-naked and jumps into the fresh, lovely blue sea for his morning wash. And by opening time, the lads were once more up for a sesh, and we make our way pub by pub towards Home Park.

Elli:

They've had a few liveners and also find out where Plymouth's pub is – 'it' being on the way to the ground.

As we make our way up a hill, on a dual carriageway, we must have been spotted because out bounds the Central Element showering us with pint glasses and bottles from a pub. When they finally run out of ammo, we charge at them – as you do. It then goes off with one Plymouth lad getting sparked and others taking a bit of a kicking for not appreciating how much trouble we'd gone to in travelling down to Plymouth.

The North End lads are bang at it when the local bobbies make an appearance. A police van had been parked up observing us and I'm now expecting our collars to be felt after we'd left a bit of carnage in the road. I'm into my pocket fumbling for the van keys wondering whom I'm going to hand them to as the police split us up. 'On your way, lads, and head up to the ground,' the copper says. Off we trotted with the police's friendly advice.

C:

It's kicked off, with one Plymouth lad taking a severe beating and Wiggie was whipping all-comers, wheeling his belt wildly above his head.

Elli:

We enter the ground in a seated stand and I drop off to sleep straight away, missing the entire match. I was awoken with the words, 'Come on, we're off.'

Great, another five hours at least of driving ahead of me! Will I ever learn?

C:

I can't really remember the game; most of us were still shattered with all the travelling and tried to get our heads down for a bit.

After the match, the bizzies escorted us back to the van and pointed us in the direction of home. We decided to get out of Plymouth, not knowing the condition of the lad who was out cold.

Stopping off in Wolverhampton for a quick drink, in a dodgy-looking disco pub, it turned out to be full to the rafters. And not wanting to upset the locals, we were swiftly back on our way.

A very, very long day out; rivet marks in our arses, sweaty armpits and stained clothes but it was well worth it. Not for the match – Preston got beat as usual – and not for the fight either. The pasties at half-time, though, they were beautiful, the best I've ever tasted with lovely pastry and a proper filling.

Oh yeah, I nearly forgot! The Leyland lad Trev never did get home that night. He woke up halfway to Plymouth and we had to inform him, 'Sorry, mate, we forgot to wake you up at Leyland.'

'I'm working in the morning,' he replied.

'Point of no return now, mate.'

On arrival in Plymouth, he had to ring his old man to inform whoever that he couldn't attend work that day! The other thing was, he had the keys to the shop with him! No one was getting a new washing machine or hi-fi that day at Currys!

D Ladd also remembers another marathon trip to the south coast the following season.

D Ladd:

Fifty-odd of us met up one Friday night and, after a few pints with the usual Friday-night fisticuffs against the local punks in Clouds, we set off to Plymouth at three in the morning.

We arrived in Plymouth at nine o'clock with a kickabout on Plymouth Hoe, 25-a-side. We expected a bit of a reception committee after one of their lads got hospitalised last season, and we weren't disappointed later on that day!

After having a good drink around town without a sniff of any trouble or sighting any of their boys, we headed towards the ground. I can't remember the name of the boozer but it was at the bottom of a big hill with a park on the other side. Anyway, the front few were about to go in when their boys bounced out of both sets of doors, tooled up with baseball bats. I was at the time just coming out of my teens and these Plymouth weren't kiddies, these were lads in their thirties and they meant business. Some lads swing bats for a bit of a show but these lads were prepared to use them. We couldn't get anywhere near and the first few of ours were now on the deck. It was getting scary – they were going to do one of us good and proper so we got on the back foot, collecting the injured, all the way up that fucking big hill. Plymouth were still after us with their bats catching a few stragglers, dishing out plenty of wood.

Then, after what seemed like an age, the Old Bill finally turned up with Plymouth doing one. The police then escorted us up to the ground and the casualties to the hospital. There were at least a dozen; one lad had a broken arm, another a broken wrist, and lads needed their heads stitched up!

This was a proper revenge attack all right.

So it's back to the pie-eaters, and another row with Wigan. We were in Louis Long Bar around dinnertime. Some lads were dining on pie, frozen chips and garden peas – lovely. Others were studying the nags or football coupons, and most nursing hangovers from the night before. They'd been to pubs and clubs spread around town 'on the pull'. Clubs like The Gatsby, a two-levelled club, downstairs would be modern soul, upstairs music of the time and old classics. The entry fee included rubber chicken and chips in a basket – yummy.

Snooty's was another, where the order of the day was either Sass – cider, lager and blackcurrant – or Green Monster – cider, lager and Blue Bols liqueur – that got you totally smashed. It played chart and dance music and I remember a good mate, Kraut, dancing to Dexy's Midnight Runners in there. Hands behind his back doing what looked like an Irish jig. He thought he was the bollocks!

Clouds was a massive club on Church Street that coach parties from out of town turned up at every week – this guaranteed an 'off'. Lads would do the circuit around the club's perimeter, either looking at the girls dancing round their handbags in their leg warmers – yes, Preston girls still wore them, to absorb the jizz running down their legs later on that night – or for non-locals, looking for a fight.

The Bull & Royal was a pub that got granted a late-night licence which was taken off them not long after obtaining it. You didn't need a collar or pants, so it attracted your 'lad' types. A report in the *Lancashire Evening Post* alleged that one night a pint of blood had been found by a glass collector left on the table. It must have been getting close to daybreak with Dracula having to do one!

The Piper was difficult to get in, and had an older element in it. The doormen were strict – cunts. The one time we did get in, it kicked off. A mate, Parky, got thrown out through the fire doors off a doorman, as well as Rambie, Kirky and a few other lads. So the brawl carried on outside. The law then turned up right behind them, and the majority of the lads got nicked. Needless to say, we never got in again.

Squires was a more upmarket club, and there was The Warehouse for Bowie and Roxy, and, if all else failed, you ended up in the Cherry Tree, the 'Blood Tub'. I think the *Star Wars* bar scene was written after a visit there by George Lucas. It had a Deep South American bar/club feel and likeness – all that was missing was a mesh cage around the DJ.

Some lads had also been to Northern Soul all-nighters around Lancashire and knew a few Wigan lads who might show.

Anyway, back to the Wigan story. The spotters were out and I think it was Bri who burst through the doors shouting, 'Wigan are here... they've just got off the train.' A la carte food was left and newspapers were dropped and the wheels were still going round on the old sewing machine tables. The lads were doing a 300-yard dash, beer swishing around in guts and last night's takeaways popping back up.

We can see our target in the distance, about 80 Wiganers, spread out in the road with Saturday shoppers going about their business. We were within striking range, and one or two Preston were already at it. Wolfie had popped up from Fox Street behind them (usual tactic) and Bami (one-man army) who'd trapped them like a greyhound. You could see the fear in their eyes by the time we'd arrived, even though they outnumbered us.

The victory was ours, their bottle had gone, and they were on the back foot. The ones who stood got a good hiding – credit for standing though. Some Preston were trying to throw one Wigan lad through Gibson's Sports Shop window in a smash-and-grab raid. It had a full display of Pringle jumpers and other sports gear on show. Other lads were trying to boot a couple of Wiganers into Thomas Cook's travel agents, I guess to have a look at what the pound was worth that day.

Anyway, we smashed Wigan all over the road, back down Fishergate to the train station.

And so to Burnley. By this time, I'd already been to Burnley five or six times, once being an evening game when 300-plus lads arrived in the pouring rain. After travelling over by train, the usual waiting committee was in place – masses of police. We were then marched round the streets getting soaking wet.

And within 500 yards of the ground, you could see just how heavy the rain was through the floodlights' beams. 'Halt!' a copper shouted, hand held up on the back of a horse at the front of the escort – everyone concertina'ing into the back of each other, lads tripping and ending up in puddles.

'The game's off, boys... you're going straight back.'

Everyone was well and truly pissed off.

And then back at Burnley, on Bonfire Night, we'd been all round the town centre with no real fireworks, just a few sparklers. We eventually got collared, herded up and taken to the Longside, paying to get in to the game at Turf Moor.

Having had a few beers, and being bored with the match, the lads started play fighting between each other – this being only a diversion to attract the attention of the Old Bill. In they came, right on cue, thinking it was going off. First they were pushed, then a helmet came off, a punch came over the top and Preston were at it with the coppers. Other lads further up the terraces surged forward towards the front fencing with all in the mêlée getting squashed or knocked over.

Reinforcements soon arrived, just about forcing through a half-open gate. The lads backed off, forming a gap. The police started readjusting uniforms and looking for tit-shaped helmets on the floor, with me and CP getting lifted. Arms up our backs, we're led round the pitch then taken to a long, narrow cell under the stand. They squeezed us into it – good job we weren't the size we are today, otherwise they would have had to get the Fire Brigade to cut us out. It had long bars that ran from floor to ceiling; it was more like being on show at the zoo. They must have thought we were wild animals.

Another officer then brought in a young Preston teenager and started to process him straight away as he'd thrown a 'banger' into the Burnley fans. 'Do ya have to tell me mam and dad?' the spotty-faced kid asked the copper. While having his photo taken, he asked, 'Do I get a copy to keep?' He wasn't clued up at all.

Years later, the same spotty-faced kid became a doorman, with him and four of his bouncer mates giving out a severe beating to a good friend and work colleague, Aussie Dave, breaking his cheekbone for no apparent reason. What a bunch of hard cunts!

Then entered a puffing, baby-faced PC, still sorting himself out, buttons popping off his uniform with a crumpled helmet under his arm, minus his badge. Sarge said, 'Can you ID these two suspects?' pointing our way; the officer was now looking at us. We were sat there all innocent like.

'Sorry, Sarge, I can't, I had my head down to protect myself.'

We were then dragged from behind the bars and shown the exit door, so I asked, 'Can we go back on?'

The look sufficed. 'No, do one. And don't let me see you again today.'

Yippee! The days before CCTV – not that we'd done anything anyway!

Lesson that day: never play with fireworks, you might get burned.

* * *

It was at Scunthorpe that I learned another lesson: never underestimate any team's firm. We did, finding out the hard way. It was a game over the festive period and I'd been picked up by Elli – driving again – early and into the back of the van I went.

I was terribly hungover, one of those hangovers that feels like someone is banging a hammer inside your head. I'd been out the night before and then back to a mate's on his homebrew. I threw that very same homebrew up, all the way to Scunthorpe. The van stunk of stale ale, Brussels sprouts and Christmas pud. If anyone had lit a match, the van would have gone up. Destination: not so sunny Scunny – who put the cunt in Scunthorpe!

A few carloads had been there for the FA Cup in November, having no trouble with the locals. Saying that, they'd had a bit of a run-in with Blackpool on the motorway services. I asked Rambie for his version of events of what happened that day but he was concussed after a kick to the head. He's got a memory like a sieve at the best of times and doesn't remember a great deal now that he's a granddad! So C takes up the story.

C:

Ten of us went to an FA Cup game away at Scunthorpe, and on pulling into the services on the M62 we notice three cars – a Jag, a Granada and a Vauxhall Viva – emptying their contents of lads. Who, then, was running a coachload of other fans? Our two cars pull up 'Sweeney style' and attention is drawn to us. It's Benny's mob from Blackpool. It then kicks off and Pia gets knocked down as usual and a good old toe-to-toe, tit-for-tat takes place. One of ours goes down, one of theirs goes down. Then a Blackpool lad produces a blade... we back off slowly towards our motors and help Rambie who is concussed, with the rest of the lads getting tooled up. The service staff must have alerted the coppers; they arrived just before it really got going again. Both us and Blackpool jump into our transport, Blackpool shooting off quicker, in a better class of car!

Not much to report about Scunthorpe, a 1–0 defeat early exit (as usual). There's always next year!

On the way back, we stop at the same services, but on the other side of the motorway, bumping into some more

Blackpool, a vanful plus a carload. Also on the services was a coach full of Preston... they totalled the car with the van escaping with bricks bouncing off it.

We followed the van 'til it pulled off at Wakefield or somewhere like that. It was last seen going up a slip road with its lights off. You know when they've had enough.

Getting back to the season of goodwill, 20 lads were in the back of the van plus two carloads and we pulled into a big boozer's car park just off a roundabout in Scunthorpe. We were informed by the landlord that it was about a good mile's walk to the ground, so we settled in. No walkabouts today; the lads fancied a rest and a bit of banter, and I was still drinking pop and honking up. Then the yearly ritual started, 'Who got you that jumper?'

'Have you got your dad's shirt on?'

'Did your gran knit you that?'

(One lad, not present that day – Micky P (Mad Dog) – once got a bright-yellow, chunky Stone Island jumper for a pressie at Crimbo. There were four of us in a pub in Preston having a pint when his sister's boyfriend, who wasn't a footy lad, said, 'Mick, did ya mum knit ya that for Christmas?' If looks could kill! Me and Rambie holding it in like Roman Centurions.)

We're all in jovial spirits, when some bright spark comes out with, 'Who's up for a bit of boxing on Boxing Day?'

'You dickhead. It's the day after Boxing Day!'

'Well, who's up for taking their end anyway? It should be a laugh.'

And I was thinking that the Seventies thing of end-taking had well and truly gone.

It was approaching three bells so we drank up and made

tracks, leaving two greedy cunts, Rambie and Kingy, as they fancied 'one for the road'.

We're now facing a hill that resembled Mount Everest with not a drop of Bovril in sight. Lads were blowing out of their arses at the summit.

There were no waiting coppers so we paid into the home end full of Christmas spirit, still taking the piss out of each other. Unbeknown, we'd been clocked by Scunny's lads and, by the time our 25 had walked into the stand, an un-welcoming committee was half assembled. We got in position at the back of the stand and before we could get into carol singing mode – CRASH... BANG... WALLOP – what a picture.

The mighty Scunthorpe launched an attack; they caught us off guard when we should have been prepared for action. Boys, lads, men and women were laying into us. One bloke in full motorcycle leathers was crashing his helmet down on to our heads. We had to retreat towards the pitch side over hoardings, slugging back on the move. The locals looked well pissed off! They must have got some shitty Crimbo presents that year, and, with us being in their end, it was the icing on the Christmas cake. The turkey stuffing was well and truly knocked out of us, as we were spilling over the barriers trying to hold it together – not a chance.

A cheer went up from the Preston fans on the away end: 'Preston aggro... Preston aggro... hello, hello!' I wish.

The police got a grip, escorting us round to the away end. Our egos were well and truly bruised and the trudge round the ground is a long one. As we passed the dugouts, both teams' benches gave out dirty looks. 'Done off little Scunny' I was thinking! Who would have thought it? Heads bowed, and into the away end we went.

Playing in the game that day was a legend, not a football

one, a cricket legend – Ian Botham. He got stick all through the game. 'You fat bastard... you fat bastard...' And other songs about his rounded physique.

Preston went 5–0 up away from home, something I don't think I've witnessed since. Not many could ever say that they either have or ever will do again. 'Beefy, Beefy, what's the score?' The Irons pulled a consolation goal back to chants of: 'What's it like to score a goal?'

A radio presenter reported next day: 'Perhaps England all-rounder Ian Botham should stick to cricket after he was hit for six, I mean five, by Preston footballers at the Old Show Ground.'

What a sight Beefy looked that day: long mullet hairstyle, a big 'tash and a couple of stone overweight. His knees were bandaged so much you could have wrapped an Egyptian mummy in them.

Oh yeah, the two lads who we'd left in the pub having another pint had arrived just before half-time going on the home end! Kingy, through gritted teeth, had grabbed hold of a lad saying, 'Get ya, boys!' Luckily for them, a copper collared the two, and brought them round to us before they had some serious damage done to their persons.

Game over, strike while the iron is hot, revenge was uppermost on everyone's mind. There were running scuffles all around the car park, which ended with CP and Rambie getting nicked. Rambie was rugby tackled into a lamp-post, banging his head. There was definitely no festive spirit that day as he was told, 'I've been after you all day, you little runt.'

We were moved on and started our descent, which was a bit easier than it had been coming up the hill. Our priority now was getting the two lads out of the nick and home.

Halfway down the hill, the sound of breaking glass was heard all around us. We were under attack, lads coming out of gardens, unloading milk bottles. Hands over heads to protect ourselves, we started moving a bit quicker. The noise stopped, their ammo gone, and we turned round to have a go back, only Scunny had disappeared quicker than they'd appeared – the ghosts of Christmas past had gone.

Now loaded up into our transport, we headed towards the police station but we were told on arrival, 'Not a chance of them being released. It will be tomorrow.'

We then headed home with our tails well and truly between our legs.

Don't judge a book by its cover! We thought Scunthorpe would be a throwaway, paper-bound, cheap read. It turned out to be a right hardback, violent thriller.

* * *

We were on our way to Port Vale, and disembarked a train in Crewe at about half-ten with a need of a livener, so off we headed to a nearby boozer. About 40 Preston lads made the trip with a couple of ICF – a lad called Bri and another lad who'd been in the Army with our mate Ste.

As we entered the pub, we clocked that it was already full with Nottingham Forest. They had had the same idea as us, a quick one en route. There wasn't any rivalry between us, just small talk and not a hint of trouble. I suppose both parties wanted to get to their destinations. Goodbyes were said and we caught a train to Stoke.

We arrived in Port Vale, and it was the smallest station I've ever had the pleasure of getting off at. Out we went on to the streets and it was getting hot – the sun had got his hat on. Sun, beer and football – what more do you want? 'How far is it to the ground, mate?' I asked a bloke.

'Couple of miles that way,' a local informed us, pointing in the right direction.

With a good walk and plenty of hostelries on the way, liquid refreshment was required. Some of the lads even thought about having a dip in the canal next to one boozer we were sat outside. No Vale were yet to be seen.

At about two-thirty, we set off to the ground walking down one side of the road, when we noticed some boys hanging around what looked like a club or some sort of pub. It had a glass door plus two massive glass panels either side in between a row of shops or houses. 'Come on, they're here!' a shout goes up from them, with others piling out.

'Let's 'ave 'em!' Preston roared back.

There was a busy road to negotiate while dodging what objects were thrown from either side, and it ended in a good 'set-to' in the middle of the road.

Wolfie:

I remember the day well, not that I'm a big drinker anyway, but I had chicken pox so no beer at all that day for me.

We were getting closer to the ground and, as usual, I was on the other side of the road to the lads mingling in with the Port Vale. So, when Preston came across the road into their lads, I stick one right on the button of a big mouthpiece at the front. Now, I'm no grass but when the fuzz arrives he only goes running to one of them holding his broken nose pointing me out. I got nicked.

'He started it, officer,' I say, being pushed into a cop car. The Vale lad also gets lifted for not playing by the rules.

While all this was all happening, an innocent lad walked

towards us on the same side of the road as the pub and got mistaken for one of ours – Preston. They steamed right into him, giving him a good 30-second kicking, followed up by him being thrown through one of the big windows. It quickly flashed through my mind, 'I hope he's all right.' Sirens were wailing, and cop cars screeched up with a couple of Preston getting nicked.

We made our way to the turnstiles trying to pay into their end after splitting up into ones and twos – old habits die hard. I had just handed over my money when my collar was felt with the copper pulling me back saying, 'You're nicked.' I was thrown into a meat wagon. Not to worry, though, I had plenty of company. About half-a-dozen of the lads were already in.

We were then taken to the local police station and booked in. By now, there were a good 15 of us and we were put into one big cell, minus our trainers. What a lovely foot aroma wafted through the air – one lad had a big hole in the end of his sock with his toe sticking through. There was also plenty of farting and belching.

We started wondering what charges we'd have coming our way, knowing that they could be serious, and then the cell door opened and in walked the sergeant.

'Why?'

'What's the craic?'

'We haven't done 'owt!'

Questions were being fired at him left, right and centre.

'Quiet!' he shouted.

Then one of the lads squeaked out in a quiet voice, 'What you charging us with then?'

The sergeant cocked his eye with a stern look. 'How does attempted murder grab you?'

'What?' fifteen voices say in unison.

'Yes, you heard. And you will be in here for some considerable time. So, have a really good think about the events that went on before.' He left, slamming the door.

Talk about the shit hitting the fan! You could see the colour draining from some lads' faces; they've turned white as sheets. We were now all at each other.

'What did you do?'

'No, what did *you* do?'

Our heads were well and truly battered. If we knew anything about what went on, we were tight-knit and wouldn't buckle.

An hour passed with us preparing for the worst, when the bolts were pulled back and once again in walked the sergeant.

'Right, I've just been to the hospital and the lad who has been thrown through a window going to the match...'

Oh, for fuck's sake, I'd seen it. Is he on a life-support machine? Will he live? All sorts of possible scenarios flashed through my head.

'...says it wasn't you lot.'

A surge of euphoria came up from my toes, colour rushed back into my cheeks within a second, and a collective sigh of relief was expelled from 15 lads.

'He says it was his own Port Vale fans and some young kid who drove round in the police car picking you lot out backs up his story. We know you were up to no good, but we now know you didn't do it. But the kid also says you were scrapping...' – Who cares? Happy days are here again! – '... but I've also had a word with the landlord and if he gets paid for the window he will be willing not to press charges and you'll be let you out in a short while.' – Get in, my son! – 'I will give you five minutes to think about it.'

Five minutes? Five milliseconds was all I needed. Get me out of here.

'How much?'

'Three quid each.'

The sergeant left.

'Yes. That's a right result,' I said.

Then one cheeky fucker said, 'I'm not paying... I didn't smash it.'

The lads went berserk at him.

The five minutes were up. 'Are you paying then, lads?' the sergeant asked after pulling back the hatch on the door.

'Yes!'

One by one, we were taken out into the waiting room for the escort to the train station and handed our trainers. They'd been looked at for glass, as evidence. The two Preston lads who'd been nicked before us were kept in and a charge sheet was spotted on the desk. It read: 'One Preston lad was seen doing a flying headbutt from behind a bus shelter.'

Fucking hell, I didn't realise that we had Superman in among us that day!

We were then let out into the escort back to the train station with the other Preston boys, Port Vale being on the other side goading and gobbing it off – full of hot air. Like I've mentioned before, some police treated home and away fans differently and Ste got lifted for informing the dibble about such things!

Once again, it was a long day out for a few hours in a cramped cell. It was nearly one of the most serious offences I'd ever been charged with to date. I do hope the lad made a full recovery, whoever he was, and hopefully Burkie 'Holier than thou' got some new socks – bless him.

Back in the rough and tumble of the 1984/85 season, we had four wins out of the first five games, then eight defeats on the trot, so Alan Kelly handed in his notice after 27 years at the club; he must have had a crystal ball. Tommy Booth then got the *Mission Impossible* task.

Relegation was confirmed with PNE getting beaten at home 5–2 by Wigan Athletic – and we'd voted them league status. A *Lancashire Evening Post* reporter wrote: 'Spineless, gutless, heartless and perhaps worst of all without any resemblance of pride!' Preston even conceded their 100th goal in the match. North End's leading scorer that season was John Kelly, who had put the ball in the net just seven times.

But before a ball had been kicked in anger that season, we had our regulation friendly against Blackburn. We took the train this time, as we fancied being able to breathe, rather than the usual tranny van. Into the town centre we went, in and out of pubs, no problems.

We were a few beers in, only to be stopped. Not by Blackburn or the Old Bill, but by young ladies handing out flyers for the opening of a new gym. The young ladies talked us into joining, not the gym, but the free cheese and wine. Chit-chatting away, we found out they weren't even from Blackburn, but a model agency from Manchester. At the ripe old age of no more than 19, we were wine connoisseurs in the making. Swirling, sniffing and slurping our wine... by the bottle. It didn't take long for the gym owner to start throwing daggers our way. We then started milling around looking interested in the equipment; we were really weighing up what could be used as a form of defence 'if' Blackburn did make a show.

Two hours later, conversation, and the wine, had run dry; we went out into the bright sunshine. We were now discussing the finer points about wine, what year this, what aroma that, it had a touch of plum in it. Bullshit – we were pissed.

Taxis to the ground were ordered, as I don't think anyone could manage the walk. We then paid into the Riverside because they were never on the Blackburn End. Wrong, they were, and a few PNE kicked off. We tried to get over the fence to help out, only to spot the cavalry arriving and they were heading our way. Our lot on the fence jumped down, trying to mingle in with the tweed jacket, flat cap, 60-odd-year-old blokes who were trying to trip us up. 'Bloody scum, you lot.'

C:

Bill gets rugby tackled by this copper who proceeds to drag him round the pitch backwards, arm round his neck.

Next time I saw Bill, he told me what went on. After being photographed and put in a cell under the stand, he'd asked the arresting officer, 'What's the charge?' I'll put it like this: Have you ever watched the films Kill Bill 1, which were the questions, and Kill Bill 2, the answers? In between were a few scenes from the film which were re-enacted. Bill later looked at his reflection in the shiniest pair of Doc Martens he's ever had the pleasure of coming close to. His image scared him half to death, and it does me to this day!

Later, at half-time, he was put in a police minibus to be taken up to the station. Sat down, cuffed up, he was nudged on the ankles from behind by another copper saying, 'Did the Blackburn fans pick on you, son?'

The copper was told, 'No, mate, just ask the PC who removed me from the terracing. I tripped up or something I think.'

When Bill had his day in court, for the said offence, he must have had amnesia after falling. PC Plod gave his evidence and it was all very enlightening to him. Bill said he must have done it if the officer of the law said so! Plus, a photo from the ground had been mislaid, although the one taken at Blackburn nick turned up. His head was the other object visible from the moon after the Great Wall of China! It must have been a well dodgy fence he'd got his nut tangled up in!

At home to Derby, we'd no joy before the game and up into the seats we went to the away end – our manor for years, apart from when the 6:57 were in town. We parked our arses on the filthy, wooden benches dirtying pale-blue jeans and designer clobber.

Five minutes into the game, Derby appeared in the same stand at the opposite end, next to the Kop. I presumed they were late arriving. We tried making a move but could see the police had already sussed the DLF, stationing themselves all around them. It was a waiting game and a plan hatched up.

Ten minutes before the end, we would make a move exiting our end and entering their gate – party time. The plan was put into action, and out we went – fine. The lads were chomping at the bit. I was halfway up the stairs when there was a stampede; boys were coming down, not liking what awaited. It was some big Rams wanting to shear some sheep – us. A spotter of the time, S.C., knocked me over fleeing! I was trampled all over, finding myself minus a trainer. I'd rolled down the steps creating a hole in my yellow Tacchini bottoms – bastard.

Derby were out, fronting us – it was men against boys. To add insult to injury, they threw my trainer at me and it was a direct hit on the bonce. Quick as a flash, I pulled my Puma California back on. 'Stand... stand!' I was shouting, while thinking, 'When are the rest going to get their acts together?'

Our numbers were down to a few as they ran at us; we backed up, and then it was into jogging mode. I wasn't up for running, nor are a few of the lads, but we had to as there were too many to handle. Our golden fleeces were being hunted that day and we weren't hanging around.

I'd never been run that far before in my life; they really did want us. I can only think there must have been history somewhere along the line. Round the ground, past the Kop we went; down Lowthorpe Road, right into St Stephen's Road, on to Deepdale Road, left down to the prison; across the Ring Road and up Church Street, turning right towards the Cenotaph in the centre of town. Some jog!

We were looking over our shoulders going past Man at C&A – that we were certainly not. Derby had stopped and the few who were left, about ten of us, were blowing out of our arses with an inquiry going on in between deep, deep breaths.

We started heading back up towards the Ring Road and were parallel with Saul Street Baths when ten Rams appeared. We were goosed but wanted some action. Next minute, we're bang at it because they wanted some fun as well. Backwards and forwards we went until our friends in blue arrive, dispatching us, day over.

Our legs were pumped up to the max, like we'd just done the London marathon, and we struggled to walk back to the bus station. It was a long one that day, but that's the game, isn't it?

And from one long day to another – in Hull. We nearly didn't make it after an incident on the motorway, and we were late arriving, parking about a mile away from the ground. Two cars and an Escort van – about 15 made the trip. Getting to the turnstiles just after kick-off, we noticed on the way in a couple of Hull lads really giving the local dibble a mighty hard time. 'We are going in,' they were saying.

'You're not... you're banned from home games.'

'Tough, we are going in!'

Leaving the psychos arguing with the police, we paid in the away end. Preston lads just wouldn't get away with that if it was with Preston bobbies.

Stood on the terracing, the Hull lads were congregating to our right in a small stand behind a supermarket. Preston won 2–1 that day, both cracking goals that were entered into the goal of the month and one going on to be in the running for goal of the season, the scorers being Jonathan Clark and Dave Jones.

The problems started when we left. The home fans exited on both sides, with every Tom, Dick and Harry wanting a piece of us. It was tit-for-tat, punches being thrown from both sides in between shirters. The police moved in, forcing us towards where the coaches were parked as we informed them we were in our own transport parked down the road. The lads were a bit edgy, not wanting a repeat performance of the previous week against Derby. There were quite a few Hull hanging around so we moved off tightly together, circling-the-wagons style.

We were a couple down. I found out later the missing two had jumped aboard a coach for the final scores before catching us up, missing out on our treat. The police were telling the Tigers, 'Move on, get home...' I could sense their boys were after a bit of T-bone for tea. 'You'll be all right... the traffic bobbies are parked up at the roundabout near your cars,' we were told.

We slowly moved off; on our right, there was a launderette with a record-breaking amount of lads squeezed into it. I don't think they were doing their dirty washing, more like waiting to give us the 'stone-washed' or 'tumble-dry' effect. It was either that or a Levi jeans-advert audition!

Two minutes later, the launderette door burst open, and it was backs to the wall time. Over they came and we were as close as we could get to holding our own – windmilling time. We couldn't move and we didn't move, with both sides bang at it for a good 30 seconds 'til the Old Bill came running back up the road. Two German Shepherds were ragging both sets of lads. Hull retreated for their final rinse. It had been like Custer's last stand – again.

The police escorted us away up the road, leaving us again after a couple of hundred yards. We carried on walking towards our transport with no real casualties apart from ripped jeans, a torn coat, a fag burn to one lad's lip were he'd had it stubbed out after just lighting it, and the funniest thing of all was a pair of smashed glasses belonging to a lad called Tony G. Why was it that funny? Because he was the driver of the Escort van and he was as blind as a bat without them.

The two pools panellists finally arrived, laughing their heads off. Specky-four-eyes – minus two – had to drive home with a co-pilot giving him instructions: left... right... next junction, etc. He'd not been to Specsavers, and thank fuck I was in one of the other cars!

The lads were a bit upset with what had gone on two weeks running, and just as we were setting off – BANG – a brick hit the side of our car. It seems some Bengal Tigers were still not full. 'Stop!'

Boot open, the old baseball bat comes out – we used to play on Sunday afternoons! They didn't fancy a bit of wood for supper so off they scarpered.

Back in the car once more, we were well and truly pissed off, and every little set of lads we see, 'Stop!' out we go to ask the way home!

Not put off, we went back later on in the season for a shitty Mickey Mouse Cup game, this time going on the supermarket end. It wasn't long before we were swinging at each other and on to the pitch we went. There was only one car this time – the others just didn't fancy it!

Payback time eventually came, though. The game at home against Hull, we were ready and waiting for them. It was a night match, and they arrived late, making an entrance on the Kop but were soon moved off, helped on their way by the police.

After the final whistle, Preston tried to stop their vans for an explanation about events at their place. One big Preston lad pulled open the back doors asking them to 'come out and play'. They really didn't fancy it now the boot was on the other foot. Why not? They gave it to us when they'd numbers in their favour.

Preston then launched everything and anything they could lay their hands on into the van while they were stuck in traffic. They came up on the pavement, nearly running everyone over, lads jumping out of the way, the driver never once putting the brakes on. Foot down, and away they go, just black diesel smoke and fumes for Preston lads to chew on. They had some serious injuries and a few Preston lads were arrested for the damage.

The local paper reported the following evening: 'After the match, police say the drivers of the two vans full of Hull fans ignored their request to wait for an escort.'

At their own peril!

While we may not have known who those ram-raiders were from Hull, when we played Burnley, it was different. We played them that often we got to know lads' faces and most nicknames. Saying this, we never got invited round for cocktails and aperitifs.

Meeting up at the Hesketh Arms car park on the outskirts of town for the vans to take us to the Land that Time Forgot, we had a good turnout and the lads ended up being squeezed into all the available transport. The dozen or so cars were already carrying five or more.

Setting off at about ten, we got no further than 200 yards when a cop on a bike pulled us over. 'Can I have a look in the back? You seem to be a bit overloaded sir,' he said to the driver.

Overloaded? I think we were trying to break the world record for footy lads in the back of a tranny van! He opened the back doors and his jaw dropped on to the tarmac like the Nutty Professor. 'Right, you lot, out now.' Biker boy then proceeded to inform the driver that he was only insured for three people in the front.

Arrangements were made to meet the driver a couple of miles away at a hotel en route. Lads slunk off in different directions, taxis were rung and a couple of the fitter ones ran up and down two steep inclines to the meet, Shanks' Pony style. By hook or by crook, we were back in the van within 20 minutes. 'Hey, ho... Let's go.' (How times have changed! Now it's either, 'Are you coming in my BMW or are you taking your Porsche?' And for the long-haul hikes to London we sometimes use the big metal bird. Gone are the days of thumbing, jibbing and the little one said, 'Roll over,' to get in the old works van.)

On arrival in the wonderful town of Burnley, we parked up behind the main shopping area. The doors burst open resembling a scene like the January sales; lads were dying for a piss after being nudged in the groin every time the brakes were touched. We went straight into the Bridge pub and it didn't take the Suicide Squad long to find us. The boozer emptied, dispatching them up an inclined road back on to the High Street. Once more, lads had snapped long aerials off parked cars, whipping their victims as they fled. One of the lads had done the same against Tranmere earlier in the book. He was game as they come but liked to use unusual items in combat.

Twenty minutes later, Burnley were back, being moved more easily than the last time. Three times this happened, yo-yoing up and down. It came to the final charge; Preston's numbers had been swelled by other cars that had turned up, and they touched 100. Glasses and bottles were flying about with half of us making it up on to the High Street. It was partly a trap and the coppers had arrived, blocking the rest off. Burnley, sensing our numbers were down, steamed into us, with Preston moving on the back foot, dodging in between Saturday shoppers. The lads were launching bins, sandwich-board shop-display signs and even baskets full of shoes. A line formed, offloading the latest cheap imitations of stylish shoes. Pickers and Kods were bouncing off Burnley heads only for them to be thrown back. I bet a few local tramps thought they'd won the lottery that night, then they probably woke up the next day with two left-footed shoes on.

Little running battles took place before and after the match with the police, as usual, gaining control.

Three carloads of us made the same trip a year later entering the same pub just after eleven. The rest of the Preston lads were to arrive later after being picked up in and around town.

Burnley knew Preston might try the same move again, and entered the boozer a couple of minutes after us. Our 12 now didn't look good against their 50. There was only one way in, so there was only one way out and we tried to leave discreetly. The first six managed to get out, then I got a dig to the side of the head and C got a brolly over his. Burnley spilled out and we realised there were four of the lads left inside. We were trying to get back in to help – no chance. The lads soon joined us after having a severe bollocking off Burnley's main faces and a kick up the arse to help them on their way. Luckily, CP knew one of them after he'd lived in Clitheroe. Respect to Burnley for not filling them in.

I know attendances at Deepdale were well down, but that game in season 1985/86 saw just 3,787 watch the 1–1 draw at Turf Moor. I bet, if asked, double would say they witnessed it. I did, I'm a 'proper' fan.

And talking of proper fans, we were ready, willing and waiting for the arrival of Bolton. We knew Bolton would show, they always do. Preston had small mobs milling around town with information exchanged between each group. Then we heard some Bolton had been spotted down Meadow Street, which was a drinkers' heaven with 13 pubs in and around its side streets at the time – distances of no more than the time it would take to pour a decent pint of bitter between each other.

As we entered Meadow Street, we spotted a mob coming into view that were quickly on their toes because Preston's numbers were too big for a change. One Preston lad ran ahead to see where they were heading, then back he came, saying, 'They've gone to the King's Arms.' This was another pub just over the main junction into town where endless roads interchanged with each other. A few Preston lads were coming the opposite way down Meadow Street from the County Arms putting the confirmers on it: 'Bolton are mobbing up in the King's Arms.' Game on!

The Trotters were found. Later, we found out that the landlord was originally from Bolton and used to run one of their main boozers. If only that information was known earlier, we could have laid on a welcoming party for them!

A plan was needed. We found out they numbered a good 100-plus, with Preston's firm growing by the minute to nearly equal that. There was a grassy area with a small mound running along it across the road from where Bolton were massed.

Crookie took control. 'Right, lads, keep low... we don't want to fuck this one up!'

Preston were on all fours and their bellies crawling into position; ribcages expanding in and out with deep breathing, there was also a strong smell of barley and hops filtering through the air, some still fresh from the last hurried pint, other smells stale from last night's session. Oriental and Asian belches, burps and farts also added to the aroma. Eyes were stretched wide open or half shut, especially from lads who'd been at the regular all-nighters in and around the red rose county – uppers, blueies, dexters, speed... all of them now taking their toll. For the majority, adrenalin is the drug of the day. Preston lads know it's a 'big one'. This is the one that gets you through the mundane working week while daydreaming, doing your job. Everyone knows Bolton are no mugs, so it's not for the faint-hearted when the war cry goes up.

Here's a bit of history for you: the pub is called the King's Arms because one of Britain's kings stopped off for a piss and a pint there. Which one, I don't have a clue. Before entering the said boozer, he tied his horse up to a tree outside; it's the biggest tree left around Preston town centre. I bet any other would have been chopped down by now. Its position would cause damage and destruction if uprooted in a storm... or it might just be bullshit!

Anyway, back to the action. Crookie was keeping watch like a meerkat, informing on a need-to-know basis. 'There are 30–40 outside having a pint... the rest must be inside. Just keep it tight for a bit longer.' Everyone was wound to the max like coiled springs, busting for action.

It was hard for Bolton to notice us, apart from the lonesome nutter talking to himself on a grassed area. In between both parties, besides the distance, is a 3ft-high railing and Saturday shoppers in cars going about their business. I bet there were a few pissed-off husbands inside them with a wife who'd gone back to the first boutique for her *Saturday Night Fever* frock after visiting ten other shops – I know, I've been there! Council buses were also driving past, going to the Gamull Lane and Moor Nook estates. These were the areas where, a few years earlier, I'd been hanging around on street corners kicking my heels at nights and getting up to other things. Don't blame the youth if you give them fuck all to aspire to when leaving school. Maggie Thatcher was the Prime Minister of the time – and she was the only cow not to give milk – but be warned: those kids will only turn out like us lot behind the mound!

We'd been there nearly 20 minutes with a few lads starting to get itchy feet and frustrated; cramp was setting in. 'Come on, let's have 'em. There's enough of us now,' a shout goes up to Crookie.

'Just give it a couple more minutes... they look like they are going to make a move and they won't be able to get tooled up from the boozer,' was the reply from the acting general. This job was being led with military precision!

Twenty more Preston arrived, joining us, like Russian dancers on bended knees, with the odd dance trooper having a peek-a-boo.

'They've spotted us, they're pointing over here,' Crookie said.

Preston rose in unison, like a scene out of the film *Zulu*. That moment, I wished I could have been over the road to witness it; it was impressive from where I was, never mind in the eyes of the Wanderers.

I found myself shaking Tenpole Tudor's 'Swords of a Thousand Men' lyrics out of my head. Right, ready for action. A quick glance over towards Bolton – you could see worried and shocked looks on their faces. They were a mass of harlequin-clad lads in Pringle jumpers – Northerners behind the times – definitely not out for a round of golf. Tracksuit tops and sportswear on others, not wishing to enter Wimbledon Centre Court. Designer-wearing, wafer-thin models – that's me – not waiting to parade on the catwalk. I wouldn't fancy it either, pent-up aggression at boiling point with Incredible Hulk, pumped-up veins popping out on the side of heads.

The bullet had been fired at the Preston Races. The lads' faces were grimaced, bulldogs chewing wasps, distorted, gurning champions in the making, G-forced cartoon characters.

I couldn't hear diesel engines, blowing exhausts or car horns; it was a blank canvas as we set off. Everyone was jockeying for position based on weight, size and running style. A noise entered my head, a sound not too dissimilar to wildebeest on migration with roars of 'Come on, then!' mixed in.

Most hit the railing moving like gazelles or horses in the Grand National at the first fence; others vaulted to the side. I didn't look back but I knew that the slightly cuddlier-sized boys would have to swing their legs over or look for a gap!

Bolton had fully spilled out of the King's, and were beckoning us on. We went slaloming in between cars and it was pouring down. Not rain drops, but bottles and pint pots! Arms over heads for protection, to sounds of breaking glass with dull thuds when hitting bonnets and hoods of cars. Plus the odd windscreen going through. Traumatised drivers were transfixed to the spot. Traffic lights were going through the colour sequence, but it was totally gridlocked. We were Scud missiles locked in on target with 30 yards to go before total destruction.

Bolton's hand-held missiles had been used up, so they tried to funnel back into the boozer through the single door frame, it being the only opening. Forty or so make a stand, it then seems to go silent for a second... fists, boots and an assortment of tools are exchanged at a rapid rate. People who've experienced such a fight can relate to such muffled sounds – skin on skin, weapons on flesh, time stands still.

The rest of the Bolton lads were back out with more ammo; we moved back under the barrage using cars for shields. There were one-on-ones, two-on-ones, two-on-twos, groups are fighting all around. Their arsenal was empty, so everyone was at it again. No side was giving an inch.

During the onslaught, a catering shop on the junction had been raided of a few of its implements and outside the shop there were a dozen crates of empty milk bottles. Preston lads returned fire, and it went absolutely 'mental'. Lads were running over cars, diving into action, flying kicks and other surreal events happening. I couldn't name who was doing what, I was wrapped up in my own world. A beer crate was thrown in my direction which was quickly picked up and crashed down on a few heads.

Three Old Bill arrived on the scene, trying to keep order with truncheons drawn. Not a chance! It was as if they were invisible. In between all the roaring from both sets, you could hear distant echoes of sirens en route, not being able to get anywhere near the scene. The junction was full of stationary cars, a complete standstill – good job Michael Douglas wasn't in one of them.

Crate dropped, my preferred weapons of choice were put to use – my fists! It was the longest, biggest and roughest encounter I'd ever witnessed and been involved in with Preston. Bodies were laid out, blokes bleeding. Backwards and forwards, the ruck went on. Lads were starting to get exhausted with a need for half-time oranges passed round.

'Two, four, six, eight... who do we fucking hate?'

The police were arriving, time to make tracks. What remained of each mob regrouped, lads limping off or being helped by others; Bolton back into the pub, Preston back down Meadow Street, both sets needing to patch up their wounded troops.

You could now hear clanging and banging from not too far away. It was the not-so-innocents residing at Her Majesty's Pleasure in Preston's prison. They had a great view from their high-rise, deluxe cells, which overlooked the battle scene, ironically next to the Imperial War Museum. They were banging with metal cups and anything that came to hand on their cell-window bars in appreciation of the afternoon's entertainment. Cheers, shouts and whistles rang out, with 'Go on, lads!' adding to the din.

To this day, I don't know if anyone was even nicked in the chaos – I don't give a toss. Preston wouldn't claim a major victory or accept it as a loss. Having had the lion's share of a feast of fighting, our bellies were full, and ale was needed.

After the game, hunger pangs soon returned once on Deepdale Road and in the surrounding streets after exiting the ground. It wouldn't live up to what happened before the match, but needs must!

* * *

We'd been looking for Millwall all afternoon around town with a few having had a good kicking on Fishergate. You could spot the 'cock-a-knees' a mile away; their swaggering walk, with a *Sun* newspaper in their back sky-rocket, ready to use as a Millwall brick. The few I mentioned didn't have time to use their origami skills, Preston having left most of them folded up on the pavement, the others running off. Apart from that, we thought it would be a no-show.

We were nearly at the ground, around 20 of us, when a line of taxis pulled up on Moor Park Avenue. This was a cinder road adjoining and running parallel to the park opposite the ground. The doors opened, emptying out some tasty lads. We told them to come down the road, out of the sight of the Old Bill. Off we trotted and they followed. I was thinking, 'I might get some revenge,' then another taxi pulled up down St Thomas' Road, its doors opened and five lions spilled out.

I went straight in, not wanting to wait like a kid in a sweet shop. Fast and furious, a one-man 'supernova' with arms, legs and head. The rest of Millwall started arriving and I tried to back off, but they were holding my Kappa jumper – no escape. I tried to undress myself with 30 lads surrounding me, all wanting a piece. They started to kick and punch the crap out of me and whatever else would come out! Bent over, jumper over my head, I fell into the side of a car, and it kept me up. Fuck knows what would have happened if it hadn't. The car had to pull over, with the road full of lads, all at it. It got some nasty dints and dents with wayward feet crashing into its panels.

I know it was my own fault but I started hearing, in between thuds to my ears and head, cockney twats – yes twats – saying,

'Kill the cunt, kill him, do him, let him die!' All is fair in love and war, but not to them extremes. Come on! Also, I got told later that my mates were trying to save me, pulling them off while having their own battles. Wolfie told me later, 'I pulled one off and sparked another trying to help get them off, Bill. They seemed like they were on a "kick-to-kill" mission.'

I broke free just before the Old Bill arrived; both sets were off in different directions. We went to the Deepdale pub; Millwall to the ground. I couldn't see through one eye and the other had double vision. I'd been absolutely pulverised.

I got cleaned up in the boozer's toilets; good job there were no mirrors because I was a right mess. The police then came in. 'Right, you lot, outside.'

We were lined up against a wall – names, addresses and details were taken. One copper said to me, 'What hit you, a bus?'

'I can't remember,' I replied.

'We will be needing a statement off you tomorrow about an incident that happened on Deepdale Road.'

They finished up with us, we headed up to the match and paid into the seats. I was getting some funny looks as I was a dead ringer for Quasimodo.

During the game, Millwall were pointing up at us with words being exchanged.

Game over. A big police escort was waiting for Millwall to take them back to the train station; Preston couldn't get anywhere near them. Not that I wanted to; I wasn't feeling too game!

I headed off home, having to cancel my night out with the missus once more. My face was in a right state, and my bonce was banging more in anticipation of the ear bashing I was going to get off her! No pain without gain, really.

The alarm was set early and I rose when the sun was just

coming over the rooftops. I went in the bathroom to relieve my bladder and what a state I looked as I caught my reflection in the mirror! I struggled to wash, with aches and pains in places I didn't know existed. It even hurt to brush my pearly whites in between still spitting blood.

It took me nearly half-an-hour to get dressed, the missus having to give me a hand. She even had to tie my New Balance 577 trainers; I wish I'd had them on the previous day. I then tried to put the son into his pram, which was a harder task than facing up to the 30 Millwall. It doesn't get any easier over the years; he still spits his dummy out now and then.

The missus had planned a family day out in Blackpool, along the Golden Mile. Slot machines, bingo, the smell of candyfloss mixed in with fish and chips. Then up to the Pleasure Beach with wristband on to the boy for unlimited rides on the roundabouts. The joys of Blackpool!

We caught the train back at dusk, key in the door and I checked behind it for a note with a Lancashire Constabulary heading – nothing. They never did turn up; why, I don't know.

Monday night's *Evening Post* read, 'Soccer knife man hunted. Detectives were today hunting a Preston North End fan...' All the details followed, and police said it was the only trouble at the fixture.

I found out some time later that a lad, unbeknown to anyone in our party, had run across the road and jibbed one of the Millwall mob, then did one. Like I've said, I couldn't focus properly and everything was hazy, so this must have been the incident the police mentioned. They'd got a description off the Millwall lad and from the woman driver, who'd been traumatised, trapped in her car. Perhaps they'd got the perpetrator?

I've never used a blade; it's bad enough witnessing what they can do, and I've seen some unpleasant sights.

Millwall clearly occupied a special place in our hearts. And such was our hatred, and respect, of Millwall around this time that we always tried to have a pop at them when they were in our neck of the woods. We had axes to grind and Millwall were our acid test.

One such time was when Millwall had a game against Burnley, with them having to change at Preston Station. One lad, Carl, did a bit of spotting for us, although I never saw him actually getting involved. Carl was the world's biggest exaggerator – halve anything he told you, and then halve it again. The sightings he would bring back about the size of opposition numbers would be bigger than any fisherman's tale. What whoppers he'd tell. If you had one, he'd have two bigger and better, even if you were on about your knob.

Well, we didn't have to wait long. He came running into the Vic & Station pub where we were, having a quiet pint while waiting for him to report back. He shouted at the top of his voice, 'Millwall are 'ere... Millwall are 'ere!' He then did a lap of the boozer and went back out, still ranting, going up Fishergate the opposite way to the train station. His arms were aloft as though Preston was being invaded by aliens. 'Millwall are 'ere... Millwall are 'ere!' he bellowed, bemusing shoppers as he went by.

The eight of us in the pub hot-footed it down to the station – still none the wiser on how many lions awaited. We just knew 'they're 'ere'! Down the concourse we went and on to platform 4.

We spotted about a dozen or so, and they spotted us at the same time. Then we started bouncing down the platform. 'Come on, Millwall!' We were like eight apprentice Zebedees, although this wasn't *The Magic Roundabout*, it was for real.

To our disbelief, Millwall started backing off, arms outstretched beckoning us on. 'Fackin' cam on!'

We were moving the infamous Bushwhackers with hardly a punch thrown. We moved them 30 or 40 yards up the platform, full of ourselves, thinking a result is coming our way. Wrong! They were more clued up than us. They stopped with a good old toe-to-toe just about to start, but what we hadn't noticed was that 20 others had scarpered on to platform 3 and were now behind us. It was suddenly pantomime season. 'They're behind you!' with a lion's roar going up.

We were well outnumbered, odds of 4:1 and 'up shit creek without a paddle'. Some lads scattered on to railway lines and others ran through the waiting room pretty sharpish. Wolfie decided to vault over the entrance barrier but he got gripped by the Jamaican ticket collector just as he was about to.

'Where's your ticket, man?'

Before he could explain the situation or pay the 2p for a platform ticket, a Millwall fan helped Wolfie out. Not in the form of 2p, but a kung-fu kick in the back and he was hoofed through the barrier in a flash.

We were stood looking back down on to the station; half of Millwall had given up the chase, the rest giving it 'wanker' signs and shaking their heads. 'Fackin runners!' one shouted. Millwall were quality, we'd a lot to learn.

We decided to go back to the pub where there was an inquiry between ourselves. 'We've got to get things sorted,' being top of the agenda.

Settling back down to the next pint, we laughed about the events. 'Carl should be at Deepdale by now,' I said.

'I wonder if he's still shouting, "Millwall are 'ere!"' one of the lads said.

Smiles replaced once tortured-looking faces. We got off lightly; you should learn by your mistakes. After all, you wouldn't put your head in a lion's mouth without expecting it to get bitten off, would you?

Back on the pitch, things were just as ugly. The 'Mission Impossible' had gone up in smoke after getting smashed at home by the Pie Men 5–2.

Preston had conceded over 100 goals that season and were already down by the time they played York City. It was the last game of the season and, with nothing to play for, it was a day out for the lads – we needed to go out with a BANG! It would be Preston's first ever time down in the fourth tier of English football the following season.

We caught a train, changed at Manchester, then on to York. One of the stops on the way is Leeds and, to our surprise, Pompey were en route somewhere stood on the platform with their backs to us. Preston steamed off the train, dished out a few slaps, jumped back on, and away we went – waving at the 6:57 with different hand signals.

A few weeks earlier, Burnley had played at York City's ground, Bootham Crescent, causing chaos with mounted police sent into the ground. We were down, so Preston lads were saying, 'Can't let the Dingles outdo us at anything, we'll go for it big time.'

What a lovely, historical place York is. The cathedral, York Minster, its ancient walls and buildings spread along cobbled streets. The fine city's public houses were enjoyed by the lads all day. There were no 'Yorkie Bar' kids to be found so Preston went on a mini rampage, throwing anything and everything through shop windows that were then looted. Even a pair of extension ladders went through a pub window. The bloke must have gone for a piss, and come back to find them stuck through his local boozer's stained-glass panel. Lads were bored; it's not the norm usually.

Entering the ground, you could at that time pay a pound extra to gain entry into the seats. Before doing this, the lads were going mental fighting with the coppers and stewards. An inspector was trying to keep order with his walking stick and, for his troubles, he got headbutted on the nose. The lad who did it I'd gone to school with – tut, tut!

The majority of the Preston lads made it into the seats to cause as much damage and mayhem as possible. Now I don't know who'd fitted the seating into that section of the stand, but it just started to fall to pieces! What bad workmanship; it must have been done by some cowboy builders.

But, on a serious note, we did hear some really upsetting news while we were at York. C remembers, 'Quite a few lads got lifted and a nice long weekend in York was had. The big downer on the day was that the police kept coming up to the hatches informing us how many deaths there'd been at Bradford. The fire had claimed many a life in the disaster.'

I was in a cell on Saturday night when they put this pissed-up young lad in with me because the majority of cells were already full. He kept papping on about how he'd drunk eight pints and he wasn't even leathered. I was just trying to get my head down. He then started to piss himself. Then a few minutes later, he started farting loudly. There's no way I could handle having this 'Bobby Sands' prodigy in with me – shitty pants – so I hit the buzzer and a copper poked his face up to the grille. 'There's something wrong with this lad, officer, and I don't know what it is.' The door opened and I jumped out.

'What are you doing?' the copper blurted out, grabbing my arm.

'He's shit himself,' I say, as the foul smell was starting to rise.

'You dirty little... You'll rot in it 'til the morning,' the copper said, shutting the door. 'Right, I'll find you another cell, you've been up to no good but you've not been bad enough to stop in there with him!'

By now I'd spent plenty of time in cells but what a drag that weekend was after hearing the bad news about Bradford. Counting tiles, press-ups, pacing up and down endlessly, and even reading a cowboy story book. That was the first bit of writing, apart from charge sheets, I'd read since leaving school!

C:

In the holding cells at court on Monday, the coppers are trying to wind us up saying, 'Looks like you're going down... the judge on duty today doesn't like trouble in our lovely city – just you wait and see.'

Before us, up before the bench is a local tramp for vagrancy. They throw him into our cell and he's received two weeks for his crime. I think they were trying to rub our noses in it.

Now it's our turn, and we're not looking forward to it, as one of the lads with us had eleven previous convictions for football already! The first sentence handed out was six weeks to the lad who'd done the headbutting, and then they deal with us.

'You attended a football match at Bootham Crescent where you caused criminal damage to the seating area and you are also charged with a breach of the peace. Have you anything to say in your defence?'

The on-duty solicitor stands up and goes into Bill's

defence first with a right spiel. 'Mr Routledge has followed his team all season and was stressed out about their fall into the bottom division. At the said football match, his team, Preston North End, scored a goal and, like I say, with all the stress and worry his team had caused him, he cannot remember how he came to have a seat in his hand while celebrating. In his shock, he threw it away on to the pitch in a moment of madness – an action he deeply regrets. For this, he is really apologetic and is willing to pay for any damage.'

I hear this from a bloke with plums in his mouth; I nearly repeated the performance of the young kid on the Saturday night.

I got a fine as well, no ban or jail, which would have done us a favour – not having to follow Preston next season.

The train journey home was spent reading about the Bradford fire, which started to make you think whether all this shit was worth it for a game of football. What a waste of life. RIP, the departed at Bradford.

And just as you think it couldn't get any worse, it did. The 1985/86 season was a shocker: two managers went through the revolving door (Booth, then Brian Kidd), leaving Jonathan Clark as a temporary manager. Some of the other stats included:

Away: Northampton Town 6, PNE 0
Home: PNE 3, Chester City 6
FA Cup First Round: Walsall 7, PNE 3
Average Home Attendance: 3,502
Highest Attendance: 5,585 against Burnley
Lowest Attendance: 2,007 against Scunthorpe United
Final Position: 23rd in Division Four

The famous Preston North End had to go cap in hand for re-election. Luckily, this was the last season this system was used, with the play-off system being used for a couple of years. Enfield applied for our place in the league; and I thought 'Enfield' was a motorcycle.

The only silver lining that season was knocking Blackpool out of the League Cup – gee whiz!

And as far as glamorous away venues went – Crewe was not one of them. However, travel was undertaken one Saturday. It was a place we'd changed trains at on many occasions and, rather than going by the obvious, we set off in two minibuses. (You sometimes ended up in vans with lads from different areas around town, not knowing their backgrounds – today was one of those days.)

First port of call was Warrington town centre. It had just gone half-ten in the morning, and we needed liquid refreshments. Entering a large pub, one vanload went in one side and us in the other, gagging for a drink. The landlord was busy on one side serving up the lads and everyone was waving notes in the air to attract his attention. I got told later a lad dragged a high bar stool over towards the TV that was fixed to a bracket on the wall. Witnesses presumed he was going to switch it on for the back end of *Tiswas* or *Swap Shop*. Wrong! He reached up and unplugged the video recorder on the shelf below the television, stepped down with it under his arm and exited sharpish. His parting words were: 'I'm off... I'll get a hundred nicker for this back in the Red Lion in Preston!' with the pub door swinging shut. He was last seen, machine tucked under his jacket, lead hanging out, with the plug trailing on the pavement!

After finally getting served, pints were sunk in one, not waiting for the landlord to notice while switching on the TV for

Football Focus or the first race at Kempton that his precious VHS was missing. He would no doubt alert the police.

Arriving not long later in Crewe, we parked in the centre and headed off to find a pub. The town seemed quite hectic with shoppers out for a bargain, a sparse spreading of police and certain areas cordoned off. A lad asked a passer-by, 'Is there some kind of carnival or procession taking place?'

'No, mate, it's a National Front march,' was the reply as he scurried off.

The NF are in town. What a lethal mixture! Football and politics! Football lads – white, black and Asian – with the far right nationalist party present that day. A cocktail for violence in the making, whether shaken or stirred!

We found a pub to sort out plans with another two carloads of Preston swelling our ranks to just under 50. What happened next is very blurred and hopefully Seedy remembers it all slightly better than I do.

Seedy:

We'd had a flyer en route in Warrington with a lad allegedly relieving a public house of its video machine, so we did one rapid.

Once in Crewe, we're in a pub just plotting up when it goes off. It was manic and events happened spontaneously! I think the NF march had started coming past and Preston just seemed to steam out throwing pint pots and pool balls at the parade. On the other side of the pub, it now became noticeable that there was a large contingent of black lads who also bolted out on to the street. All hell had broken loose.

For some reason, me and Dave T had managed to get

locked into the boozer. And we could see fighting with weapons being used through the leaded windows. A pool ball then makes a reappearance through the glass. I found out later not only were Preston at it with the NF, they were having it with the black lads thinking they were Crewe! The black lads thought Preston were NF, until one of their ranks shouted, 'Stop, they've got blacks with them, they're not NF!' The NF were more confused than any of the sides!

After nearly five minutes of rucking, it seemed to have calmed down and the door was unlocked by the landlord. A few black lads filtered back in to join up with a small mob of Crewe lads. They'd been undetected in the mêlée. One lad proceeded to pop his head out of the studded oak door – WHACK. A Preston lad, Mad Jack – and he was mad, take it from me – smashed him full force with a pool cue in the face, sending him reeling back in. The lad's boat-race was well fucked up and I think Jack had shouted for us to 'Get out!' Even the Crewe lads' white faces had turned black as thunder as they surrounded us. I was shitting myself when a black lad recognised Dave. Luckily, or unluckily, he'd been in jail with him and to our relief he got both of us out untouched under a barrage of threats. A quick 'Thanks', and we jogged on to catch up with the rest of the boys as more police arrived to help their colleagues amongst the chaos.

Was I glad my mate Dave T had done a stretch in prison with the Crewe lad! The day was more befitting a sketch out of a black comedy than your normal Saturday-afternoon football fight. One you want to forget but on the other hand remember and reminisce about. It still remains a somewhat grey area and haunts me to this day.

A night game at Stockport was the norm due to having illustrious neighbours like Manchester United and Manchester City. Usually, they played on Fridays or Mondays just so they would get a couple of thousand in.

A fleet of cars and vans set off following the signs to Manchester Airport, as Stockport was not much further along than the end of the runway. Even the older lads among us had never been and we didn't know if they'd be up for it.

After parking up in the town centre, a couple of pubs were visited with some fine ale sunk, that being the only pleasure sampled before the match.

We then paid into the seats and ended up sitting near big Joe Corrigan. He was that big in the flesh he cast a shadow over the pitch. Another norm that season was us getting beat, which we duly did, 2–1.

Heading out after the match, a few Stockport got moved on by the police. So it was quick foot into the transport and a close bumper-to-bumper drive around the surrounding streets. Our scouting mission turned up a blank so it was back into town.

We were doing a 10mph crawl in half-a-dozen cars and two vans and, as we went past a boozer, some snidey Stockport launched bricks at the last car. Its back window went through and the driver hit his horn and brakes. Drivers and passengers in the rest of the vehicles were hanging out of rolled-down windows pointing and shouting to take the next left.

With the transport parked up, Stockport might have thought Preston had gone the wrong way. Everyone was out and loading up with a selection of missiles, some lads armed up to the hilt. Preston took a left then another left on foot. A surprise element was wanted for the inflicters of damage to the car, sneaking up a street; the pub was less than 50 yards away when a Stockport spotter clocked Preston. He gave it toes into the pub.

With the plan up in smoke, and no time to waste, it was full steam ahead towards the target. It was then a matter of get in, do the occupants, exit and home. Preston were nearly at the pub's front door when it was banged shut and bolted. Lads started deploying the assorted missiles they'd been carrying for the last couple of minutes – litter bins, bricks, bottles and 'owt else they had went right through the acid-etched windows that had probably been in their frames for over 100 years.

A couple of lads jumped up on to the pub's stone sills, taking a peek inside. The public house now resembled the *Mary Celeste*; not a single soul was seen, which was odd as it had had a head count of over 30 a minute earlier. Both the landlord and the barmaid had gone as well, just half-filled pint pots and smouldering fag ends in ashtrays. The only sound was of the odd fragment of glass falling on to the pavement and heavy breathing from the lads. If you're going to give it out, you should expect something in return, shouldn't you? A last brick was thrown, smashing into the optics, and it was back into the transport before the police turned up.

The final view looking over a shoulder at the aftermath was of red velvet curtains flapping and billowing in the wind.

And from the quaint image of a newly smashed-up pub to the history-laden city of Chester. And even in places as nice as Chester, you can get the odd spot of bother. We'd been a few times before, the only trouble being getting into the pubs either en route to Wrexham or playing in the lovely, picturesque city itself. You usually had to break into groups of twos or threes just to get a bevy. This year, it was my 21st birthday and we were having a good day out until a Preston lad, not in our company, brought a lump hammer crashing down on to the bar demanding a drink. We did one rapido, not wanting any attention. I do wonder sometimes if he ever got a drink or service with a smile?

With plenty of ale inside us, we headed up to the game, getting there just after kick-off. We were walking round the ground when we spotted about 30 lads ahead coming towards us; no worries, we had about the same numbers. Now nearly nose-to-nose, it went off, but they had half-a-dozen Old Bill in tow and the fighting was soon stopped. Reinforcements arrived, and one from each side got lifted. The police put us on to the ground, with us wondering exactly who they were, because Chester never seemed to have any lads when we'd turned up previously.

When we'd visited a couple of years before, at the final whistle we'd gone right across the pitch and right into the Chester end, chasing what lads they had out of the ground, sliding in the mud as we went.

The match ended with a 2–0 defeat – again – and we headed back into town. Rambie wouldn't stop going on about this burger shop and the egg burgers that were served up. As we were leaving the fast-food joint, we noticed 30 other lads walking the same way but on the opposite side of the street. A Black Maria was trailing them with another one parked straight up ahead. It wasn't the same mob from before the game. I then recognised a couple from run-ins over the years – it was Tranmere. We crossed over the road and started walking side-by-side and got chatting. 'What you doing here, lads?' I asked.

'Looking for Wrexham... have you see 'em, la?'

It suddenly twigs! 'I think so... we bumped into 30 lads outside the ground and I don't think they were Chester. Why them?'

'They slashed one of ours up badly and we said we'd meet here the other week to settle a score.'

'They must have fucked 'em off after our little run-in.'

There was no chance of any action, even if both parties were interested, with too many Old Bill watching our every move. We headed for the train station, Tranmere to their vans, goodbyes said.

There was always someone out there wanting to settle a score, with us getting caught up in the middle. Our mate confirmed it later that they were Wrexham, after getting out of the nick.

We headed back to Preston for a night out and the mates got me absolutely smashed. I ended up talking like a clanger after drinking all the Soup Dragon's soup!

I went for a piss in the Red Lion pub and someone gave me a right twatting in the face, then did one. I didn't know what I'd done to upset him. It could have been the Soup Dragon himself!

Another jumper ruined! What a waste of sheep's wool – thanks for the 21st-birthday present, mate.

* * *

For the 1986/87 season, we had a new manager – big John McGrath, a well-known lad from Salford who had made a playing career out of booting quick wingers! A plastic pitch was laid to raise funds by hiring it out to the community. Perhaps, just for once, we had a season to look forward to!

Preston finished second in the league with a club record of 90 points and, in the process, turned over Burnley 4–1 away, and 2–1 at home. Also, 16,456 fans turned out on a Friday night at Deepdale to witness Preston beat Northampton Town 1–0, the eventual league winners. Things were starting to look up! It was a game in which Gary Brazil scored the only goal with end-to-end stuff from start to finish.

Once again, PNE knocked Blackpool out of the League Cup. Preston also had an FA Cup run, beating the likes of Bury,

Chorley and Middlesbrough, then going out to Newcastle United at St James' Park in the fourth round. The only downside was the transfer of the lethal John 'JT' Thomas to Bolton Wanderers.

The legend Frank Worthington – on and off the field – also arrived at Deepdale at the back end of the season.

So there we were, off to Northampton in a 50-seater coach, only it was full, so two carloads of us set off as well. We met up with the coach at the services near Birmingham to arrange a meeting if possible when we arrived in Northampton, as we'd never been before.

We parked up in the town centre and went straight into a boozer. It was just before midday and drinks were ordered for the ten of us. We'd not been in long when faces started to appear at the front 'olde worlde' leaded windows. Enter Northampton's boys – 10, 20, 30, 40, 50 or more – we had no way out and no chance against those sorts of numbers. It looked like it was going to come on top.

A lad in his late twenties then came walking over humming 'The Boys Are Back in Town' by Thin Lizzy. Call it foolish, but I went straight up to him and said, 'Is there enough of you yet? I'm sure we could handle a few more.'

He just looked at me strangely.

I then said, 'We've got no chance here, mate, but a coach full of Preston are in town... they might be up for it?'

Wolfie:

I'd been on my walkies, one of my usual tricks, to find the coach and also to see if there were any lads about. I didn't find either! I then headed back to the pub to inform the lads.

And on rounding the corner I'm greeted with a sight of 80 unknown faces, half pressed against stained-glass windows, the others trying to get in. I can't let the lads down so I run towards the door full pelt, doing a high dive over lads' heads and crumpling down into the lusher [pub]. I'm up on to my feet quickly with no time to waste as the mates are well outnumbered.

The Northampton lads started to leave, telling us, 'I can see you haven't got the numbers... we'll try and find the coach.'

The landlord was also on the blower to the police station in the background. The colour started coming back into the lads' faces and unusual smells faded away.

At this stage, it was respect to Northampton for the walkover; we'd have done the same. Another beer was ordered to calm the nerves and Ste said, 'Right, we'll keep it together and we'll move off in a few minutes and try and find the coach. They might be up near the ground if they've had a police escort and, if we run into Northampton and get cornered or anyone goes down, we'll all help out.'

Ale finished, the pub door was pushed open, the coast was clear so we headed on out. We left on tenterhooks looking in every direction.

We had been walking for about ten minutes and our composure had returned as we headed over a bit of grass wasteland when someone shouted, 'Fackin' get them!' It was an area with more points than a compass and the Cobblers came from every direction. Northampton must have been waiting and now had us surrounded. Hurriedly, we circled our wagons into a huddle – it seemed to be becoming a regular occurrence. We formed a tight circle and the first one arrived on the scene – BANG – he went down, same to the next and the next one. Great! We seem to be doing all right.

I noticed a mate was hitting one on the head with a pint barrel. It wouldn't smash and nor would the lad go down. There were 25 of them into us and we were holding our own. I don't know if you've been in a situation like that, but it gets the ticker racing. It's times like this you'd rather be out with the wife shopping, it's that scary – only kidding.

'Run!' was shouted loudly in a Preston accent. This usually means the Old Bill have turned up or something nasty was about to happen. A gap appeared with more Northampton arriving on the scene. I also thought that some of the lads' arses had gone with the old turtle's head making an appearance. The ten of us started running as if our lives depended on it with the 70 Northampton behind us, and I didn't think they wanted to cobble our shoes. Going full pelt down a high street, we then went across a junction when a Ford Capri came tearing round the corner. It looked like the one off *The Professionals* by the way it was being driven.

It threw out the anchors but Rambie was out in the road in front of it and it clipped him; he went down. I grabbed him by the back of his dungarees – fucking dungarees. He thought he was cool in them, like someone out of Dexy's Midnight Runners. I'd just managed to get him up on his feet, and saw the rest of the lads disappear into a shop 30–40 feet away. The Northampton lads were still hot on our heels and we just about made it in before any serious damage was done.

As we got into the shop, there was a hysterical woman shop assistant screaming at us. The three members of staff thought we'd come in to rob the shop. A bloke was on the phone straight away to the police and another picked up the till and bolted up the stairs with it; the other two soon followed him, locking the door at the top.

'Where's Burkie?' I cried out.

'He must be still out there,' someone else shouted.

We found ourselves in a car-spares shop, cans of Castrol GTX, car batteries and a large selection of air fresheners surrounded us. Out the lads went, letting loose with everything; there was plenty more where that lot came from. Lads were bumping into each other game-show fashion, unloading their wares.

The Northampton cunts were trying to put our mate through a shop window with him bouncing back off. It was back in for a quick oil change and MOT. By now, the shop's two front windows were totalled and so was the glass door. The locals were trying to restock the shelves and there was oil all over the floor with everyone sliding about on shards of glass. Everyone attacked them for one last time and we started to move Northampton, while also hearing sirens in the distance.

Northampton's lads were running everywhere and a couple of lads managed to get back to Burkie. He was sat on the floor with his coat over his head. A quick dust down and everyone headed in the opposite direction, not waiting around for the police to come. On doing so, we passed two couples in their mid-forties saying, in Yankee accents, 'Are you soccer hooligans?'

They got a reply from all ten of us: 'Fuck off!'

Just before we got to the ground, the coachload of Preston lads came out of a boozer and one said, 'Where've you lot been?'

'Don't ask,' was the reply.

We paid to get into to the cricket – I mean football – ground and what a shambles of a stadium it is. Stands on wheels pulled into position around the county cricket ground. We weren't a happy bunch of lads.

Just before the final whistle, Preston went round to the

home end 80-strong. Preston lads, arms folded, waited for the gates to open. And when they did, anyone who looked up for it, or wanted it, got it for the next ten minutes. The rest of them wouldn't come out. They found themselves on a sticky wicket; funny how things change. The Old Bill and undercover started turning up with quite a few getting arrested. It was day over and home we went. At least they got some payback!

Next day, at Sunday football, one of the lads was sat in the changing rooms before the game telling his team-mates what had happened. 'We emptied the shop. I even picked up this big starter motor off the counter and launched it into them.'

A lad chirped up, 'Bet that got 'em going?'

The team was rolling about on the floor laughing. Laugh now... cry later!

When Preston played Northampton in the return fixture on a Friday night, we beat them in front of a full house. The NAT (Northampton Affray Team) never returned the favour; they never did travel up to ours. Preston had a good size mob out, eagerly waiting, only for it once more to end in inter-feuding at last orders.

And so to a little local skirmish. Who'd have thought it? Little old Chorley drew Preston in the FA Cup. It's a hop, skip and a jump from us, just down the road. We'd had a couple of run-ins with Chorley lads on nights out ruffling a few feathers. The locals were never too keen on 'Preston Townies'. The Magpies had knocked out the mighty Wolves at Burnden Park, the home of Bolton Wanderers, in the previous round. Chorley fancied a big pay day so, this time, Ewood Park was their option, not fancying Preston's 'plastic fantastic'. For us, we hoped for a double header! Fingers crossed that Blackburn and Chorley lads would be out. Have our cake and eat it.

A fleet of cars met up at the Hesketh Arms pub to take the short trip down Preston Road to Blackburn. No matter how many times we'd been to Rovers, it had always been a non-event, but expectations were high that day.

Over the years, we've had bits and bats, usually chasing their mob for hours on end. Once, they did launch an attack off a railway bridge near the town centre then got off. A few lads ended up having to go to hospital for stitches.

We arrived early and drank in nearly every Thwaites pub in town looking for double trouble. The only action witnessed was a group of other Preston lads doing all the bandits and fag machines, many being dumped in the pubs' beer gardens. We got the backlash from irate landlords with the police on our cases.

The long hike from town was undertaken half-an-hour before kick-off. It was still pay on the day so someone came up with the idea of trying the Blackburn end to see if there were any lads about. We rounded the corner behind the stand to be confronted with a line of the boys in blue, as fans were walking towards turnstiles, some being stopped and questioned about which part of Lancashire they were from. The 40 or so I was with started chanting, 'Chorley...Chorley...Chorley!' The majority of us got through; the odd lad who got stopped and questioned generally knew a street or road in the Chorley district. It was that close.

In we went, regrouping on the other side, making our way up the steps into the packed end. It was going off straight away. Running battles in a swaying crowd took place with lads not knowing who was who. The major 'off' was between two sets of Preston lads!

The action was caught on camera and shown on Monday

night's local news. Police moved in and started arresting, managing to move the majority of Preston round to the Darwen Road End. Three of us got our heads down, mingling in with the black-and-white scarf-wearers, waiting to see if more Preston had the same idea. There were only two more lads that I recognised, one being a face around Preston, a real hard case, and he was well pissed. The five of us made our way into the middle of the singing Chorley, where the man about town started singing Preston songs. Anyone who was brave enough to confront him, and the other four of us, came out second best. All-comers were sent packing.

They shut their cake-holes; it was a piece of cake!

Eventually, in the second half we decided to leave, due to the boredom of the match and no one bothering us. We made our way into town. Surely they must have some lads? It's the law of averages! No, there were none to be found.

Later, we met up with the rest of the lads after having a good look around, before returning to Preston, gutted as usual.

* * *

After surviving a trip to Middlesbrough in the last round, we'd been pulled out of the velvet bag against Newcastle away in the FA Cup fourth round. St James' Park, here we come!

Preston were on their best Cup run for many a year and, if an underdog like North End were ever going to win the Cup, it would have to be the hard way. Two coaches were booked which were top quality – the lads on board, not the transport. The heaters didn't work and they did 50mph tops! Everyone shivered all the way to Newcastle. The only warmth we got en route was stopping off for a few beers in a little village boozer and all huddled round the open log fire.

On arrival, our 100 spilled off the coaches into the freezing conditions. The lads fancied a good, brisk walk round the ground to get their blood circulating. It was already busy with large queues forming at the turnstiles with a big crowd expected. Preston's turnout that day was second to none. The only problem was there were no Geordie lads to be found! Not that you could spot them by their clobber. Donkey jackets were still regulation dress of the day.

Our lot decided to get into the ground, not fancying missing the match due to being locked out. We weren't used to doing well in the league, never mind in a Cup competition, and the lads were football fans above anything else, plus there was always the post-match entertainment.

On entering the stadium, what a sight greeted us – there were over 5,000 North End supporters in a crowd of 30,495. Preston averaged that season just over 5,000 at home, and the opening home game had attracted less than we'd brought to Newcastle that day. Talk about people jumping on the bandwagon! Fifty-four coaches made the journey that day.

The game petered out a 2–0 defeat; it was not going to be North End's year once more. The sheer size of Preston's travelling army that day took the police by surprise and they kept us locked in for nearly an hour. On our exit, all the Magpies had flown home – either that, or gone celebrating in local working men's clubs; there were none to be found.

It was the biggest following Preston had taken anywhere in my time and I never witnessed a punch thrown. Perhaps we were in the wrong place at the wrong time or the right place at the right time. Who knows?

We heard the following week, when we travelled to Halifax Town, that a few Preston did have to visit Newcastle's Infirmary after not answering the question, 'Have you got the time, mate?' Their silence was met with an iron bar across the old grey matter! Pity we weren't around to defend them. The attendance that day at The Shay Ground was 2,968, with only a couple of hundred Preston making the trip. Where had they all disappeared to?

There were many such trips when we wondered where all our fans had gone. But when we travelled to the capital, we managed to muster a decent turnout, particularly when Preston needed a win to regain Third Division status as runners-up in the league. On that trip by train, we had plenty of ale and a pack of cards on board our 'Orient Express' to keep us occupied on our journey south.

We arrived at Euston and met up with several Preston lads who'd moved down to London and the surrounding areas over the years. We had a nice firm out that day with over 100 lads having made the trip. Then we headed on down to the Underground and, to most of us, it was still Double Dutch. Central line this, Northern line that, with colours not meaning a thing. Finally getting sorted and on our way, we had high expectations on and off the pitch. Talk about looking for a needle in a haystack – it was hard enough to find a boozer round Leytonstone, never mind any of their lads.

At the game, there was a bit of a kick-off in Orient's seats; a few Preston lads had decided to go in them instead of the away end with the police having to move them out.

The ball was pumped forward to Les Chapman, the old man of the team; he looped a shot over everyone's heads, which ended up nestled in the onion bag. It was fairly late on and it secured the points. At the final whistle, there were scenes of joy and jubilation, with hugs and kisses between grown men.

The only action I saw that day was when I climbed over the

fence and dropped on to the pitch. My promotion present was a truncheon round the head delivered by one of the Met's finest. I also ripped my clothing that day, not through scrapping though! On the way down on to the pitch, I caught my new Hawaiian shirt. I took it the officer didn't realise what promotion meant to a North Ender, so I held no hard feelings.

The police finally gave up trying to stop Preston lads getting on to the playing surface and opened the gates – if only I hadn't been so impatient. Preston fans were carrying round players on their shoulders and singing their heads off in celebration. Most had never experienced anything like this, with it being nearly ten years since we'd tasted any sort of success.

On leaving the ground, Orient's followers had faded into the evening. The only thing to look forward to was if we bumped into any other firms at Euston, next year's fixture list and the Donkey Lashers.

Naturally, Preston were on the crest of a wave as they entered the Third Division in 1987/88, but it turned out to be a great anti-climax – a total wipeout. And this despite Preston having, I thought, the three best strikers in the league – Tony Ellis, Gary Brazil and the young Nigel Jemson. We also had the most skilful midfielder ever to grace our plastic pitch – Brian Mooney.

North End stuttered in the league, finishing 16th. The highs were a Freight Rover Trophy run which nearly saw Preston reach Wembley for the first time in 24 years. A 0–0 draw at Turf Moor against Burnley took North End back to Deepdale all square. In front of a 17,592 crowd, the Clarets won 3–1 in extra time.

Off the pitch, we knew we could rely on Blackpool to give us a decent day out. A decision had been made not to go on the train to Blackpool, as we would get clocked getting on and off

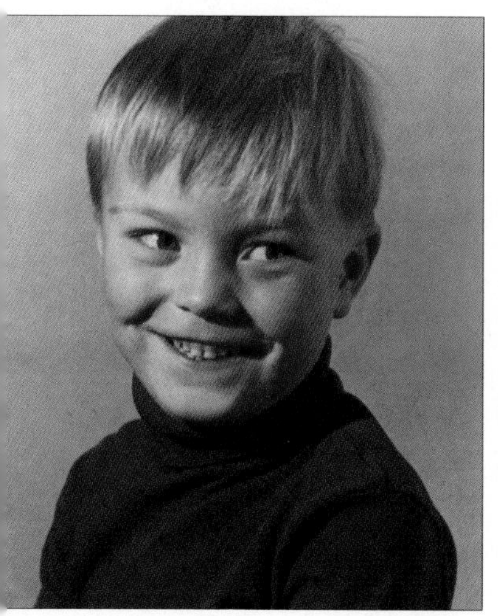

Above left: 'All things truly wicked start from innocence.' Me as a young lad, looking as if butter wouldn't melt …

Above right: Young, dumb and full of 'Come on then!'

Below: SMG Cubs; League and Cup double winners of season 1975/76, undefeated all campaign. We are pictured here with North End legends Mike Elwiss and Roy Tunks.

Above: Birmingham coming over the Town End fences at Deepdale in 1979. This was my first hands-on engagement in hostilities on the terraces

Below left: The boy about town. With a few of my school chums – that's me in the middle.

Below right: An assortment of north-west lads on the ferry to Northern Ireland in 1984.

Top left: Italia '90.

Top right: Rave on, baby. On holiday with the better half in the early nineties. Wacky shirt, ponytail – those were the days.

Middle: All aboard the Orient Express – London bound!

Left: In the Smoke – Wembley 1994. A day out from the asylum for some of the lads present.

Above: Striking a pose – NOT! Ready for action.

Below left: One of our many days out away from the footy. These trips could – and did – end up messy to say the least.

Below right: A penny for them. A million and one memories. Here, I'm sitting on the old Pavilion Stand players entrance steps at Deepdale just before the stand was knocked down to make way for the final piece in the jigsaw of PNE's new stadium. It's a whole new ballgame at Deepdale nowadays.

it, so it was decided on cars and vans. The convoy set off going down the 'A' roads, using the back way via Poulton. We stopped off for some light refreshments bang on eleven bells at the Wyre River pub, left just after 12pm, and managed to get into Blackpool undetected, parking up in back streets just past the North Pier. A good 100 of us were on foot, making our way along the front and everyone was well up for it.

Preston turned left to head up Talbot Road; hopefully, Blackpool would have a lookout to run off to the Ramsden or the Hop Inn pubs informing Blackpool of our arrival. Wrong! Blackpool were in Yates's and out they came. The problem was that our friends, the police, had set up camp outside. Nothing was going to stop Preston's surprise attack and spoil their fun.

The lads ran towards the pub and you could see that most of the Tangerines didn't fancy it and were on the back foot. A few game lads started mixing it and I was scrapping with a bloke nearly twice my age when I felt a clamp on my forearm. Looking down, I saw the rabid German Shepherd that I'd described earlier, who'd decided to use my arm for lunch.

Preston were steaming in all around and the doggy plod let me go. I did a quick change and I was a new man – Mr Benn. It then went pear-shaped with more Old Bill arriving and rounding us up as they tried to regain order.

We were then escorted up to the ground – well, it was more of a dump than a ground, even worse than ours. Their owner of the club at the time – who ended up sewing bags in the nick – had not splashed the cash yet.

You could see a few Blackpool down side streets taking a nosey as we were moved along, and five of us managed to peel off from the escort. Their main lad was too busy trying to clock ours, Taz, so I ran up from the side managing snidely to land one in the side of his head. Stunned, he staggered backwards and did one with his mate before I got any chance of more action.

I have read their account about the events before the match that day – ambiguous, equivocal and enigmatic!

Game over and we got the usual treatment, kept in and then escorted back up to the train station. We managed to drift off in twos and threes in different directions and got mobbed up back at where we'd parked our transport.

We waited for a bit and then made a move towards the Ramsden pub down the back streets. En route we bumped into the Bisons! Now fanning out into the road, we slowly walked towards them; they were bouncing about, beckoning us on. Getting within 10ft, their main actor came running towards us shouting, 'I want Taz, leave him for me.' The lads made a gap to let him through – big mistake. We had Blackpool back-pedalling and a few punches were thrown, but, with their top boy at it with ours at the back, they managed to get it together moving forward. Preston lads were spooked by this and started back-pedalling, leaving about 20 of us to make a stand. We stood no chance and Blackpool got well on top and we had to do one – nightmare! Preston were moved good and proper by the Lashers, all because of one man, their top lad. Every credit.

The police arrived on the scene and we were rounded up once again. This time, we were escorted to our transport and sent on our way back home. Preston were left licking their wounds and I was dropped off at the hospital to get a big prick up the arse, a sharp reminder of a not so good day.

The return fixture was on Boxing Day and, by all accounts, they were coming en masse. By the time both sets of lads had made any sort of contact, it was on the ground – eye and verbal. Arrangements were made for the Red Lion pub in town later, when the crowds had died down, so we were set to get our festive knees-up after all.

We set off to base camp, the Red Lion, after the final whistle, and it was soon solid right up to the doors. The beer was flowing and it was a waiting game, with no news coming through on the hoolie grapevine. Lads started to think after an hour it was going to be a no-show. Then news arrived that our main faces had been attacked on Deepdale Road, having been well outnumbered. The rest of us gave it another hour and called it a day. Blackpool must have been rounded up and escorted out of town. Once again, inter-feuding started over lads wanting to get home to their young families. That was why Preston, in my eyes, never really swelled into a formidable force – too much bitching and falling out.

Cold turkey, flat balloons and more Christmas pud... that was all there was on offer for the Christmas derby that year.

I've heard Blackpool claimed a victory that day. Their prize was our top lad's belt. Someone got hold of it and apparently they hung it over the bar in their local. They should have waited 'til they got to the Red Lion instead of jumping the gun. That's when a proper result would have been sorted!

Years later, I bumped into some of their old heads in Poulton while having a Christmas drink. Sound lads and we'd a good chat about the old days.

It's frightening how much a man can mellow in his old age, isn't it?

Vic:

Don't volunteer to be the driver – it's never a good move but it was my turn, so I had to agree.

C and me hired a van; not a nice minibus with seats like we would all like, just a standard transit. 'We're moving house' was all we'd to say to them to get the van on the hire.

Saturday morning came and I was up early, not realising what I'd let myself in for. I picked C up and then called for the Leyland lads that were making the journey. We had the usual suspects on board – Crookie, Scotch, MB, EM, among others. Then we headed over to Preston. When we picked up Crookie. he was skint but we weren't going to leave him behind so he was on a freebie. What he did have as collateral was a sheepskin coat he'd acquired the night before! So it was up for sale at £40, with no takers.

When we arrived at Preston, we were met with a small but tidy mob of good lads that were up for a laugh and were reliable. The total number for the van was three up front and about twenty in the back. It was a struggle but they squeezed in and we set off on our merry way with the back arches touching the wheel. It could only get better.

Many things happened that day but I'm only going to touch on a few that stand out. Also, RIP to three of the lads on that trip that were too young to be taken away.

We were on the M62 and everyone was in a merry mood with the beer and the chat flowing freely. When you're driving, it's hard work, listening to everyone getting pissed and you're sober.

As were driving along at 80mph, a car came up alongside with five young men in it. They were staring our way. We returned stares, now noticing that they were Burnley supporters. So the abuse started between the vehicles. We went past a sign saying 'Birch Services one mile'; this prompted hand signals to pull over at the services and we'd sort things out there. The three of us in the front were laughing and told the lads in the back to keep quiet when we pulled up and we would give our new friends a nice surprise. Now don't get me wrong, the odds weren't stacked in their favour, and we're no bullies, so it was just going to be a laugh to scare the shit out of them.

Anyway, they indicated, pulling off the motorway, and we followed. They parked up and jumped out really keen and well up for it. I parked up just ahead of them and the two other lads and I got out. The two mates headed towards our foe as I went to the back doors. The Burnley started to bounce towards us looking at me funny, but not as funny as when the doors came open and the rest spilled out on to the car park. It's a shame there were no camera phones in those days – it would've been a classic picture! Their jaws dropped, scraping the floor as they turned to run. A couple made it back into the car but it was too late as we now had them surrounded. It was apologies galore and they didn't really want any trouble. Good, nor did we, just a laugh at their expense and their food, booze, fags, mags and newspapers.

With all our freshly acquired contraband, it was time to head on to Grimsby and, while I was driving still at 80mph, the lads in the back started acting up. They were having a bit of a sing-song and decided to blow pepper in little sachets from the motorway services into each other's eyes. Then they started diving about and the van began to sway. There were some big lads in there; MB was one of them. If you put a couple of handles on his waist you could have mistaken him for two barn doors. He started swaying, which in turn made the whole van sway. It wasn't easy keeping control. From the middle lane to the other two, we swayed back and forth with the central reservation looming. Luckily, I just about managed to avoid it. 'Any more and the van goes home. You can all calm down because, if the Old Bill go past and spot us, we will get fucked!' I said. The rest of the journey to Grimsby went without a hitch if my old memory serves me well.

Signs for Grimsby centre were spotted and we exited the motorway and on to the 'A' roads, everything A-OK!

Everybody in the back was happy and boisterous when up ahead the traffic was building up and grinding to a stop. The Old Bill were checking cars and vans and obviously this wasn't ideal, so it was everyone out and walk. The lads turned a corner heading for the back of some buildings to find a way round the police so I could pick them back up past the checkpoint.

We were now at the front of the queue with the head of a dibble popping through the open window asking us where we're going and what for.

'We've come to collect a suite that we've bought off someone in [a random street] out of the local paper.' (I had that one noted down – I'd done a bit of research.)

'OK, mate, on your way, have a good day.'

'We hope so, officer.'

The rest of the lads appeared down the road so we parked up near a small industrial estate and walked into town. Grimsby had a few spotters hanging about who flew off when they saw us marching into their manor. There had been no action and it was getting late, so we set off to the ground, where we met a small reception committee. The dibble were there as well so we had a bit of a run towards each other which was met with the Old Bill intervening and they put us straight on the ground. We now hoped that it might go off after the game; they knew that we were here so they had time to get sorted and no matter what their numbers they would be met with 25 lads that wouldn't move.

The game passed without any incidents and Preston won!

It's out into the open again. And as we walk up the road, Grimsby come out from a side street – great! It's going to go off and we're stood there, willing and waiting. It's a skirmish, nowt major and we don't move so they're on their toes with us in hot pursuit. They stop and rally with a few more punches thrown, then the usual sound of sirens. We stay put as Grimsby do one into side streets only they know best. The police line us up against the wall and would like to take a video and some photos for the record. They also ask for the drivers of the cars or minibuses. No one steps forward; they ask again, saying, 'If you don't come forward, then you all spend the night in Grimsby nick.' That doesn't sound too appealing so I step forward, having had my details taken. 'Who else is driving you shower about our town!'

'Just me in one transit van.'

This is met with 'You're joking!' which is passed down the radio: 'You won't believe this, Sarge...'

We're then escorted by more dibble than you could muster for a G8 Summit back to the van. They still can't believe we're just in the one. But they want us in it and out of town, ASAP.

We're back on the road with police to the front and rear 'til we're out of town. Eventually, there is no more police, so we make a steady pace for home. Then the lads in the back want some beer and nibbles.

Wakefield, that's what the sign said, so there will be an off-licence to be found. We find a little shop and park across the road. The van empties with the lads getting cans and going to the counter to pay, when the door opens and two long arms stretch inside grabbing a tray of ale. Then they both disappear. With that, everyone grabs what they want, running back over to the van. All the doors slam shut and it's go, go, go! I drive left, right, left and down a side street. Anywhere really, just to get away from the shop. We park up down an alleyway between some houses with not a sound to be heard. The silence is broken with the unmistakable sound of a can opening and one of the lads saying, 'It tastes better when it's free.' Everyone cracks up and joins in the drinking.

'Where's Scotch? Is he up front with you lot?' a voice booms out.

'No, he should be in the back with you,' I reply.

'No he ain't.'

Shit, we're a man down. And the last time he was seen was in the offy. (He hadn't made it out and they had locked him in the shop, ringing the police.) As we are running through what to do – 'Leave him, he's only a jock' – even we wouldn't haven't done that! – a woman went past walking a dog taking a long, hard look at the van. The lights are out with a lot of noise and movement coming from inside. The nosey boot was probably head of the local neighbourhood watch scheme! Twice more she went past. Bollocks to her, we needed to get back to sort the Scotch problem out. Once more she went past but stopped and pointed at us.

The next thing, blue lights appear and, with nowhere to go, we sit tight as a patrol car pulls up. I wind the window down and lean out noticing that in the car are two dibbles and Scotch in the back with a big smile on his face. If he was going to get locked up, at least he wasn't on his own now!

The police inform us that they have struck a deal with the shop owners and, if we give them back what had been taken, we get Scotch back and we'd to do one. Now that was a good deal. About ten unopened cans of lager are passed out with the dibble asking, 'Is that it?'

'Yes, officer.'

With that, Scotch is released, hops into the back of the van, is handed a can and we're off home with another escort, this time a car at the front and a riot van to the rear all the way back to the motorway. We're told not to stop 'til we get back to Preston, as police would be looking out for us all the way. If we did, we would all be nicked and charged.

At nearly every turn-off on the way home, a patrol car was parked up making sure we didn't get off anywhere. We finally pulled off the M6 at the Tickle Trout Hotel on the edge of Preston, where we were stopped by the Old Bill. They'd kindly been waiting for us and made everyone in the back get out and start walking up the hill with us in the front told to head home. That was that, day over!

We had to turn the van's engine off and roll into the hire centre when returning the Transit. The engine was knackered.

Two things that ring out about that away day were: Don't drive a van unless under orders off the lads! And don't bother to bring a woman's sheepskin coat that's for sale into a van full of lads, you've no chance of getting a result.

It might not have been as violent as we might have liked

in those days but it's just one of the many days out we had. At Preston we were a tight bunch that liked a laugh and a drink – we weren't just thugs!

1988/89 was a roller-coaster of a season; I saw Preston getting smashed away at Wolves 6–0 – who went up as champions – and a 5–3 home thriller against Brentford in March.

North End's up-and-down season was epitomised with the return game against Wolves in the May with Preston already in the play-offs and Wolves crowned champions. One up, then 3–1 down, then Tony Ellis tapped in a second and then, in the dying seconds, Patterson got an equaliser. A classic football match in a sun-swept Deepdale.

Preston were well up for the two-legged play-offs against Port Vale. In the home leg, North End dominated the first half, going a goal up. Vale then took control of the second half, pulling one back, with it ending 1–1.

Away at Vale Park, Port Vale took the lead early on, although Preston pulled one back within minutes. Then a dodgy penalty decision against North End saw David Brown save the spot kick. Hopes were high at half-time; these were soon shattered six minutes into the second half. North End went 2–1 down, and then another Vale goal with a quarter-of-an-hour left on the clock made the score 3–1. Preston didn't give up, but all efforts came to no avail. No Wembley, no promotion – you get used to it being a North Ender.

You also get used to running with the wolves – and, in this case, it was at Molineux. Preston and Wolves were now up to the dizzy heights of the third tier, and a fleet of vans and minibuses were booked, meeting up en route. It was the best away turnout for a few seasons but we still couldn't get things sorted. Too much fannying about and stopping off at too many boozers made us arrive late, just before kick-off. Over 100 of us exited our transport and headed to the ground. Molineux was in a state of disrepair and a new stand was being developed.

Preston marched round what's left of the famous stadium, looking for their boys with the gates being tried to be kicked open. Then a decision was made to pay on the Wolves end. Preston had caught the police unaware and the plan nearly worked but the lads who paid on got sussed straight away. The Old Bill radioed through for back-up and sent in the horses with heavy-handed tactics, lads getting lifted. They finally pushed us round and into the ground.

Eventually, we witnessed one of Preston's biggest ever defeats. Preston had six put past them; a certain Steve Bull scoring several and his mate Andy Mutch helping out by chipping in with the rest.

After the match, Preston spilled out and even managed to lose most of the waiting police heading for the nearby pub. I cannot remember the name of it but the lads thought that there were bound to be some of the Subway Army in out of a 13,000-plus crowd.

On arrival at the said boozer, lads tried to gain entry but the locals weren't having it, throwing a few glasses then bolting the doors. Preston tried to force their way in, with half-a-dozen coppers trying to control the situation. Wolves didn't want to play for the second time. Some lads trapped round the back were booting in the fire escape doors shouting, 'Come on!' with no takers. Wolves that day had met their wolves in sheep's clothing. Preston were finally dispatched by the Old Bill.

We set off back, stopping off in endless towns and villages to be moved on by the local dibble.

Another minibus that went to the match – but not with our convoy – had picked up a local Wolverhampton girl. She'd decided to come back to Preston with them, only to get fired off for being a pain in the early hours. What did she go and do? She only went to Lawson Street Police Station. The lads who were in the van nearly lost their jobs, dignity and relationships after being arrested. She retracted a statement some time down the line. There was no truth, or evidence, in the said matter.

Saying that, a rumour went round that a few lads who were in the van that day picked up a similar type of girl in Burnley at one night game. Their mode of transport this time was a camper van. This lady was up for a laugh and very accommodating, letting the boys have some fun on their return journey to Preston. One lad who didn't participate kept a watchful eye on proceedings to witness lads share her 'company' twice. By the time they'd reached the Tickle Trout Hotel on the outskirts of Preston, she was physically exhausted and the two-timers were worn out. They had a quick whip round and booked her a taxi. The lads gave her a peck on the cheek and waved her goodbye. She was last seen propping up a petrol pump, bow-legged after thoroughly enjoying herself.

A home game against Bolton saw us drinking before the match just off Meadow Street in a pub called the Stone Cottage. A few Bolton made the mistake of coming in, so they got a slap and were sent packing.

After the match, Preston had clocked two vans from Bolton turning up St George's Road. Another mob of lads, not with us, started launching bricks into the vans further up the road. The brakes slammed on, pulling up into a side street. The Preston rubble boys did one, leaving us to mop up their mess. Some big

Trotters emptied out and the half-a-dozen of us were on the back foot slugging away. Meanwhile, the fuzz had been alerted by the noise of bouncing bricks and a lot of shouting going on.

The Big Fella:

Bill and me got collared, and just at that moment when the police are having a word with us, the Bolton lads who'd taken a pasting before the game walk over and grass us up to them. They have a right good moan at the Old Bill about us. The police also thought we'd smashed the van up, so we got arrested. Later, we're charged with criminal damage and breach of the peace. We thought both were in connection with what happened to the van.

Four times we went to court pleading 'not guilty'. And on our fifth appearance, the Bolton van lads are told they've to turn up to give evidence. We enter the courts that morning to be informed the witnesses might not be able to make it. But also we're told the breach of the peace is to do with an incident – a fight – outside a certain pub. We hadn't been anywhere near the said pub that day, so it was two different incidents we're up for.

On the first charge of criminal damage, the prosecution approached the bench and informed the judge, due to the adverse weather conditions and snow on the train tracks, that the witnesses could not make it. They cannot proceed with the case so the judge dismissed the charge.

On the second charge, breach of the peace, PC such and such approaches the bench and whispers something into the prosecutor's ear. He then informs the judge on the second charge they can offer no further evidence too. Case also dismissed, we are free to go. British justice at its best!

Don't get me wrong – me and Bill were no angels but either the PC in question thought we had doubles – I can't imagine anyone else being as ugly as Bill – or he had bad eyesight, or we'd taken a trip in a TARDIS, or Scotty had beamed us up or it was a complete case of mistaken identity. Anyone can make a mistake, can't they?

We'd both had five days off work without pay, and even paid witnesses out of our own pockets to turn up. We had all that stress knowing we really hadn't done anything. This time we were squeaky clean, pure as the driven snow!

A few days later, the Old Bill turn up on my doorstep about another incident that happened at Port Vale in the play-offs. This was when the police were attacked at the end of the game. I'm taken to Preston nick and asked if I can help with the police's enquiries into this and other incidents and give them a few names. Put in front of me is a 3ft-high stack of black-and-white photos and a large selection of coloured ones. It took me over three hours to go through them while being asked question after question. I didn't know a single person or a name.

'Are you sure?' I was asked.

'Honestly. I don't!'

Once in the play-offs, the most exciting thing that happened at home was a fire scare on the away end with the police putting Vale fans on the pitch for 20 minutes.

For the return leg, we met up at Knutsford Services after work, jumped into a box van and off we went. In all the time we'd travelled to Stoke, the only real trouble we'd had was with Port Vale, not the 'Naughties'!

At the match, we were squashed into an open away end, and

I'm sure they sold more tickets than they should have done. At the end of the game, there was a lot of pushing and shoving going on with the stewards, then the plod turned up. Preston were penned in the away end 'til celebrating Vale fans left the ground. North Enders started to have their own spot of entertainment with the police and their dogs.

The newspaper men were busy the next day with the headline that read: 'Search for PNE fans after attack on police'.

A little incident once at Port Vale still makes me laugh to this day. About 15 of us had paid into Port Vale's seats with their lads clocking us but not making a move. At half-time, we went behind the stand half expecting them to attack us. What we didn't expect was all the supposed 'proper fans' joining in. A bloke in his fifties smashed the Big Fella over the head with his red flask full of coffee. It only lasted a few seconds 'til the Old Bill were on the scene. We were moved into the away section with our mate rubbing his head and all the lads taking the piss.

* * *

In 1989/90, John McGrath resigned after an appalling first half of the season, leaving his assistant Les Chapman in temporary charge. His first game was a visit to Reading, ending in a 6–0 thumping.

Preston exited the FA Cup at the hands of a Northern Premier league team, Whitley Bay. And then the fans' favourite John Thomas returned, and survival in Division Three was only confirmed after the final game of the season at Shrewsbury Town which Preston lost 2–0. Luckily, both Fulham and Cardiff City, below Preston in the league, also lost. The main highlight of a dismal season was not getting beaten by Blackpool home and away.

Off the pitch, though, there were plenty more highlights! It had been over ten years since we'd last played Birmingham in the league. You would have thought that ten years on I should have been older and wiser – wrong!

There was a good turnout, with lads in all the town-centre pubs, and we met up with our Leyland mates in the Black-a-Moor Head. The Zulus had been spotted in an escort going up Deepdale Road, so Preston moved off to have a look, weaving in and out of back streets and alleys in small pockets of 20 or less. This was to avoid arousing any unwanted attention.

We found our 20 turning right on to St George's Road, noticing horses outside the Deepdale pub. On closer inspection there was a group of lads stood outside with plenty of black faces mixed in. It was definitely the Zulus, their name and reputation going before them, having a handy firm. We were into 'job mode' and the lads knew they had to hit hard or they would come unstuck. There was hardly a word spoken on the move but a mounted officer clocked us when we were within 30 metres of the pub. The Zulus also clocked us and started moving towards our advancing party.

Pia:

A Preston 'lad' flies in butting one and he goes down with the coppers trying to get between the two factions. I spot an Old Bill on a horse has hold of the mate by his hair, dragging him away. I distracted the officer and shouted, 'Run!' to the mate – which we both did, but in opposite directions. I went down back alleys then hid under a footbridge for a while before doing one and going home. The day was now over for me; I didn't want to get lifted.

The mate had run off, ending up on Blackpool Road,

tying his jumper round his waist and then heading towards the Kop to go on the game. He's trying to look calm and casual by the time he's reached the turnstile only there's a bizzie stood next to the turnstile door. And as the mate is just about to pay on, the copper grabs his arm. He's now asking over his walkie-talkie for an ID description of the individual who'd run off from outside the Deepdale pub. The copper gets an ID. 'Can you come with me?' he tells the mate. The mate pleads his innocence on the way to the cells under the stand to no avail.

Later, he's transported to Preston's Lawson Street Station to get booked in and the desk sergeant asks him, 'So you don't like PC such and such?'

'Who?' the mate replies, thinking he meant the Mountie.

'PC such and such... the officer who you headbutted earlier on outside the Deepdale public house.'

He'd only stuck one on a plain-clothes or an off-duty copper. All I can say is what a dickhead the mate was for going back to the ground. Also, I missed out on a good run-in with the Zulus on Moor Park after the match. Would the mate ever learn?

Leyland Lad:

Matches against Birmingham City in the early Nineties were always eagerly anticipated. Despite being in one of their lowest league positions for years, Birmingham's Zulus would always turn out. Not just for the bigger clubs but also for teams like Preston, who they knew would rise to the occasion at home but not necessarily make the effort when making a visit to the second city.

A lady friend-of-a-friend had been seeing a

Birmingham lad for a few months, Big T, who was a good lad and had soon been accepted by all the boys in Leyland. A few weeks before the game, he'd mentioned to one of the lads that a few Zulus were coming up for the match and meeting in Leyland beforehand. Somehow wires got crossed; the news spread like wildfire and became a little more exaggerated.

A few days later, the news on the Leyland grapevine was of an imminent invasion. The town has always been a PNE stronghold and on the Friday night before the game our friends from the West Midlands were discussed at great length – would they really come to Leyland? Or would it be just Big T and a couple of his mates?

Next day, the landlord of the Railway pub must have thought Christmas had come early. Ten-past-eleven and it is standing room only as the entire Leyland firm and 30 or so lads from town filled the main bar. Half-an-hour later, the pub's buzzing like only a pub can on Saturday mornings before a 'big 'un'. The beer's flowing and there's not a female in sight! Just 'laddy' chat and the sound of nondescript chart music on the continuous-play jukebox.

Two pints later, a face from Preston arrives by car. The Zulus are in town, but not this town. A good 150 have been spotted getting off the train at Preston. It's now nearly midday, it's time to 'sup up your beer and collect your fags' and the pub empties. We cross the road and enter the adjacent train station.

On platform one, our tidy mob numbering about 100 waits for the 12:07 to Preston. The journey only takes five minutes and soon we are out of the station and on the way to the Black-a-Moor Head to meet with the rest of the

Preston boys. The pub offers a fine vantage point as to the right is the Ring Road and main route to the town centre, and to the left Stanley Street with Yates's Wine Lodge opposite the T-junction. More of Preston's mob arrives at our town centre HQ. The pub is 90 per cent lads, with a few local pissheads moaning they can't get served.

News comes through that Birmingham are near the ground under a small police escort. The shout goes up and we leave in groups of a dozen or so. We cross the bus station and go undetected in splinter groups all the way to Meadow Street. Meadow Street still had all its pubs and has a few lads in each of them with mounted police patrolling the area.

We know the Zulus are about but it's the wrong side of two o'clock. At first it's a trickle, but now the pubs are emptying and soon there are 200 of us negotiating the traffic on Deepdale Road. Crossing, and then making our way into the back streets. The Deepdale pub comes into view; there's a few lads outside and two police vans up the side street. The mounted police should still be on Deepdale Road as it's quarter-to-three, but where are the Zulus?

'They're 'ere... they're 'ere!' The voice is in a state of shock, the voice has panic in it, and the voice is flushed with pure adrenalin! The first Brummies appear on the corner of Falcon Street. It's 100 yards long and we're at the other end. We've only been separated by a row of terraced houses and back yards for the past 200 yards or so. No one from either mob realised they'd been parallel in their movement and are now about to clash. It's us at one end and them at the other as Falcon Street cobbles are covered in trainers worn by the sides of two very willing parties.

It must be about 200-a-side and the mobs are 40 yards apart. This is a massive turnout for us, while they could probably put out five times this number for their big games. The enemy is multi-racial, and there's even a couple of Asians with them; we've also got our black lads out. 30 yards... 20... 'Come on!' The war cry goes up and we're into them, windmills are flapping. This is the main event and neither side is moving! Then – BANG! The lights go out for a few seconds, the mounted Old Bill arrive. I've taken the full force of Trigger's arse as he backs around. The lads pick me up; I think I know what's going on but my eyes suggest otherwise. It's like being on a roundabout as a kid, seeing everything in a blur, there's horses all around. Long truncheons enter my fuzzy vision, people are going down, and both sides retreat in opposite directions, job done by the Lancashire mounted constabulary.

It's lasted less than two minutes and I'm propped up against a wall trying to get my shit together with more Old Bill arriving on the scene.

Preston and Birmingham: nil; Lancashire Constabulary: one!

I've come to a bit by the time we reach the ground, but to this day I don't remember much about the game. Afterwards, I heard it went off on Moor Park just across Deepdale Road. Equal numbers played at Grand National with the horses. Some of the lads spoke to Big T a few weeks later; he said the Zulus had been most impressed with our turnout and one day the main lads might make the visit to Lancashire!

They did a few months later but, fortunately for us, they were playing Blackpool!

Preston won their last home game against Swansea 2–0 so the never-ending relegation story was put on ice until the results had come in from the last games. The end-of-season ritual of a jolly was to be had regardless, and Shrewsbury was our destination, the train our mode of transport.

As we pulled into Shrewsbury Station, a mob of Shrews were waiting. They got dispatched, on their little, tiny toes they went, with us in hot pursuit. Finally, we gave up the chase and went into a boozer, only to find them in there and all out of breath. With looks of shock on their faces, they did one once again. We just got the beer in while laughing.

A good drink was had with different groups having the English Border Firm off throughout the day. Banned lads were turning up in end-of-season fancy dress, avoiding the plod's attentions.

Preston fans were squeezed in the away section of Gay Meadow and it was party-time whether North End stayed up or went down. During the game, reports started coming through on anoraks' radios of other results. Preston got beaten 2–0... but stayed up.

The gates opened at the end of the match and Preston once more scattered the EBF all over their town.

H Butt:

A football injury meant my ankle was knackered so I could hardly walk, but I wasn't missing this for anything, as we might not go down. I limped round Shrewsbury all day. Preston had a massive following and took over half the attendance that day in Shropshire. We were fuelled up on nearly a month's supply of cider and the loony juice soon took its toll.

Preston went mental after the game, rampaging

through their quaint little town. I just hobbled behind watching the mayhem unfold and the destruction they left behind.

I ended up with Rambie, CV and a couple of other lads in a wine bar, sampling the grape 'til 7.30pm, also thinking we might be the last ones in town. We decided to make a move to a pub near the station and soon found out that we weren't! A few hundred yards down the road, about 100 of the lads were stood outside a boozer in full song mode. It didn't take long for the local bizzies to turn up wanting Preston to sup up and leave town. By now, they'd had enough of Preston on this wonderful, sunny day. We got moved up to the train station with some lads managing to break off looking for another drink and to see if the EBF were a firm worth bothering with.

Eventually, the train left after the driver had spat his dummy out. Thinking it was day over for some fun, the lads just wanted to get off somewhere or back to Preston for a bevvy as lads excitedly talked about the day's events. We then noticed a heavy police guard on Crewe Station as our train pulled in. The police quickly put us on board the connecting train when someone shouted, 'Look at what we've got here!'

There were about 40 Wigan lads in the end carriage who also had a police presence with them. So the day's festivities were possibly not quite over yet! About eight police were guarding the door to the end carriage as the train pulled out of Crewe; I bet the Pie Men were glad. It was a waiting game until we arrived at Wigan Station.

Everyone had the itch and was full of anticipation as the train pulled in at Wigan with lads on the edge of their seats. Greater Manchester Police were waiting on the platform; I suppose they wanted to get rid, soon as possible. Wigan were off, walking past the windows giving it 'the big one' with one-finger salutes and 'wanker' signs. 'BOOT' – a door flew open and Preston steamed off, straight into them. Truncheons were drawn and the boys in blue weren't afraid to use them... but there was no stopping the lads today.

CV:

Someone grabs me by the arm saying, 'No, let's get round the back,' then drags me along the train to exit one of the back doors right into the Wigan in a pincer move. Lads from both sides were being knocked down and bouncing back up quicker than a whore's knickers. In general, Wigan got a good hiding. That will teach them not to pull faces and give signs again.

H Butt also remembers that moment when the train pulled in, saying, 'We all piled off the train and gave it to the pie eaters. I was doing all right, even on one leg, knocking a lad all over then – WHACK. I felt a thud to my left eye and claret started to run down my face.'

Lads were at it all over the platform with Wigan and the police. There was even scrapping going on on the train tracks and it took a good five minutes for order to be restored with the police gaining control – spoilsports. Preston were back on the train after a job well done. We laughed our heads off as we carried on on our journey home. Happy days!

Pia also recalled a bit of the aftermath. 'Two of the lads who travelled with us that day were banned and turned up as Tweedledum and Tweedledee! What a sight they looked. After all the violence and rioting up and down the country that day,

I remember hearing a local radio station announcement: "The police in Shrewsbury are still looking for two Adolf Hitlers and various farmyard animals!"'

A statement released later went along the lines of Preston North End fans being branded 'animals' by a police chief after they rampaged through the streets of Shrewsbury. There were clashes between opposing fans but the majority of incidents seemed to be aimed at the police – it was appalling!

That weekend, the papers were also full of stories about 'the beautiful game'. Fans were 'rampaging' all over Britain that day but also in Europe. So it wasn't just an 'English disease'.

12

TOPPING UP THE PENSION

It was getting well on top and I 'had' to start calming down or the cell door would shut and not reopen for quite some considerable time, if I didn't change my ways. It wasn't just my escapades at football that I had to worry about. There were nights out with the lads, out-of-town events and weekends away, but that's a whole lorra different stories. I was really trying to sort myself out when yet another tasty treat came along – Italia '90.

The nation was gripped with World Cup fever and I felt compelled to go to the European country which is shaped like a big boot. I needed to have a gander at what English lads faced abroad, apart from the baton-wielding, trigger-happy Carabinieri police.

The rave scene was also in full swing, 'R U on one, matey?' It never really gripped me, raving – well, the music and dancing didn't. I never have been much of a mover on the dance floor. Lads from all over were getting involved in the rave scene and friendships were struck up all over the country. The only stance against it – and 'E' – was a few boys walking round wearing 'Hooligans against E' T-shirts.

Some lads, who I knew, ended up getting heavily hooked on lethal drugs such as smack, crack and just about anything they could get their hands on. Lives were lost over the coming years before their natural life span. Very sad times.

With all this happening around me, I tried to get my fix down at the gym where I thought I would get rid of some of the pent-up aggression from my system – the testosterone running riot round the veins in my body. This was after I'd been to Italy and then on to Bulgaria for two weeks. I'd a right paunch on me and looked like a pot-bellied pig. Three or four times a week, I'd go with a mate, Stu, to vent my anger, pushing iron. I just couldn't seem to do things in half measures. I do wonder if I've got an addictive gene.

Next, it was down to the local boxing club, taking my son along with me. Bobbie, a good mate who helped out at the club, said, 'Drop a bit of fibrous tissue and we'll think about putting you in the ring.'

Thanks, but no thanks, and I never went back again. A fight at football or a brawl in the street, that I could handle, but going into a boxing ring would be a totally different ball game. I wouldn't know if I could ever cope with the Queensberry Rules.

But whatever I tried to do to distract myself from what I really enjoyed, I just couldn't keep away from my beloved PNE and the lads! And there were many occasions when I wondered if I was letting myself get sucked right back in again.

In 1990/91, with 15 players making their debut for Preston, it was one of those same-old, same-old seasons once again. North End eventually finished 17th, two positions higher than the previous season.

A 6–1 thrashing of Burnley in the Leyland DAF Cup area semi-final was Preston's biggest achievement that season. And Wembley hopes were dashed when Tranmere Rovers beat Preston over two legs in the Northern Final.

Zek:

It was an early start in a box van with nearly 40 of us squashed in and we struggled to gain any speed heading over the moors, hills and inclines. As we slowly made our way to Mansfield, another van from Preston with the Avenham lads in caught us up and we signalled for them to pull over. A few of us got out and jumped into their van as there was a bit more room and space to breathe. We then continued on our merry way in slightly more comfortable surroundings.

Then we stopped off at a pub on the town's outskirts and one lad volunteered to wait outside as lookout for the other van to arrive as it still must have been struggling. It never did arrive. Eventually, with the time approaching three and with no sign of them, either because they had gone a different way, they'd not been spotted or had broke down, we supped up and got back into the van and headed to Field Mill.

After parking up near to the ground, we walked to the turnstiles only to find them all shut, but no one was giving up and we all managed to scale the gates and get in. During the game, Mansfield lads are giving it, 'Where were you before the match? Get yourselves up to the Plough after the match.'

Thumbs up and nods shown to say we'd be there. While on the match, we saw some lads from the other van, which had now arrived. They told us some of the lads had decided to stay in the boozer for a few beers, not even bothering to come on the game. Preston won the match with Basil Rathbone getting the winner and we left happy with the result.

Now mobbing up outside, we thought it had gone pear-shaped with an escort of police waiting to take us back to the vans.

On arrival at the vans, we found that Mansfield had pulled one of our old tricks, letting all four tyres down. A copper said they'd get someone to sort it and another helpful officer informed us that they would walk us down to the Plough pub to allow us a pint until it was done. They moved us off and walked us towards the boozer with the lads rubbing their hands, expecting Mansfield to be in. As we walked through the doors, the coppers seemed to melt away which we thought was a bit strange. They didn't even put a bobby outside the door. We all piled in but there were no Stags or whatever name they go under to be seen.

We're just ordering our ale when the back doors of the pub burst open. They have made a show and it goes off big time. Most people must know what happened next, so I'm not giving a Football Factory story of events. It lasted a good five minutes with us moving them out on to the car park. The next thing we know, a full squad of the boys in blue arrive with our spotter and they arrest over 20 of us. This results in a weekend in the cells and a Monday court appearance with, luckily, a lesser charge on my head than some of the other lads. The majority of us were bailed with others remanded for three months.

During my court appearance, the Preston officer informed the court that the Preston fans had been making arrangements for a meeting away from the ground during the match. There was no mention of Mansfield fans who'd been shouting over to us about where and when. I can only imagine that it must not have been heard!

Fines and jail sentences were handed out and I still wonder why the police left the scene of the Plough public house.

I couldn't be bothered going on a Mickey Mouse Cup competition at Deepdale, so Rambie and me went for a few beers. The rest of the lads went on and left us drinking round Meadow Street. Nearing the end of the game, we ventured up to the Deepdale pub to meet the boys after the match.

On entering the pub, it was quite full. It wasn't full of Preston locals watching *Emmerdale* but most of the cast. Yes, it was full of Burnley. I glanced up at the text on the telly and it showed Preston were winning 6–1. Burnley had clocked us entering and one snaked over, asking, 'What time is it, lad?'

And another shouts over, 'What's the score, lads?'

This lot are a real backward bunch if they can't tell the time and read what's appearing on the screen. Pointing at the television, I sarcastically commented, 'It's 6–1, mate. And it's nearly full-time because it's just after nine o'clock.'

A few more started coming round us, saying, 'What a shit ground Deepdale is... I wouldn't race greyhounds on it.'

'What about whippets then?' I replied.

The six-fingered ones were not taking too kindly to a bit of friendly banter so we joined another Preston lad who'd been sat in the corner of the boozer. Burnley didn't follow so we slowly made our way down Deepdale Road, waiting for the lads to come off the match.

They didn't show; they might have been busy.

We then headed back to Meadow Street. And as we were making our way, the brain surgeons, who'd been in the pub earlier, were now about 30–40 yards behind us, numbering about 15–20. Obviously, we must have upset them but I don't know how or why. They started mouthing off and breaking into a jog towards us. We threw a quick right into a little park near to the Stephenson's pub, hoping there might be some Preston about. Realising that we weren't going to make it to the pub with them hot on our heels, we decided to stand and give it our best shot. They entered the park and cries of 'Get 'em!' went up, and it was three of us against the inter-bred firm.

Just as it was going to go off, the boys in blue must have observed the Burnley mob stepping up a gear and a van of Old Bill screeched up. This stopped everyone dead in their tracks. The police only nicked the lot of them, slapping them around their double heads. 'You bullies... there's only three of them,' said a copper as they were dragged into the van.

It was a lucky escape for Burnley with what damage we could have inflicted on them. Miraculously, the police just sent us on our way without any questions. We then skipped off to the Stephenson's to find there wasn't anyone in after all, then headed off to Hartley's near the train station as the lads might have been in there. Arriving ten minutes later, we ordered three beers, and there was still no sign of anyone, Preston or Burnley. It was a damp, wet night with no one about apart from the warm log fire to lift our spirits.

A few Preston who we hardly knew then entered the pub. And then, not long after, our worst nightmare – 40 Suicide

Squad. There were ten of us in one side with Burnley in the other and a bar in between us. They proceeded to buy a couple of bottles each; I think they knew we were in. We weren't hiding but we made sure the exit was clear.

Burnley had been in for about ten minutes when a glass came over and they started to make an advance. It was time to leave the building and on to the street where we stood a better chance with pint glasses taken as souvenirs. We'd just got through the doors when the 'Burnley Express' steamed out with 40 on board. Pint pots and bottles were unloaded by both sides. Burnley had the advantage of numbers and a downhill gradient on this dark, wet night. Our new mate from the Deepdale pub got his directions well mixed up and ran straight into a wall. He slid down half-unconscious and, with the situation worsening, Rambie and me managed to get him away from the fighting before he could come to any more harm. Burnley seemed to give up the cause very quickly – or maybe their train was due.

We then sent the now double-visioned lad home suffering from one hell of a headache. And if I'd have been him, first thing the day after, I'd have been going for an eye test. You don't want to be running into solid objects like brick walls too many times.

Rambie and I headed back into town and, glancing through pub windows, we finally spotted our mates in the Stanley Arms.

'Where've you two been? Have you seen any Dingles about? We can't seem to find any.'

We just looked at each other, shaking our heads. If only they knew.

A few weeks later, the Burnley rocket scientists were in court. The judge, on hearing the police evidence, told them how disgraceful it had been to attack three young teenagers. The judge then proceeded to hand them all big fines.

What a good job the old face cream had done at the time! Alas, not any more – you should see the wrinkles on Rambie's face nowadays, the old git. I only wish I'd kept the newspaper clipping!

* * *

Groundhog season was 1991/92 – in my eyes, there wasn't a game worth a mention. The attendances at Deepdale proved it and Preston finished 17th... again.

Having kept my head down for most of the season, which was really a case of having to, the last away day came along and this one was not to be missed. With a promise to myself to keep out of trouble, I joined 30 lads and caught a train to Birmingham New Street. Other lads had gone down in different modes of transport to West Bromwich Albion.

We landed in the centre of the Black Country around noon, going for a few beers in and around the Bull Ring before heading up to the Hawthorns. And for some reason, we ended up in a bar adjoining a hotel where you had to press a buzzer to gain entry. Entry was allowed after the barman had run his eye over you and considered you were sound enough to come in. He studied us for a few seconds, must not have minded what he saw, and let us in.

Halfway through a pint, we observed a couple, then several, then a dozen or so, and eventually up to 20 black lads milling about outside, glancing, then gazing, through the barred window inquisitively. 'Are them lads waiting to come in?' someone asked the barman.

He examined the lads, replying, 'No – a couple of them aren't welcome in here.'

A prolonged stare was now being delivered from them in our direction. Words were exchanged between themselves with much finger-pointing our way. 'I wonder what their problem is,' we mused.

'You... you... you... you... out here, now!'

It wasn't difficult to lip-read their comments or confuse their forward and backward moving of fingers and thumbs thrown over their shoulders. 'I think they want us to come outside,' Pia said.

Pia then silently mouthed back through the glass to them, 'If you want to get it on, go and get the rest of your lads.'

'For fuck's sake,' I was thinking.

'Roight then... roight then... wait there, wait there. We'll be back in a minute.' They then do one.

I hurriedly informed Pia that we were in their manor; they'd probably get double or even treble our numbers and I wanted to get up to the game in one piece. Additionally, I couldn't afford to get into any trouble whatsoever and there were cameras all over the place. I think he took the hint and we all left the scene pronto. I bet the Brummies were mad as wasps when they arrived back and we'd all disappeared.

We quickly grabbed directions to a taxi rank as we said our goodbyes to the barman. He'd directed us as the crow flies which meant going through a department store.

A lad with us, whom I hardly knew, was well intoxicated and, as we were leaving by the swinging glass doors of the store, he placed a hat on his head, with the price tag still attached, dangling down. Outside, all of a sudden two 6ft-6in burly security guards pounced on the lad, bundling him to the floor. Arm up his back, knee in the base of his spine, one of them was on his walkie-talkie and five more steroid-filled wannabes arrived. 'I'll pay, I'll pay,' the lad on the chewing gum-splattered paving slabs was pleading.

While this was going on, the boys were asking them to let

him go and it was only a joke, as more security guards joined their colleagues. The lads started pleading for their mate but it started taking a turn for the worse, as more guards were spotted running through shoppers in the distance. The muscle-bound Popeyes started pushing the lads and, when one raised his walkie-talkie as though he was going to club one of them – BANG – the caveman's legs crumbled and he staggered before he hit the deck. He'd given one of the lads no choice but to strike first.

The restrainers waded into the boys – big mistake. Within seconds, there were more casualties on their side and they started to retreat. The pinned-down lad was up off the pavement and we got off, with the offending item, a pork-pie hat, left where it lay. I know it was out of order but they never gave the lad a chance to hand it over, walk peacefully back into the store or pay.

We then managed to flag down taxis and headed up to the Hawthorns through the streets of the multi-cultural city. On arrival at the ground, outside a pub, we bumped into some Preston lads, who'd just had a bit of a rumble with the Section 5; they had then vaporised.

Never mind. We went into the ground to witness Preston getting hammered 3–0. During the match, one Preston fan with his young son had been voicing his opinions. This was about North End's fortunes that season aimed at the team, manager and directors for letting the fans down once again. Pure frustration! For his barrage of complaints, he got lifted, getting dragged round the pitch with his son. Nothing seemingly had changed there in over ten years.

Coming out of the gates, the joys of spring were lost on Preston fans in general and everyone was having a right old moan. Sluggishly, we made tracks on to the main drag back into town, scanning the Baggies, hoping that some of the happy crowd bustling by were Section 5. Not even a glimpse! As we were crossing the dual carriageway, hoping to flag down taxis in the busy traffic lanes, one Preston lad was idling at the back, when a car nearly knocked him over. He just about managed to jump out of the car's path and instinctively gave it the 'wankers' sign. The driver hit the brakes and the passengers emptied out, with the nearside traffic grinding to a halt.

Five Asians were closing in on the lad and he was looking over to us for back-up. Of the cars which had braked behind the now empty one, three of them had opened their doors and the rest indicated that they were moving to the second lane to carry on with their journey. Twelve other Asians stood watching events unfold. The three from the first car were behaving in an aggressive manner towards our mate, who's on the back foot, but not for long. The lads joined in proceedings with things soon sorted. The passengers from cars two, three and four were back inside pronto, revving their motors, ready to go, and all four left the scene, burning rubber on tarmac.

'For fuck's sake! What have I told you today?' I berated Pia again.

'It's only a bit of fun, mate,' Pia said, arms outstretched, shrugging his shoulders as we jumped on to a passing bus back into the city centre.

Luckily, there was no more trouble with bus conductors, train staff, police, the Zulus, Section 5 or any other boys on New Street Station.

Relaxing back into my train seat, I eased up on the lads, remembering the things I'd got up to over the years. I loosened up, slackened off and started to giggle, amused by their childish, naughty-schoolboy antics. And it was not long before someone suggested that we got off at Wigan for a drink.

'Just a drink?' I said with a knowing look.

'Yeah, come on, we'll have a laugh,' was the reply.

We got off at Wigan and headed up to the Bee's Knees pub in the town centre. Approaching the entrance, we saw three burly doormen wedging themselves into the doorway. One had beads in his hair like he'd just got back off his Caribbean holidays. 'Sorry, not tonight lads,' he told us.

As he was doing this, another 15–20 doormen were quickly heading in our direction. Once, twice, three times, not a lady in sight, the lads had fronted trouble without a fellow hoolie being involved. Four if you count the black geezers in the Bull Ring. 'I doubt if you'll get in anywhere else in Wigan tonight, lads. You're better off leaving town,' he told us as he stood there playing with his beads. Looks like it might be another red rag to the boys.

'Where you from anyway?'

'Preston.'

'Definitely no chance then!' he said, as he changed his slothful stance to bolt upright. 'I was inside with [X], and he told me that you lot have got a bit of a reputation [compliment taken], so, boys, it's a no chance in town tonight.'

More doormen were arriving and a passing police car was taking a look, so we headed back to the train station. Was I glad!

Back in Preston, it was into the same old same pubs. You'd think I'd have given the lads a wide berth, wouldn't you? Well, put it this way, just ask that geezer Adam about that forbidden-fruit lark! Friends in need are friends indeed, and it was my funeral if I got involved again in the following seasons.

And finally, in 1992/93, Preston managed to get into Division

Two! But only because the Premier League had been formed! Exit manager Les Chapman with Sam Allardyce given temporary charge. This was until John 'Long Ball' Beck was given the post. Big Sam has now gone on to bigger and better things – apart from Blackpool.

Preston's game of snakes and ladders returned, seeing them slither back down to the basement league. A 1–0 defeat at Burnden Park saw Bolton promoted and North End relegated. This left Gareth Ainsworth in floods of tears – Gazza style – with fans throwing away their flat caps and whippets. I personally was left sulking over a pint. In all my time of following Preston, it's the only time I've failed to get on the match due to a sell-out. I was locked out and not locked up as usual.

Preston didn't get beaten by Blackpool home or away with a cracking 3–2 win at 'Gloomfield Road'. A certain Tony Ellis, having returned to Preston from Stoke, scored a hat-trick. This put a dent in the Blackpool home record, which read before Preston played them: P–41, W–33, D–7, L–1. The mighty whites doubled their losses!

Zek:

We've turned up late at Stoke's Victoria ground with Preston having brought quite a following. The away end had shut its turnstiles and, on asking the stewards, one informs us that there is probably room in the seats in the side stand. On paying in, it's only rammed full of Stoke's lads. Luckily, we enter a seating area above the 'Naughties'; unluckily, we're clocked straight away.

We then start to play musical chairs, moving closer and closer towards Preston's away section when Graham Shaw takes a dive for a penalty – maximum 10 on the scorecard. There's only a few of us so it's backs to the wall with the Potters raging at the referee, giving them cover and a signal for an assault on us. We've got the upper hand as they have to climb over seats to get to us but they have vastly superior numbers. Fortunately, the police arrived to our rescue. We think that they're going to move us out; no, we're nicked instead. However, when we're being led away, we notice more Preston entering the stand.

Pia:

We've queued up only to have the turnstile doors shut in our faces, and a decision is made to go into the seats at the side. A steward informs us on the way in that we won't last long in there. We took no notice, very rarely did.

Ten of us enter the stand and sit down at the front, now knowing why the steward had given us a word of warning. A lad with glasses comes over, asking us to come to the toilets under the stand and to 'get it on'. Toilets are usually confined areas and looking back up the seats I didn't think that that amount of Naughty boys would fit in them. We preferred to have it where we were so we could give a little show rather than try to match the firm they had.

However, the police had clocked the little meeting and, realising that we might need a hand, they swiftly removed us into the away end before any serious damage was done. We were up for it but knew really it was a lose-lose situation.

After the match, a good-sized mob of Stoke were waiting behind a strong line of police. We managed to get to our cars but one of the starter motors was knackered and it took a bit of time to get the engine ticking over. For the second time that day, we were lucky as we just got off before Stoke got to us. Major respect to Stoke as they had one of the firms of the Nineties and, boy, was I glad to get off.

It was the last game of the season once more with Preston needing to win to stay in Division Two, with Bolton also needing a win to gain promotion to Division One.

We met up early for the train with bacon butties and coffees in hand. A good 100-plus of us boarded the train with other Preston fans. Preston Station had been crawling with police, with a good few joining us on the train to Bolton. A rumour was also going round that we would be escorted straight up to the ground. So plans were hatched to get off at Lostock, the last stop before Bolton.

Just before the train set off from Lostock Station, there was a mass exodus, done to perfection by over 100 lads. The police ended up staying on with the shirters. There were only two or three pubs in the village which were just opening their doors. Licensees were not so glad to see over 100 lads on their doorsteps, but were usually glad to see their money.

With two hours of drinking inside of us, it was back on the train, arriving at about two-ish, spilling out on to the streets and scattering the waiting Bolton. The police were in attendance and some Preston lads got lifted. We were then herded down towards the ground and on to the car park outside Burnden Park when Preston fans started passing us saying, 'No chance, lads.'

'They've shut the turnstiles.'

'It's a full house.'

'You won't be getting on.'

This didn't put the lads off; they're always up for a challenge. Preston then tried to boot the turnstile doors and exit gates open. The plod were soon on the scene, calling for back-up and trying to surround us. 'Right, you lot, there's no room left on the ground and there's no way we're leaving you to roam the streets of Bolton. We'll be putting you on the next train home to Preston.'

Everyone was of the same opinion. 'Fuck that for a game of soldiers.' We were off down an embankment and on to some train lines, full steam ahead. A few police followed, the rest not being able to leave their posts. All the while, more and more Preston were arriving in droves.

A mile or so down the tracks, we managed to get back up into the middle of town. We found out that Bolton's lads, nicknames galore, had gone up to the match. The lads fancied a drink, so we enter Yates's for a few shandies. There was no bother at all until the landlady declared, 'No more drinks. It's getting near the end of the match and Bolton fans will be coming back in soon, so please leave.'

Some lads didn't take too kindly to her words after taking their dosh for the last two hours.

'If you don't leave shortly, I'll ring the police.'

Preston began to leave, with a few windows getting put through just for the hell of it. Idiots, I know, and now we'd get the unwanted attention of the police. We quickly moved a short way up the road and dived into the next boozer.

The police did arrive at our new base camp with a senior officer having a word with the landlord and stationing a few officers on the pub's main door outside. Just as he was doing this, the final score came through – Bolton 1, Preston 0, with their goal being a 75th-minute penalty. The lads started feeling a bit down, thinking of going back to shitty old grounds. To me, it was the same-old, same-old.

The pub's door was locked by the landlord and more beer was ordered. A row of police was formed two-deep outside the pub as Bolton started filtering past giving it 1–0 hand signals and other verbal shite through the windows. Preston's lads' noses are pressed up to the glass, putting two fingers up and giving it, 'We'll be back in town shortly.'

Thirty minutes passed, and so had most of the Bolton when the pub door reopened. The senior officer said, 'Right, you lot, five minutes to drink up and go!'

This is met with a volley of 'Fuck-off!'; 'Fuck you!'; 'Kiss me arse!'

It was like water off a duck's back and out he went.

Then on the dot, five minutes later, he reappeared. 'Right, lads...'

'Fuck off!'

'Fuck you!'

'Kiss me arse!' Before he could even finish.

Everyone just carried on drinking and laughing, fancying a night out in Bolton. I was chatting away to a mate, wedged in the corner of the pool room, keeping an eye on events outside through the window.

Very shortly, two riot vans arrived, joining their colleagues. I couldn't see who or what was inside them but I soon found out. I carried on with the small-talk, supping my ale, when the next thing the pub's back doors burst open. Enter 'Robocops'.

They stormed in and, if you've ever seen any cyborg or robot films, well, these could have starred in them. They took no prisoners, whacking the fuck out of everything with their big batons. Lads tried to start fighting back, but got the full force of the mighty stick. Me and the mate were giggling like mad. Why? I don't know, as it was a really serious situation. We were trying to make our way to the now open front door, but this wasn't before we got our share of wood about the head and other parts of our bodies. The lads outside were having a right go at the police with the storm troopers still moving the rest out. The senior officer was shouting at the top of his voice, 'You were told you only had five minutes to leave.'

There were injuries all round; one lad was holding his broken arm, others had cuts and claret oozing out. All of us had lumps and bumps with egg shapes starting to form on our bodies. One lad had been on the toilet at the time and the door was booted open and a helpful riot cop proceeded to curtail his visit – sharpish! He didn't even have time to pull up his pants before exiting, kecks round his ankles. They were machines – no names, no numbers, snarling and spitting orders. I guess they'd say they were only doing their job.

They managed to move Preston to the train station with lads getting cracked all the way. On the station, there were only three transport bobbies left to deal with the situation. Even they couldn't believe the heavy-handed tactics that had been dished out. The riot coppers were stood at the top of the ramp, some with arms folded, others tapping batons into their hands. Bins, benches, fire extinguishers and anything else on offer were being given to them as a farewell present. By now, the lads knew that there was no way they were getting back out, so we boarded a train to Chorley to drown our sorrows.

On arrival, the few gobby Bolton who were in Chorley were soon sent packing. And the usual suspects relieved the takings from the fag and bandit machines, and even a DJ's record collection. This left the rest of us to drink the night away.

* * *

After a 2–0 home defeat by Crewe on the opening game of the 1993/94 season, my thoughts that the future's white quickly turned into 'Is the future shite?' No, Preston put the loss behind them and the only way was up with five wins on the bounce. However, a season-long routine of ping-pong, meaning the ball being lumped up in the air too often – I really got pissed off with the long-ball game, making excuses sometimes not to go on – did mean that Preston made the play -offs.

The first leg was at Torquay United's Plainmoor ground. I didn't make the trip for the first leg; PNE got beat 2–0, vindicating my decision. Wembley now looked as close as the moon but I purchased a paddock ticket, ever the optimist. Never say never! Preston were also ripping up their 'plastic fantastic' pitch after the game and I fancied a piece for the back garden.

What I witnessed that night was a match which not only initiated my grey hairs, but also put the pride back into our sorry footballing club. The 'PROUD' was well and truly back in the team's badge.

An early Tony Ellis header gave Preston both a 1–0 lead and some hope. The 'Gulls pulled one back in the 16th minute. North End fans started to think that there was no way back with the aggregate standing at 3–1 down and they had an away goal advantage. Then a turning point; Paul Raynor hit the deck under an alleged punch from Darren (Bruno) Moore. This happened right in front of where I was standing with the lads. A red card was pulled out and off 'Bruno' went. This saw Raynor get up and wink at us! Game on. And just on the stroke of half time, 'Captain Fantastic' David Moyes headed home and it was 2–1.

Half-time came and went in what seemed like an age. And seven minutes into the second half, number 3 hit the net – another header from Stuart Hicks. The long-ball game was paying off! With a nail-biting finish to the 90 minutes, extra time was needed. If I hadn't been through enough watching Preston over the years, I had to endure another 30 minutes of torture. It was end-to-end stuff with both teams missing numerous opportunities.

Then with extra time nearly over, 'super' Paul Raynor popped up and a fourth header went in. Preston fans went absolutely bananas. Raynor, more or less, had to come straight off with a mixture of cramp and exhaustion. It seemed like an eternity before the little pea was blown around its metal casing. When it was, the lads were over the fences with players aloft on shoulders. Preston fans were hugging and kissing each other with tears rolling down their cheeks. Thirty years of hurt was wiped away and even I nearly shed a tear! Wembley once more beckoned for Preston North End. If a game like that had featured in *Roy of the Rovers*, the readers would have thought it was too far-fetched. The Twin Towers, here we come. My mate Wayne got the match ball and hundreds of jubilant fans left with AstroTurf rolled up like carpets under arms and on shoulders, including myself.

While we'd have to wait for the joy of that day out, there were plenty more to be had elsewhere, with one of them having been a trip to the England–Scotland border. The last time we'd played Carlisle was over ten years earlier, but the lads wanted a good day out and a good day out was to be had.

A morning train up there, and we came out of the station

with two dodgy-looking CID on our tails. The 50 of us went straight into the first pub and sat tight, waiting for the next train in order to get mobbed up. We were followed into the pub by our two new friends. The towels were just being whipped off the pumps and it was eyes down for a good session. And another 50 joined us shortly after; we then spread out into two or three pubs. The two CID kept an ever-watchful eye on us while playing pool, and every time they bent over to take a shot a walkie-talkie came into view in their back pockets. Masters of the undercover, they were not.

Preston were in Carlisle's manor; let them come to us was the idea. A few did, sticking their heads round the door, then doing one, sharpish. What, no welcoming committee off England's number-one, self-acclaimed hooligan and his Border City Firm? Come on!

Just after two bells, we moved off to Brunton Park with little pockets of Carlisle popping up down side streets which were quickly dispersed. Dods was allegedly spotted by one of the lads; he never did have a chance to introduce himself. We ended up under a heavy police escort until we reached the car park and were then allowed to wander off.

J:

I was on a banning order at the time but thought 'fuck it' and travelled anyway, not wanting to miss out. I tried to gain entry into the ground but got collared off a Preston police spotter along with six others. They marched us off and put us into a sweat-box, parked up behind one of the stands. A Preston officer of the time then came into the mobile cells and, give him his due, he got us out, telling us to do one and try not to be seen again for the rest of the day. With a big sigh of relief we did as he'd asked, but probably ended up missing out on one of the biggest kick-offs ever. It was caught on CCTV with both sides at it, over 100-a-side with no one giving an inch. I was absolutely gutted about missing out.

We got to the ground just before kick-off and a few of us went for a walk, stumbling on an open turnstile door. You don't look a gift horse in the mouth, do you? We should have done.

Inside the stadium, there was a flight of stairs and up we went to find a long bar area at the top. There were only four of us and we tried to order up four pints but last orders had gone. We didn't know if we were in a supporters' club, a hospitality suite or a lounge area as there was only a few old blokes finishing up their ale. We then trotted up some more stairs into a stand and daylight. Holy shit! We were in Carlisle's stand and it was full of their lads. How is it you can spot the opposition a mile away?

A copper stopped us and asked us for our tickets. We started to play the game, checking every pocket and blaming each other for losing them. 'Sort it out, lads, and stand over there until you find them,' the officer says. We did so, moving to one side.

The BCF then began clambering over seats to greet us. Between 50 and 60 lads were heading our way, with a lad at the front asking, 'Where you from?'

We were all dumbstruck.

Again, 'Where the fuck you from?'

One of the lads, whose nickname was Scotch (RIP),was actually Scottish and, if he'd spoken a few words, it might have confused them long enough for us to get a head start of a couple of seconds. Alas, he didn't.

'You're fucking Preston!'

BANG! They're into us, more or less fighting among themselves to get a punch in, like a pack of hyenas wanting their supper. We're moving backwards, back down the steps, windmilling, trying not to fall down the stairs. Carlisle seemed to get wedged in the exit as we tried to hold them back. Then Rambie shouted, 'Into the toilets!'

However, I wasn't quick enough and the door was shut before I had a chance to get in – cheers, lads. Visions of Millwall started to flash through my head as I was trying to hold off about 30 Carlisle, shouting, 'Let me in... let me in.'

I was in Superman survival mode, arms and legs lashing out and, luckily for me, the boys in blue arrived to save my skin. One of the few times that I've been glad to see them. The Carlisle lads started getting dragged away and I started banging on the toilet door. 'They've fucking gone! Open the fucking door, you cunts.'

I was covered in blood from my once-again broken nose. The door opened and I called them every name under the sun and all they did was burst out laughing, saying, 'We didn't realise we'd locked you out. Everything happened that quick.'

I got cleaned up in the toilets and checked out my Stone Island jumper that was ruined, while a copper stood on guard. The police then escorted us out and we had to pay into the away section of the seats. The three so-called mates were still laughing. Who needs enemies with mates like mine?

Half-time came around and it was down to the fence, making arrangements with the rest of the lads on the standing section behind the goal to meet up outside the gates just before the end of the game.

Our gate opened bang on full-time and over 100 boys were

waiting, chomping at the bit. 'Right, come on!' Preston moved off with the attitude that Carlisle were going to get it. No more than 50 yards gone and the roar went up. The Border City Firm were in front of us and Preston spread out, about 30 lads across and 3–4 deep – it was battle lines drawn.

It was the second biggest mob fight I've witnessed, after Bolton. It then went 'off' with the fighting occurring in a snake-like motion, starting at one end and moving down to the other, almost like a hooligan Mexican wave. 'In out, in out... you do the hokey-cokey and you knock one out, that's what it's all about.' There was fighting going on all around, with lads at it in between parked cars, and about six coppers with batons drawn were trying to keep order.

During the mass fight, I had my Henri Lloyd woolly hat pulled off and it was murder trying to find it while all the scrapping was going on. I remember when I purchased the hat at a local boating shop, the assistant asked me, 'Where do you do your sailing?'

'Pardon?'

'What kind of sailing do you do, sir?'

'Sorry, mate, it's fashion. The only boat I go on is the one to France.'

The shop in question soon found out something the hard way. Having nothing tagged up on its rails or shelves, it was robbed blind by the local Preston shoplifters and pirates.

H Butt:

If you've seen the video on the Internet of Preston and Carlisle, it doesn't show the full extent of the events. Preston were well prepared because, if you fail to prepare, you prepare to fail. The lads went at it hammer and tongs.

Preston moved through the police and I had one of the best toe-to-toes ever in my life. It seemed to go on for ages but, in reality, it probably only lasted five minutes. I'd this lad in a Burberry jacket over the bonnet of a car giving him a right hiding when I felt someone grab me from behind. At first I thought I was nicked, but it was our kid warning me the snatch squad had started lifting lads and I hastily moved on.

The fighting finally got split up and Carlisle got moved on after nearly five minutes of action. In the dark, 30 of us found ourselves on a street corner which, if you threw a right, led you into town. All of a sudden, Carlisle came again, double our number. We took the initiative, advancing towards them screeching like banshees. For some reason, the BCF didn't fancy it, back-pedalling against a flurry of fists and boots raging in on them. The odd few, who did make a stand, got totally annihilated, hitting the deck with others scurrying off. More and more coppers arrived on the scene moving us on our way – the victory was ours.

Preston regrouped, walking back to the train station under police guard. Carlisle didn't make a show in numbers again that day, but small groups of Preston, who'd splintered off in different directions, took severe beatings off superior numbers.

J1, a close mate, got knocked unconscious and the hyenas proceeded to put the boot in while he was laid out on the pavement. He ended up in hospital and has had to endure years of cosmetic and constructive surgery to his face and teeth. When a man is down and out, that should be enough, shouldn't it?

We managed to disembark the train at Penrith for a

celebratory drink. I know I took a good kicking in their seats and maybe it was a score draw on the car park; on the day in question, however, raves, Ecstasy and old age had not taken their toll on the Preston boys and they were able to move England's number-one, infamous BCF. Long brass horns were taken off a pub wall with a rendition of the Viking cry trumpeted out. All the lads were up on their feet singing out loud – great days.

The next season, only 30-odd of us managed to obtain tickets for the match due to ground improvements, and the same two CID were on our case following us pub-to-pub like the previous year. This time, though, policing had toughened up with cars being stationed outside the boozers. A heavy escort had been arranged to the game with lads getting lifted for stepping out of line. Probably because the law didn't want a recurrence of the previous season's antics.

After the match, on the same corner, we again encountered the BCF with numbers touching 100; it was our turn to back off as we were down to only 20 lads. The victory was theirs.

I found in both return fixtures at Preston, Carlisle turned up but on the whole wouldn't stand. They would unload bricks, bottles and missiles with the odd little scrap, and then do one. Encounters such as behind the Black Bull pub in town and the Charnock pub are good examples, and they were 'gone within 60 seconds'.

But one way of restoring pride to the club was performing well on the big occasion – both on and off the pitch – and Preston now had a chance to do exactly that in the greatest footballing arena on earth – at Wembley. We finally had something to celebrate, and it was a day out for our family, the lads. Southward we went in the early-morning sun on our coaches. Was Saturday, 28 May 1994 going to be a day to remember, or not?

The boys were enjoying themselves drinking and singing round London, absorbing the atmosphere before the match. And I must stress that under no circumstances would any of them be involved in any way, shape or form in any shenanigans whatsoever! They were Preston fans, through and through.

After lashings of flat ale and southern shandy, we walked up Wembley Way to enter the famous stadium. I was amazed with the sights that greeted me. There were nearly 25,000 Preston fans among a crowd of 40,109, and they were about to witness Preston North End stroke the ball around on the hallowed turf – the original field of dreams.

I was bumping into people who I knew weren't the slightest bit interested in football, let alone PNE, my club. There were blokes, women and children wearing replica shirts, scarves, silly hats, painted faces, waving flags and holding aloft banners. The secure units in and around Preston must have released all their patients for the day!

I took a minute to survey my surroundings, thinking to myself, 'I bet I won't set eyes on the majority of these here today on Deepdale for the opening fixture of next season... or, come to think of it, ever again!'

The whistle went, with one of the founder members of the Football League against the Football League's newest club, Wycombe Wanderers. Despite being under the cosh, Preston managed to go 1–0 up with a superb bicycle kick from Ian Bryson. Within 30 seconds, it was 1–1. A short while later, Preston went 2–1 up from a majestic header by Paul Raynor. At half-time, Preston went into the dressing room with a lead and expectations were high.

Not long after the interval, Wycombe equalised and then dominated the remainder of the game, putting another two goals into the onion bag.

The final score was 4–2. Oh well, it wasn't to be; shattered dreams are made of this. What was hard to swallow was that Preston actually played football instead of the long-ball, kick-and-run, over-the-top ping-pong that got them there over the season. Would they revert back to the long-ball game next season? I truly hoped not as I couldn't handle it.

If my memory serves me right, there was only one arrest that day, and it was no one connected with us. Who said we're not football fans?

CV:

A coach had been booked for most of the lads' first ever trip to Wembley, it being the play-off final after we'd beat Torquay in a nail-biter. We managed to get plenty of ale on board and it was inevitable that a good skinful was to be had.

Upon arriving in the city of Westminster, plenty of southern beer was sunk with the odd can or two on the numerous Tube journeys.

On entering Wembley, I plonked my fat arse down into a seat, striking up a conversation with Crookie. 'If Preston score, do you fancy a trip on to the pitch?'

'No. But if you make it on to the pitch, I'll give you a tenner. Plenty have tried, only not many succeed.'

The lads are sat close by; on hearing me strike up the bet, they also fancy a flutter and they are obliged to flash the cash.

The whistle went and I'm sat there thinking, 'I've got to do it now... there's no turning back.'

Goal! Fuck me! I'm off down the seats, up and over the fence, across the racetrack, on to the pitch and into the centre circle. By now, the game has restarted with players running around me. Shit! What do I do now? The stewards quickly run on, grabbing me by both arms and leading me off. This was to loud boos with just a small pocket of cheers coming from one section – who else but the lads? It's one of those surreal moments in life. My thoughts now change to 'I'll be needing all my winnings for the forthcoming fine.' Luckily, I'm just thrown out with a warning not to come back on.

While being shown the exit door, one steward informs me they'd managed to prevent Chelsea, Everton, Man United and plenty of other teams from entering the playing surface. So for my cheek alone, which got me on the pitch, that was the reason why they only threw me out. I'd already sorted for one of the lads to be waiting at the turnstile, if it was still open, with a change of top and cap. It was, and I was back in to collect the prize money, rubbing my hands.

Some time later, the PNE club shop released a video of Wembley '94. And the commentator said something along the lines of, 'Oh no, there's someone on the pitch. It's a small, fat, bald guy and he looks more like a bouncing bomb.' Cheeky git.

I was correct – only 8,337, including a couple of hundred Lincoln City fans, turned up for Preston's first home fixture of the 1994/95 season. It was the fifth game into the season because the newly laid grass pitch wasn't ready for the start. The game saw Preston win 4–0 and, yes, they were back to the long-ball tactics.

North End then went from 17 September to 5 November before picking up a point with seven defeats in a row. John Beck went soon afterwards, on the end of a long ball. Gary Peters, another one of the Crazy Gang, took over. He brought in two midfielders – Simon Davey, and a certain David Beckham – on loan. Both made their debut against Doncaster Rovers on 4 March 1995. Davey scored the first and Becks came off the bench at half-time to score Preston's second directly from an inswinging corner. The match ended in a 2–2 draw.

The week after, away to Fulham at Craven Cottage, Beckham notched one of his future trademark free-kicks to earn Preston a 3–2 win. Preston managed to remain unbeaten during Beckham's five-match stay, only Fergie whisked him back to Man United for him to make his Premiership debut. The rest, as they say, is history.

So, really, Preston launched the legend that is David Beckham with his CV reading: 'Teams played for: Preston North End, Manchester United, England, Real Madrid and LA Galaxy.'

PNE finished in the play-off positions but once more fell by the wayside against Bury. Bury beat North End 1–0 both home and away, watched by Beckham and the Neville brothers in the stands at Gigg Lane. No Wembley this year.

But there was still plenty to enjoy off the pitch that season. While we were still in with a shout of the play-offs, we had a trip to Lincoln to look forward to, the home of the Imps. And I was determined to keep my nose clean.

Lincoln was also home to a firm called Lincoln Transit Elite. I've no idea how their nickname came about. Maybe it was because they used vans for transport to away games, or maybe because their entire mob could fit in one! (Not really, lads... where's your sense of humour?) Recently, I've heard they've still got an active little firm. Travelling to anywhere around the country, you need to be on your guard, having myself slipped on many a banana skin and come unstuck.

We met up in the Hyde Park pub which is no more than a pint-pot's throw from the town centre. And by eight in the morning we were blowing the top off the first beer of the day. Just after nine, the coach pulled up and, with limited companies left on the list, it wasn't a brand spanker. A good carry-out was taken on board with the driver sorted and we set off at 9.30am. Taking a scan round, it was a good mixture of old and young 'uns. There were also plenty of lads present who I hadn't travelled with before. The seen-it-all and the up-and-coming – what a lethal cocktail.

Our first destination was a village en route for a couple of pints and then on to Lincoln. I was out for a few beers with the mates and I knew there were plenty of good alehouses in that neck of the woods, having had the pleasure of visiting them quite a few times.

In addition to cans, bottles and hip flasks being raised to the lips, other substances were making an appearance which were also starting to be consumed – each to their own. The bus started to resemble a mobile chemist's with an unlicensed pharmacist. Queues quickly formed and prescriptions handed over which looked remarkably like Bank of England notes. I was about to witness the joys of chemistry, the science of the properties of substances and the combinations with the reactions that follow – lads getting totally wasted. The air was thick with the smell of skunk and poppers were being passed about – just what the doctor ordered.

We'd been on the road for just over an hour and the atmosphere started to change too, becoming a rather charged one. I was leaning over the back of my seat having a chat to a mate, when I glanced over to the back row noticing a lad who was totally transfixed. He was staring out of the window, zombie-like. The eyes of the lad in question were the size of footballs and he seemed to be gazing at nothing rather than taking in the scenery or the cars roaring past. What a window licker!

'Fuck me, Bill; I didn't know that gear was that strong! Look at the boat on him,' the Wee Man sat across from me said, pointing at the boy stuck to the window whose lips had turned royal blue.

I knew the lad slightly from the match and he always seemed on one. That day I think he'd overdosed on certain dietary substances or had had more than the recommended daily intake of 'E' numbers. Other lads could have out-talked any sports commentator, hands down. There was also a bad case of 'flu going round with lots of sniffing going on. I might have been mistaken; the coach's radio was blasting out Grandmaster Flash and Melle Mel's 'White Lines' through the speakers!

Arriving in a little village, whose name I cannot remember, we found a selection of pubs. We then split into small groups, not wanting to frighten any of the locals with the amount of space cadets travelling that day. A decision was made to meet back at the bus at twelve to head on. This was achieved nearly on time which was a first, as you will always get someone wanting one for the road or needing a piss after having two hours to have one.

We'd just set off, in what I said before was not your top-of-the-range transport, when the bus broke down. The driver jumped out and lifted up the engine hood, shaking his head like all mechanics do when you take your car into the garage, tutting and sucking in air through pursed lips. The look on his oil-streaked face after five minutes told the story – it was fucked. Arrangements were made with him either to meet us in Lincoln or sort out another coach company to take us home after the match.

The main objective now was to find some transport to get the rubber-faced crew to Sincil Bank. Local taxis and a minibus were booked, which started arriving around 2pm. It was pay up-front or don't go, and I could understand why after they saw our motley crew. We paid with the promise of a good tip for the driver if he got us to the match on time. The driver would have given Nigel Mansell a run for his money, racing down country lanes and 'A' roads with us bouncing around inside the taxi. He missed out by minutes, pulling up outside the ground just after three. The lads gave him his tip anyway as he'd been a nice chap – the tip being 'don't eat yellow snow'.

We'd paid on and I can't really remember much about the game! The match finished and the gates were opened with 50 lads not knowing where they were heading or how exactly they were getting home. The lad who'd organised the coach was trying to get something sorted.

Twenty of us had been wandering about for a good 30 minutes, with the rest of the crowd having dispersed. Then turning a corner, we spotted a pub sign 50 yards ahead with a couple of lads entering it and looking in our direction. We'd only advanced another 10 yards when out of the boozer spilled 15–20 lads, who started to launch pool balls, bottles and glasses, catching us unawares. The arms went up to protect ourselves and, after the initial unloading, we had time to take a proper look at what was going on. Two lads had pool cues in their hands, with others beckoning us on. 'Come on, then!'

Without any prompting, everyone surged towards the perpetrators of this action. Being a betting man, I wish I could have had a flutter on the 5.15 at Lincoln. They trapped like greyhounds that had been fed boiled eggs. By the time Preston lads had reached the pub, its big oak doors were bolted shut. A big PPS lad set about kicking them in with all his might and others did likewise at a side door. Then a Preston lad shouted from down the road after stumbling on the situation, 'The Old Bill are here.'

Within seconds, the police arrived and lads were walking off casually as if nothing had happened, some crossing over the road and entering a newsagent's. The bell above the door rang again. It was Preston's intelligence officer with other fuzz stood outside. 'Right, you lot, your replacement coach has turned up. And, if you're not on it within 15 minutes, it's going without you!'

I could see steam coming out of lads' ears milling about the shop. Everyone was still coiled to the max.

Herded on to our second luxurious bus – well, it went, at least – we set off for Preston after the driver was told under no circumstances to pull over, or stop, anywhere en route home. The only exception was the motorway services for a quick piss-stop. They also informed him that they were radioing ahead and patrol cars would be checking his movements.

The coach door shut and off we went. Within minutes, the pharmacy had reopened even though the green-cross sign hadn't been switched back on! And, by now, Blue Lips' lips had changed colour to post-box red, which went beautifully with his pasty complexion – Blue lips, then red lips, and a white face... he was a walking, talking Union Jack. Not to worry, as he was quickly back in the queue for a pick-me-up.

* * *

A new striking partnership was brought in during the summer for the forthcoming 1995/96 season, which consisted of Andy Saville and Steve Wilkinson. Expectations were high, although Preston got beat at home by Lincoln City on the opening day of the season! North End then went on a 21-match unbeaten run.

A new stand was built to replace the old West Stand, named after the Preston legend Sir Tom Finney. A 6–0 defeat of Mansfield Town, with 'Sav & Wilko' getting hat-tricks, was one of the highlights of the season. In the run-in for promotion, a 2–0 win at Leyton Orient saw the Lilywhites gain just that. And another 2–0 success at Victoria Park, the home of Hartlepool, saw Preston lift their first title in 25 years.

A promotion party was to be had at Deepdale the following week against Exeter. It was a full house with home and away supporters, including season-ticket holders, locked out. When was the club going to get its act together regarding ticket allocation? Again, it was a 2–0 win. One scored by the hero of the season, Andy Saville, with his partner in crime getting the other, Wilko... over and out.

Pia:

We're coming back from a non-eventful tea-time kick-off at Bradford in the FA Cup and pulling in at a Burnley Station, when the Suicide Squad come bouncing out of the waiting room. They then start doing some kind of tribal dance with their disarranged faces contorting into gruesome images, like the New Zealand rugby union team. Their lips were moving without anyone being able to make any sense of what they're trying to say. Someone mentioned they might be from a local nut-house or inter-

bred, when it finally clicks! They're inviting us off for a dance. I've since read in the Burnley book that we wouldn't get off the train. Would you get off with all these nasty-looking creatures jumping up and down, frothing at the mouth? Yes, we did.

Despite Old Bill being positioned at every exit on the train, it didn't stop a big lad from removing an officer of the law from his position blocking the carriage's door. The lad then bangs the door's green button and we're out, chasing a back-tracking Suicide Squad into a nearby pub. This brought out more of their mates and all they did was throw glasses until the police arrived!

Two early trains left Preston Station at 6.30am and 7.30am, and we had to change at Euston for the connection to Gillingham, for a game in the league when both teams were jostling for top spot.

The mates and I left on the 7.30, and disembarked at Euston with a very impressive 100 lads, plus other Preston shirt-wearers among the crowd. It looked the bollocks when travelling across London while changing Tubes, up and down escalators and mobbed up on platforms; it certainly sent a shiver down your spine. The connecting train was caught at Victoria which arrived just before 11 bells in Gillingham.

On filtering out of the train station, similar numbers to ours were spotted 500 yards away. Yes! Preston fanned out, filling the road with the other mob doing the same – game on. A loud 'Come on!' went up with Preston starting into a jog, hands being clapped. So did the other mob. It was less than 50 yards to combat when familiar faces were clocked – what a bastard. It's only the 6.30am train crew. Anchors dropped, hands shaken and pleasantries exchanged, and nearly 250 lads now walked to a pub with the bolts on the door just being pulled back. We were greeted with delight off a Cheshire cat-like, smiling landlord.

A good drinking session started with only little bits of skirmishes around town. The lads were on a pub crawl with a 'let them come to us' attitude. They must have known we were here but, with the amount of lads in their boozers, we had carte blanche.

We'd been informed off a Maidstone/Brighton lad, Scott R, who was with us, that they didn't have a firm worth bothering with. So it was beer, beer, we want more beer.

I, myself, did have my hands full that day; not with trouble, but with carrying my mate, the 'Big Fella', from the gateway to the lakes. He was absolutely legless. I more or less had to carry him from the town centre to the Priestfield Stadium. And at over 6ft tall and weighing the other side of 15st, did I have a struggle on my hands. At one stage, he tripped up, falling off the pavement and splitting his head on the kerb.

On arrival at the turnstiles, I was greeted with, 'You're having a laugh if you think he's getting in in that state,' said a copper.

'It's OK, officer, I'll look after him,' I replied.

'He can sit down over there 'til he sobers up a bit or you can take him home.'

'All right, I'll sit down with him for a bit as well.'

'No. You can take a walk round the ground to get some fresh air in your lungs or you will be taking him back to the train station.'

I wasn't too keen on leaving a mate but I did as the officer said, hoping the Big Fella would sort himself out. Granted, I'd had a few southern shandies, only I wasn't pissed, just knackered after my 'World's Strongest Man' event.

Lap of the ground done, I headed back to where the Big Fella had been sitting... but no one seemed to know where he'd gone. Thinking he might have gone on, I paid my money to watch an unexciting 1–1 draw, and I still didn't find him.

After the match, we were escorted back to the train station with token gestures made by the Gillingham lads from down side streets. They were soon dispersed without the lads breaking sweat. As the Preston mob marched down the road, a local stood on the other side shouted over, 'I thought the Gooners had a good mob but this is impressive, Preston!' (Compliment noted.)

The Big Fella was still nowhere to be seen.

The Big Fella:

I opened my eyes and thought, 'Where the fuck am I?' I quickly realised that I was in the all-too-familiar surroundings of a cell. Jumping up off the bench to bang on the buzzer, and try to find out exactly what I had done, I hear the sound of splish-splosh. I'm stood in a puddle – oh no, I've pissed everywhere. It's with some uncertainty that I now put my finger to the button.

A couple of minutes later, the hatch drew back and a copper's face appears. 'I won't be a minute,' he says.

He soon returns, opening the cell door with a mop and bucket in his hands. 'Right, if you get your mess cleaned up, the desk sergeant says you can go.'

Cleaning equipment taken, I proceed to clean up like Hilda Ogden. I wasn't going to question him, was I? Ten minutes later, he returns and, by now, you could eat your dinner off the floor which is shining like a new penny. I'm then taken to the desk, given a severe warning about my drunken conduct, of which I can't remember a thing, and told to leave Gillingham on the first available train. Glancing up at the clock on the station wall, I see that it's 8.30pm. I must have had a good kip because it was around two-ish the last time I'd checked when going to the bar!

I managed to get the 9pm train to London, a connection to Manchester and then a bus to Preston arriving at 2.30am, when people were spilling out of all the nightclubs. I was just thankful that I didn't have a charge sheet upon my person or something worse. I'd only a banging headache and a grazed face. The moral of the story being: 'Don't peak too early!'

A new season – 1996/97 – offered new hopes and new let-downs. A 1–1 draw at Deepdale against Spurs in the League Cup, with a lesson taught and a lesson learned at the Lane with a 3–0 drubbing. Yorked out of the FA Cup and a Division Two league position of 15th come May.

The main shout was a 3–0 annihilation of Blackpool on Friday, 13 December at Deepdale. Should a derby win be the extent of Preston's success during the season?

The match against our bitter rivals Blackpool was moved forward to Friday night so that it could be shown live on Sky. It was also our first league game against the Lashers in six years.

The majority of Preston's lads finished work at dinner and it was party time. The lads knew Blackpool would turn up, but in what sort of numbers, was the question being asked. Three drinking areas around Preston were rammed to the rafters by tea-time, tea being ten pints.

Watering-hole number one: Plungington. This being my and the mates' preferred venue for boozers that day. This is a road which has ten or so pubs along its length, with twenty more splintering off down different side streets in the area.

Watering-hole number two: Meadow Street. By now it was seeing a decline in trade, with boozers closing down monthly due to the popularity of the town centre's new 'fun' pubs. I estimated it was down to seven or eight at the time. When I first started drinking after leaving the Fulwood & Railway or the White Hart pubs, it was compulsory to head there on a Friday night. If you managed a pint in every hostelry before closing time at eleven, you'd either be plastered or you were a liar. Today, it's down to three – how sad.

Watering-hole number three: Friargate. This was the nearest area to the town centre and the most expensive. It had around nine pubs to choose from.

The booze was flowing as were the tales about run-ins with Blackpool over the years. Would Benny's Mob show? Are the Bisons still running about? Who are the new and up-and-coming Donkey Lashers? The club at the time was owned by a man who was a dab hand at sewing mailbags!

Blackpool did show outside the Hyde Park pub with a heavy police presence. Preston, having been pinned in the pub by the police, resorted to throwing stools through the pub windows as they tried to get out to meet their near neighbours.

We made our way up to Deepdale and started to queue at the turnstiles for entry. The Old Bill that night were looking for any excuse to whisk you away. Lads were getting lifted left, right and centre – plenty of them were with me!

Due to ground redevelopment – not before time – Blackpool had been given the Spion Kop, a more suitable surrounding for the Blackpool fans in attendance because their ground was also a right dump. It must have felt like home sweet home. The Kop was knocked down shortly after we'd played Blackpool. However, Preston fans kept complaining of unusual smells in forthcoming games.

Preston that night ran out convincing 3–0 winners in front of a near 15,000 crowd. It's always good to get one over your old rivals.

One of the funniest incidents I witnessed that night, apart from a mate who was a Blackpool follower being treated to a bit of polished brass to the head, involved Yatee, a well-known lad from Leyland, who'd a true hatred towards Blackpool – 'Do I not like tangerine.'

He was in the Sir Tom Finney Stand when he decided to mount a one-man assault at the Blackpool end. He started running across the pitch, arms outstretched, beckoning the Blackpool into conflict. Half-a-dozen coppers followed his kamikaze-style advance towards the Kop and it took all six of them to restrain Yatee as he wasn't for giving up on his one-man mission.

Yatee was last seen being carried out of the ground with arms, legs and head reacting to the presence of the police uniforms and the cuffs he was wearing. He was thrashing about uncontrollably.

On his court appearance several weeks later, he explained to the 'all-ears' magistrate what exactly had occurred, which went something along the lines of: 'I was queuing to enter Preston North End's ground when I felt someone brush past me. I soon realised when entering the stadium that my wallet was missing. I then tried to report this to the police but they were very busy that night. I was in what I can best describe as a bit of a foul mood, even though Preston were winning. Then when a Preston attack was broken up, I noticed a Blackpool fan waving aloft my wallet, laughing with his mates. Not only did it contain my wages which were needed to support my family and to put food on the table, but also family photos and personal details. My composure snapped and, the next thing I knew, I was being wrestled to the ground by several officers. For my actions that day I apologise but, hopefully, you can sympathise with my frame of mind at the time, your Honour.'

A slap on the wrist for Yatee and a warning about his future conduct.

Game over. We were out on to Deepdale Road with running battles taking place along its length. It was a hate-filled atmosphere which you could cut with a knife.

We then slowly made our way into town for a good celebratory drink on both fronts. It had been well earned and was well needed. Out of the original nine with whom I'd first met up earlier in the day for a drink, before we'd moved off to meet the rest of the lads, we were down to just three, which thankfully included me.

The three of us drank round town into the early hours, eventually meeting up with a large chunk of the boys in Arabella's nightclub. After a good drink, we were asked to make our way out for the tenth time by the doorman.

Finding ourselves stood chatting in temperatures that would freeze the balls off a brass monkey on Church Street, it was buzzing with lads from the match, blokes who weren't interested in footy, having been on a night out – is there something wrong with them? – and girls in white stiletto heels wearing tops and skirts made out of an amount of material that you'd struggle to blow your nose on. Everyone was also deciding whether they wanted something to eat.

Maybe it will be a kebab. Only the meat's probably been

going round on its skewer for the last two weeks but plenty of chilli sauce will hide its nasty taste. And tell me, why do they always bang on a selection of salad? After a massive drinking session, in excess of 15 pints, and a portion of chips to go with the kebab, are you the slightest bit interested in your waistline? No! Anyway, most of the shredded cabbage and greenery ends up on the pavement as you stagger home. I personally order a can of Diet Coke with mine.

Before a decision could be made on a pizza, curry or a rancid kebab, a shout went up, 'Come on, then!' This seemed to drift down from the direction of Tokyo Joe's nightclub which is further up Church Street. We soon saw heads bobbing up and down, coming our way. Take-away forgotten about for the moment, it went off outside the Parish Church. Every credit to Blackpool for staying in our town. I can only imagine they'd been after our lovely lasses in the nightclubs. And while there were plenty of clubs in the seaside resort, many of the punters in Blackpool's clubs usually wear black leather pants, white string vests and grow big, bushy handlebar 'tashes with most dancing the night away to 'YMCA' and the like.

The lads started fighting with anyone who fronted them, including the Old Bill, who were trying to regain order.

Some time later, exhausted, I managed to flag a taxi down, having been separated from the boys in the mêlée. It was well on top! And for some reason I got out nearly two miles from where I actually live. Why, I don't know. Maybe with all the excitement that had happened during the day and all the shandy I'd consumed, I was a bit disorientated. The missus and the next-door neighbour had to launch a rescue party in the wee small hours to find me. Her fella had been lifted for being a naughty boy.

They drove round for nearly an hour, before eventually finding me doing five steps forward, three steps to the side, four back, in sub-zero conditions. I was frozen to the bone.

Before setting off on their quest to find me, the missus had rung the police station to report me as a missing person – well, really to see if I'd been nicked. One of the officers had asked her, 'How old is William? And how long has he been missing?'

Later, when I was tucked up in bed giving it some zeds, a patrol car came round to the house asking if I'd turned up, with the missus informing them that I'd returned safe and sound. Was that considerate of the police or what?

Next morning, sat up in bed, the missus was giving me the old 'what for'. I meekly replied, 'At least I didn't get lifted last night. I behaved myself.' Wasn't I a lucky boy!

* * *

For the start of the 1997/98 season, there was a buzz around Deepdale with the arrival of three young Manchester United players, namely Michael Appleton, Colin Murdock and Jonathan Macken. 'You'll never win anything with youngsters...' That phrase was surely coined for North End's season.

Preston drew Blackburn Rovers in the League Cup which saw them get turned over at Ewood Park 6–0, but managed a 1–0 win at Deepdale, which resembled a training game.

The managerial axe was wielded once again with David Moyes taking up a caretaker-manager/player role. He managed to pull PNE away from the relegation zone to a final position of 15th once again. Moyes earned himself the job full-time, hanging up his boots.

We'd not played Blackburn Rovers for some considerable time as Preston were usually in a lower league, only we'd been pulled out of the bag against them in the League Cup. Not having a crystal ball, Preston didn't really know if the Darwen Mob, H Division, Toolbar & Mill Hill Mob or Blackburn Youth were forces to be reckoned with or whether they'd show at theirs in the first leg. If they did, they would be well and truly put through the mill by Preston – big time.

With a dinnertime finish for most of the lads, we hit Blackburn's lovely town centre not much after two in the afternoon. Our 100-plus headed up to the Blob Shop, allegedly their pub. After pulling open the doors, after the doormen were brushed aside, we could see it was rammed, not with Blackburn, but Preston. A good 150 had taken a full day off, with some of the older heads present having a score to settle. The majority, however, had a point to prove, which was that our near neighbours weren't in North End's league, even though they were in the Premiership. A roar greeted our entry into the pub, with friends, mates and acquaintances shouting the ale in. Preston had a mob of over 250 in town and Blackburn wouldn't be able to handle our magnitude. We were superior.

Shortly, Preston started to drift into other pubs due to finding it hard work getting served with numbers swelling to folklore proportion. There were increasing numbers as every hour ticked by, while at this stage there wasn't a sniff, stench, stink or sighting of any Blackburn firm at all.

The lads I was with started to make tracks towards Ewood Park, optimistic that Blackburn might show, despondent they hadn't. It was less than an hour to go and we were closing in on Jack Walker's ground – big boy's toy – with 40 of us having obtained tickets for the said person's lower-tier stand.

Strolling down, it went off. Preston steamed a pub near to the ground where Blackburn's lads must have been in hiding, knowing what numbers had turned out. Credit to Blackburn as they came out, but not for long. A heavy police presence had been monitoring the lads' progress towards Ewood and they managed to keep Preston back, running into them on horseback, followed by police with batons drawn. A few windows got put through and lads were getting lifted. And what Blackburn did emerge got totally turned over and smashed.

Finally being moved on, lads made it to the ground with skirmishes everywhere. Preston were taking liberties which was probably years of pent-up frustration surfacing. We lost a couple more from our 40 to the boys in blue, as we didn't know which entrance to take.

Inside the ground, we took residence in seats near to the away section thinking Blackburn's so-called firms might join us. No such luck. As soon as the match got under way, Preston were under the cosh on the pitch from a quality side and the lads started to play up and we lost one more – RIP, Tony H.

The score ended up six fucking nil. The humiliation and hurt in the lads' eyes were plain to see and the night wasn't over yet. Another one down! In the darkened surroundings, in among the Rovers fans, we made our way back towards town – the law of averages and all that!

Going past the pub where the little fracas took place before the match, it had shut up shop with over 200 Preston milling about. It was just one of those things and the lads were going to have to accept that it wasn't going to happen. Or would it?

Rest assured, though, Preston weren't resting on their laurels. One of the lads put on his thinking cap, suggesting plotting up in a pub further up the road and waiting to see if Blackburn sneaked into town. This also let the bulk move on and the lads might have some fun with smaller numbers.

It sounded good. The lads gained entry into the pub which stunk of fustiness and other pungent smells. Surprisingly, there wasn't anyone else in apart from the landlord; it was a right dump. Before ordering, the door was booted closed and the curtains drawn, making out that it was shut. Saying that, I don't think anyone else would have come in. The lads lasted 30 minutes chatting quietly while one kept an eye on proceedings through a gap in the grotty, mould-ridden curtains. With nothing much to report, everyone left.

It was plain sailing into the town centre and most pubs en route had their doors locked. The Blackburn lads must have been avoiding Preston like the plague and the day played itself out.

Preston had beaten a path to Blackburn that day and the penny had finally dropped that there was more chance of pigs flying than Blackburn's lads making a show. It had just been a pipe dream. We then headed up to the Boulevard going on eleven-ish, finding out that the rest of Preston's lads had spat out their dummies and weren't for going home. It started to get nasty with the Lancashire Constabulary trying to get the lads on to trains and out of their dirty old town. I wasn't my normal cool, calm and collected self, such was the heavy-handedness of the police. No more Mr Nice Guy.

After much deliberation and exchange of dialogue, we caught the train home. It had been one of those days. The years had gone by since we'd played Rovers and they were still like fish out of water. The number of times that the North End now get to play Blackburn come round as often as a Preston Guild and by the next Guild they might have got their act together.

The return leg a fortnight later was another no-show.

* * *

It was a whirlwind start for Moyes' boys to the 1998/99 season; only one defeat in Preston's first 12 games, losing 3–4 to Stoke at home. 'We're on the march with Moyes' army.' Over the festive period, Preston took maximum points, lifting North End to the top of the table.

In between, they drew the mighty Gunners at home in the FA Cup third round. Arsenal, the team of the moment, went one down after 17 minutes courtesy of Kurt Nogan. And then four minutes later, it was 2–0, Nogan once again. The goalscorer ended up interfering with Preston's mascot, the Deepdale Duck, behind the nets!

No fairytale ending as usual for PNE, the game ending up a 4–2 win for Arsenal, with their class showing. Not to worry, promotion was Preston's main aim. However, the chances of this went out of the window with only one win in their last nine matches. Preston were once more in the dreaded play-offs, facing Gillingham. The first leg at Deepdale was scrappy, ending in a 1–1 draw. It was down to theirs and Preston were never in it, losing 1–0. We wouldn't be walking up Wembley Way that year, but there were plenty of tasty skirmishes to relieve the gloom. One of those was a little trip to Reading's new home, the Madejski Stadium. A minibus-load of us set off early doors, with plenty of ale sunk on the way down.

The Big Fella had sorted the driver. It was a bloke from his work, who wasn't into footy. A few quid greased his palm, and he was blissfully unaware of the mayhem that was about to kick off around him.

On the way down, the service stations were full of Welsh rugby fans and one of the lads kept winding them up, shouting, 'All right, Jonesy.' We then arrived in Reading just after opening time, parking up behind the train station. This was because a few of the London lads were coming up on the train and we wanted to make the rendezvous as problem free as possible. In addition, a coach of Preston boys was en route and they'd be in touch when they were on the outskirts of town.

The Big Fella:

On parking up, I asked the driver if he fancied a shandy or anything. 'No thanks. I've got some sandwiches and a flask and I'll meet you lads outside the ground after the match. I'll get my head down here and have a bit of a kip.'

He now pulls out, from under the seat, a tartan blanket and wraps himself up.

The first four of us walked through the station and out of the front doors, while the rest of the lads emptied their bladders. We four witnessed and heard something a little out of the ordinary. We clocked the usual home-spotter, a lad in a blue-and-white, stripy Paul & Shark jumper, lurking about. Also, there was Preston's intelligence officer of the time with a local bobby, pacing up and down as we came into view. Nothing unusual yet, you might think. Then someone, who wasn't with us, tapped the said lad on the shoulder, saying, 'You'll be on your toes in a minute,' in a northern accent, to a puzzled look from the lad. 'The Northern lads are here now.'

With this he scarpered to a nearby pub adjoining the train station.

We were back to full strength with the other eight turning up. The exile, cockney Whites and the coach had not yet arrived. Only the lads didn't want to wait, and marched straight over to the boozer into which the spotter had disappeared. There was a man-mountain of a bouncer stood in the doorway, stroking his pony-tail and I reckoned he'd been tipped off that we'd be coming over. He said, when we tried to gain entry, 'Sorry, lads, can't let any away fans in today.'

The Reading boys, or whatever name they went by, were pressed up behind him, not really fancying coming out to play. 'Give us a contact number... give us a contact number,' they mumble.

'It's not a dating agency we're running! We're here now, boys!' the Big Fella said.

A few Old Bill were heading over so we moved off, making sure they saw which way we went for later reference. As we made our way to another pub, we passed (I suspected) an undercover copper looking over the top of the *Sun* newspaper, trying to conceal his identity with a baseball cap – I don't think so! It may have been a sixth sense to our lot, but the lads could usually spot an undercover OB. Whether Reading could is debatable, as they got sucked in by the undercover reporter Donal MacIntyre not long after.

We settled into a pub not far away with phone calls made, telling the rest of the lads of our whereabouts. Then a couple of police officers with cameras in hand entered the alehouse, stating, 'Your intelligence officer says you lads are OK, but we'll take a few nice pictures of you lovely boys and we'll be on our way.'

It wasn't like they didn't have enough of us already from outside the train station and previous away trips.

After an hour had passed and all the lads had arrived, there were a good 80 of us in the boozer. A young Reading spotter then came in, asking once more for a few contact numbers. (The young lad in question was seen in the background on the undercover TV report a short while later.) Lads swapped numbers with him and off he went.

The phones didn't go before the game and the Old Bill were well on the ball, getting the lads back on the coach and the rest of us jumping in taxis up to the ground. Not that Reading had a chance with the numbers they had, Preston having a good turnout of lads that day.

It was another shite new ground, situated in the middle of an industrial estate, where we witnessed Preston get beat 2–1. Worse still, the 75p-a-minute pay-as-you-go credit was soon eaten up on my mobile.

Outside, after the match, we were greeted by our driver in the minibus and we asked him to drop Scotty and Kingy back at the train station. Getting out of the car park was horrendous and we were stuck in traffic for nearly 30 minutes, which is great when you're gagging for a beer. Finally, we got moving and saw a few Preston lads stood outside a boozer, pointing and mouthing 'Reading are up the hill'. Funnily enough, that's the way we were heading anyway. Then 100 yards further up the road, Reading came at the van, 25 of them throwing bottles and bricks as we were doing 20mph in the traffic. The back doors burst open, but the driver wouldn't stop. Everyone was shouting for him to stop. Only he didn't. He'd now begun to see what a big mistake he'd made, volunteering to drive while trying to dodge all the missiles. You can't blame him as the van was in his name and he didn't know the score. He was thinking he'd done really well getting away from the situation, but he was now getting bollocked off all the lads for not stopping.

We arrived at the train station with the lads still fuming that they hadn't dished out any retribution for damage done to the bus. The Southern two boarded their train back down to the smoke, with three of us milling about near the train station's entrance. The other lads had nipped to the speed bank, shops or to spend a penny, when the same mob of Reading appeared, slightly out of breath. Action stations!

They were standing some distance away, not knowing our numbers but trying to strike up a conversation while keeping their eyes peeled. We kept an eagle eye on them, waiting for an ambush. They then started going on about Chelsea and Wrexham, which we found rather strange. Then the lads started arriving back with the last one saying, 'Right, we're all here now, we might as well get off.'

He hadn't noticed Reading hiding in the shadows just outside the doors. CRACK! A Reading lad steamed in, knocking one of ours to the floor. They must have realised that they well outnumbered us. The brother of the lad on the floor dived into the mêlée on top of the Reading lad, and it was game on. Then two more bods came flying in the ruck from behind us, but they only started shouting, 'Police! Police!' ID cards in one hand, walkie-talkie in the other, calling for back-up.

Oh no, it was undercover again – game over. Reading did one, not wanting to hang around with one of our lads pinned to the floor by the plain-clothes officers. More police arrived and we had to explain exactly what had gone on, and luckily no one was lifted.

We then boarded the minibus with a still shell-shocked driver, drove to the outskirts and stopped at an off-licence. While deciding which tipple we fancied for the journey home, a mobile went. The southern voice on the other end started wittering on about this and that – blah, blah. Over the next 20 minutes, he informed a lad that he wasn't even a Reading fan and that he followed Chelsea. I wonder if it was the same bloke who got duped by the BBC reporter? How foolish were those boys? They're a small firm and they let their guard down!

The night wasn't over. We stopped off in Stafford on the way home, falling out with the locals.

Tony R:

During the Eighties, I didn't get to many Burnley games due to my many visits to the clinker. When I did, I was normally the unlucky one. Usually it went off and, more often than not, my collar must have had 'nick me' on it because I reckon five or six times the police just did as it said on the label. The last time was a Sunday around the time of Paddy's Day.

We'd met in the Lovat pub in Preston as it had opened at nine in the morning with arrangements being made for two big Luton box vans to be hired one way with a driver. 'That's a strange job,' the hire firm had replied.

By 11am, over 40 top boys were drinking quietly, not wanting to attract any unwanted attention from any party. It was a very moody place.

By 11.30am, we were ready for the off. The plan was to sit one lad up front with each driver, giving directions to our destination with the rest of us in the back. And, as we drove to Burnley, the smell of the good old days drifted round the van en route!

Half-an-hour later, we pulled up outside the Swan pub in Burnley town centre with the first part of the plan achieved. Our naughty 40 piled into the pub undetected, with a motto – 'sit tight' and they will come looking for us; we'd no need to move because we'd only have the Old Bill on our case.

An hour passed, and I'm revved up, so Scot, a mate, and me decided on a recce up to Yates's. (We should have sat tight.)

On entering Yates's, we notice a few Burnley but not big numbers and they clock us. Drinks are ordered but we're alert to the situation as more and more Burnley start arriving. Then a Burnley lad shouts, 'They're coming!'

Burnley make a move out of the door swiftly, taking glasses and bottles. Looking out of the window, the way they're heading, I can see Preston coming up the shopping area walking towards them. Burnley let loose with their wares and Preston shield themselves, cautiously moving forward. Ammo gone and a few scuffles start. Within a few seconds, the Old Bill have truncheons drawn between the two firms, splitting them up. They'd been parked round the corner and quickly moved in. During this time, Scot and me are out into the back of the Burnley, trying to crack a few. We're missing them and they're missing us. Then a lad trips up, grabbing me and we go down. Just before close combat takes place, I'm being dragged away with not a punch landed by either party – lifted once again. I've got the video to prove it and it catches me throwing punches but not connecting. I received a Section 5, being bound over to keep the peace.

Like Tony said, the vans were booked only one way. So, after the match, we put our heads down, went past the coaches and under the bridge. Nine times out of ten Burnley gave us a show and they did this time. The police were quick to react once more, moving us on with only a few handbags from both sides.

Once again in their book, they mention handing out hidings.

If they did hand out slaps to lads getting into taxis, it wasn't us; we got on the train to finish our quiet day out.

I won't deny a couple of times over the years that they've come to Preston mob-handed, but they've been sussed off the Old Bill and been pushed into a pub. They've then attacked one-armed bandits and toilets!

I'm also a witness to them coming down Deepdale Road, one dark, wet night after a Saturday tea-time kick-off!

Soon, we were also privileged to entertain some illustrious company – the fallen giants Manchester City came to Deepdale on a Bank Holiday Monday. I decided to take the son on and I was with a mate before the match in a local newsagent's near the ground.

While I was entering the shop, I accidentally bumped into a few City lads. Then on coming out of the shop, they were still hanging around with one lad flashing his train and match ticket, wanting, I think, a reaction. 'Yeah, mate, I know you're City... what about it?'

I suddenly remembered that I was with the son and decided to leave it. We carried on walking across the road as there was Old Bill everywhere on Deepdale Road. The City lad started giving it large, gobbing it off along with his mates as we were all walking to the ground. I just smiled and nodded at the knobhead as we made our way. When we were both parallel with the souvenir shop, he shouted something at me. Silly me gave him the 'wanker' sign and I just carried on. Unbeknown to me, on my blind side, the clever cunt ran across Deepdale Road and, in full view of a copper on his horse, whacked me twice on the side of the head. My son reacted by pushing him away. The mounted copper shouted out, 'What do you think you are playing at?' The City snide simply trotted back over to his mates.

'I don't know, officer,' I said with rage in my voice, 'I suggest you ask him.'

'Just get on your way, and don't let me see you in any more trouble today,' the copper said.

The red mist was coming down and the cheeky twat over the road was laughing with his mates. Why do it in front of the Old Bill? Why do it when I'm with my young son? I couldn't afford a nicking, but...

Ten yards on, I bumped into a few Preston lads squaring up to some City. One of the Preston lads said, 'Do you fancy giving us a lift, Bill?'

'Sorry, I'm with the son.'

The mouthy City lad needed a lesson about his conduct; I give him no credit for what he did. You reap what you sow and, if he was ever to get pay-back, I hoped it wouldn't be in instalments!

A cracking game of football was then observed, ending in a 1–1 draw. This was watched by a sell-out crowd, although I noticed an empty seat in the City away section.

I'd come out just before the final whistle and put the son on the bus home. The game was over and both Preston and City started spilling out of the stadium and I joined the Preston walking past the Bill Shankly away end. I then bumped into a few City fans who I knew from Preston and arrangements were made to meet up for a drink later.

I was stood there with a City mate chatting away when a mob of about 30 City lads walked up, one a lad from Leyland who I knew. 'What do you lads want?' one said in my direction.

'Just talking to my City mate here, but if you want to meet up for a drink, we're going in the Deepdale pub and you're more than welcome to join us. Your mate there [I pointed to the Leyland lad] knows where it is.'

I set off walking to the pub, entered it and ordered a pint, informing the lads that they might have a few guests joining us.

A couple of beers later, City hadn't materialised so we set off into town to a big pub called Greyfriars. As I was walking up the steps towards the boozer, the City fan who I knew from earlier was stood next to the doors. 'Do you fancy a pint?' I asked.

'Yeah. I'll see you inside. I'm just waiting for a few lads.'

It had slipped my mind that he meant City lads.

On entering the pub, there were already quite a few Preston sat up on a raised part of the gaff, looking out of the windows for any Blues.

Halfway down my first pint, one of the lads stood up and shouted, 'City are in.'

Spinning round, the penny dropped that the mate had been referring to some City boys he was meeting for a drink. I told the Preston lads to calm down and I'd go over to see what the score was. I then noticed that it was the lads from outside the ground earlier who'd been squaring up to Preston. The bloke in question with the City I'd known for over 20 years. He'd also followed Preston in the Eighties and we'd fought side-by-side on many occasions for Preston and England. I was then joined by D Ladd, just before I asked the mate why he'd brought City in. I could also feel the Preston lads' eyes burning into my back and there were growls of unrest in the camp.

'What's the score?'

'Just having a few beers with my City mates.'

'Don't think they're welcome.'

'No, no, no... they don't want trouble, just a few beers.'

'Preston think they're taking liberties and I can't guarantee that it won't go off any second.'

'Well, if it does, they've got to go through me first,' replied the City mate.

Nightmare.

It then went off, with Preston steaming into the rest of the City. Glasses and stools were being thrown in the battle with Preston chasing City out on to the street. They were on their toes with Preston lads hotly in pursuit. Sirens and blue lights were heard on their way towards the scene and a few lads got lifted when they turned up.

I found myself taking time out to go over in my mind what I'd just witnessed.

It was day over and Preston started to drift off home with City having been moved out of town, leaving a heavy police presence on every corner.

You can't always guarantee what might happen. I tried my best and sometimes you shouldn't piss in your own backyard.

And talking of guaranteeing what may happen, we were all convinced towards the end of the season that automatic promotion was a cert with nine games to go. Er... wrong! Preston ballsed it up, winning only once in their last eight games. With Fulham left, and the play-offs looming, it was a party atmosphere on the InterCity train to the capital. Preston knew that Fulham weren't renowned for having a firm as we'd visited Craven Cottage many times before. The last time, the police were breath-checking fans before allowing entry into the ground and turning away many a Preston fan for smelling of alcohol.

Sure enough, twenty minutes into the game, police swooped on to the terracing and started lifting lads for allegedly being drunk and disorderly. A bit of argy-bargy took place with the boys in blue which didn't go down too well and more Preston were ejected.

So, before hitting the executive part of central London and George Best's local, Preston lads got off the Tube in Chelsea's manor, at Fulham Broadway. There was a bit of history between both teams and it could have turned out to be interesting if any Headhunters were about. No such luck! They must have had a tasty away fixture. A few drinks later, everyone headed over to Fulham, passing Jill Dando's house (RIP) which was still covered with scaffolding and plastic sheeting.

The cockney Whites had sorted out tickets for us in the main stand at Craven Cottage, next to the away end. I think it must have been a listed building as it was nearly as old as the antique West Stand which we knocked down years ago. Mr Mohammed Al-Fayed had recently purchased the club with high ambitions. Fulham convincingly won the title that season, achieving 101 points.

It was a near-capacity crowd with 20 of us sat in a pocket among the home fans. And it wasn't long before Fulham scored and we got clocked by what lads they did have – yes, they did have some. 'Fackin' this... fackin' that...' threats are thrown our way. 'Yeah, yeah, yeah!'

Just before the half-time break, we went down under the stand and half went for a piss, half on back-watch. Then it was a-changing of the guard. While this went on, Fulham appeared. We were stood just out of the bright sunshine, but their lads who bothered coming down spun on a sixpence, disappearing quickly back into their seats. The cockney big-mouths for some reason now didn't fancy it.

On the day in question, Fulham hammered us 3–0 and were presented with the trophy.

The lads waited outside for a bit, but the Fulham boys must have had a fitting for a Pearly suit or gone on to an end-of-season 'Knees Up, Mother Brown' with a few jellied eels thrown in – or is that only in the East End?

Also arrangements had been made for a few sherbets with other Preston lads, before they set off back home to God's town. The lads and I were stopping down in the Smoke. Everything was top-notch, and we were enjoying a few light ales, when an incident occurred. I ended up nearly covered head to foot in claret. Will things ever get sorted?

As the new millennium loomed, ever the optimist, I started to convince myself that it had got to be Preston's season eventually, hadn't it? And what better time to do it than at the turn of the century?

And yes, for once, I was right! Preston started with a few ups and downs, then went on an 18-game unbeaten run. Despite a few blips on the way, and a 2–0 defeat at Cambridge United's Abbey Stadium with two matches to go, North End still lifted the title – other results that day went Preston's way for a change.

In between winning the Division Two Championship, Preston went out to Arsenal in the third round of the League Cup (2–1 at Highbury) and exited the FA Cup in the fifth round 2–0 at Everton's Goodison Park.

There were plenty of matches I could harp on about, but, to cut it short, Preston North End returned to second-flight football with games to spare after a 19-year absence. Among the few blips along the way, one of the roughest was a 4–1 home defeat at the hands of Wigan Athletic in August. This was a distant memory, however, when Preston lifted the trophy as champions after defeating Millwall at Deepdale on 29 April.

Looking back over the season, there were a few tasty encounters, and one that stands out was Preston's tie against Everton away in the fifth round of the FA Cup. We really fancied our chances against the Toffees, and we had also heard a lot about Everton off the playing field, so Goodison, here we come.

About 40 of us arrived early by train and went straight into the Punch & Judy pub. We decided to wait for the rest of the lads to turn up and a few of the boys went for a mooch around. Being in Liverpool, they soon bumped into a young scally Scouser who asked them, 'Would you like me to do any shopping for you today, la?'

'A nice coat wouldn't go amiss, mate,' one of the lads said. 'We're heading back to the Punch & Judy and, if anything turns up, we'll see you in there.'

Just 20 minutes later, the lad's new mate turned up with three Lacoste jackets – this boy was quicker than the Internet. Liverpool's full of comedians, singers and the odd tea-leaf, and this pub was full of self-employed, help-yourself merchants. There was a wide range of swag available, ranging from socks, razor blades, fags, various items of electrical equipment and packs of boiled ham. And with beer at a pound a pint, the pub was heaving.

After the lads had snapped up a few bargains in the January sales, we moved on to the Blob Shop, then the Adelphi Hotel and other boozers in town. There weren't any Everton about so we headed off up towards the ground in taxis, stopping off in the Stanley Arms for a final pint.

Our bubble had burst. Preston got beat 2–0 with one of the goals scored by a Chorley boy, which just rubbed salt in the wounds.

Coming out of Goodison, we headed back into the Stanley Arms. One of the lads had been informed that Everton were turning up – defo.

An hour later and with no Blue-noses arriving, the lads were getting itchy feet wanting to move on. Two decided to go for a recce, but, on pushing open the pub doors, they were immediately lifted. Preston's intelligence officer informed them that they were likely to cause a breach of the peace and bundled them into the waiting van. The police then entered the pub, informing everyone that if they didn't leave within ten minutes they had enough vans for the rest of us as well. Taxis were ordered to return to the Punch & Judy for a second look at what goods were now on sale.

Five of us jumped into the first taxi that arrived and it took off past the Blue House pub. The Everton boys were just leaving and one of the lads I was with wound the cab window down. 'Are you lads looking for something?'

'Yeah, la.'

'Well, we're heading for the Punch & Judy if you fancy it.'

'No problem... we'll see you there, mate.'

They didn't realise that two minutes behind were ten other taxis with Preston lads in coming their way. The lights changed before any action had started. We were informed later that, as the taxis pulled up, Everton attacked them. The problem was that the drivers had put the cabs' locks on. This must be the standard practice in Merseyside with all the runners that are done. We'd also heard some reports about flashing steel being brandished, so things were obviously hotting up a bit.

We were all back at the Punch & Judy, safe and sound, with the lads ready for action. Quite a few were nervous of 'Uncle Stanley' making an appearance and started smashing up old pavement slabs that were being replaced outside. They'd been left stacked up near the boozer which was very considerate of the council to do so and leave Preston some ammo. Not having to wait too long, a Preston lad shouted through the pub's front door, 'They're here!'

Preston steamed out towards Everton, some launching bits of pavement in their direction. I bet, if it had hit a target, it would have hurt. Just as it was going to go off, dibble arrived to save the day. They must have been lurking in the shadows, just out of sight.

The police rounded the lads up with batons drawn, forcing them on to Lime Street Station. Preston made a few attempts to get back out but to no avail. It was day over and we retired home to the local pubs to drown our sorrows.

Another night game in the run-in for the Division Two title saw Preston take on Wigan at the JJB Stadium, and a good 100 of us caught a train at about 3pm. The Old Bill were waiting on Wigan Station but let Preston drift off into town while keeping a watchful eye. Ten of us broke off from the mob and headed into the Bee's Knees pub for a pint. The rest of the Preston lads strolled up the road into town, attracting all the attention. Not long after, a few Wigan lads entered the Bee's Knees boozer and were told the score: 'You firm up and we'll meet you somewhere.'

Wigan left, saying they would sort something out. The rest of the lads were phoned to inform them of what was happening as they moved from pub to pub. The police were pushing Preston towards the ground, informing them they'd be able to get a beer in the Wigan Pier pub.

We finished off our pints and a phone call was made to see where the lads were. As we were walking round a corner, I noticed to my left that Preston were stood outside a pub about 400 yards away and, to my right, I saw 30–40 lads coming our way. We then threw a right to meet them head on. At first, we couldn't tell who they were, because the bodies moving towards us were our age and we hadn't seen Wigan for years. We had a good 15 with no fear and we went straight into them. We also needed to be quick, knowing that the plod would soon stop the fun.

I got one right in the chops that sent me backwards into a wire fence, bouncing back like Big Daddy, the wrestler, off the ring-ropes. The only difference now was that there were no old dears hitting me about the head with handbags. It was a good full minute, vicious toe-to-toe. The police arrived with cars and vans pulling up, jumping out, truncheons in hand and dogs snarling, pulling on their leads. They managed to get between us pretty sharpish, driving both sets back. No one wanted lifting so we set off walking back to where the Preston lads had been surrounded at the pub. Thankfully, no one got collared.

The match was won 1–0 by Preston in an 'edge-of-your-seat' game.

In the darkness, the gates finally opened with Preston trying to make an advance over the bridge behind the stadium. Wigan were already on the other side, throwing bricks and rocks. There was a bit of scuffling with the police having the upper hand, eventually gaining control. They then gave Preston a tight escort back to the station and sent us on our way home.

So on to Bristol. We'd played Bristol City as the last game of the season a couple of years before, and they'd brought a good following up to Deepdale. Bristol, by all accounts – well, the City Service firm – took a good hiding around town before and after the match. There are plenty of stories about that day and some lads would rather have them swept under the carpet. This season it was Preston's turn to travel to Bristol and go a-hunting in Wurzel country for one of my favourite tipples, cider, and plenty of it.

Four of us boarded an early train with other Preston fans and we'd made arrangements to meet a minibus-load of other lads in Bristol.

When the train arrived at Temple Meads, there were already four of the Southern Whites waiting, including Scotty, so we exited the station and headed straight for a pub to sample the pleasures of the forbidden fruit. Eight other Preston lads that had been on the same train joined us, leaving the other Preston to wander off into town. Having found a nice little street with plenty of boozers, Pia and I settled into one, and the minibus lads soon turned up. We didn't want to hit the town centre as our numbers weren't really up to any sort of standards.

After a good session, we doubled up in the minibus, driving to Ashton Gate just before kick-off. To our astonishment, there were no apple-crunchers waiting.

As we were queuing up at the catering stand just before half-time for a pie, the police closed down the kiosk. They then proceeded to arrest all of the staff for what I can only guess was a dodgy case of food poisoning the week before.

Preston that day ran out comfortable winners 2–0 and we were Champions Elect. The Preston fans gave the team a standing ovation, while the coppers made sure we didn't join any of the City fans who were on the pitch.

On making our way out of the away end, to our right-hand side Bristol lads started giving it verbal and the old finger-across-the-throat signal. Once outside, the eight or so I was with got set upon by 70 CSF. The hostile mob can't have been happy with our consumption of half an orchard of their finest apples before the match. A few Old Bill tried to keep order but they hadn't got a chance. We tried to retaliate but, with numbers not in our favour, it just wasn't going to happen and the old legs had to come into action. It was as if half the core of Bristol wanted a slice of us. This was revenge time, I think, for their visit to Preston. In the mêlée, and the baying crowd, I managed to flag down a taxi, jumping into it in one hell of a mood.

At the train station, the rest of the Preston lads started to turn up; luckily, no one had any serious injuries. We expected City to make another show and by now everyone was in the same frame of mind in our 'band of brothers'. They never did, and it might just have been a good job, the mood everyone was in.

Setting off back home on the train, I was seething, as once again Preston hadn't travelled in numbers and I was finally wondering whether it was all worth it. (The answer was, yeah, even after all this time.)

To reach Preston, we had to catch a connecting train at Birmingham New Street and, while sat waiting on the Glasgow-bound train, five Stoke lads also got on. Next, some other Preston who had travelled to Bristol but weren't with us, I must stress, launched an unprovoked attack on the Stoke lads. It was plain to see these so-called PNE were totally wasted off drink and drugs, and were well out of order.

Before I had a chance to stop the assault, one Stoke lad was knocked out, with the others taking a beating. I'd been on the receiving end not too long ago, so I managed to jump in between, blocking the onslaught and any more bully-boy tactics.

It turned out that these Preston had just made a big mistake, for there were over 100 Naughty boys shuffling down the platform stairs. A look of shock and fear came on to the faces of the lily-livered Preston lads, and they did one out of the back carriage doors, just as the train pulled away from the platform.

It also looked like it might be Round 2 and the remainder of us on the train would probably get the punishment lined up for the turn-tails.

Within minutes, the carriage started to fill with Potters going potty.

'Is it these?' one Stoke lad said to another who was holding his face.

'No, it isn't them.'

Then another Stoke lad said, 'All right,' to Pia.

He replies, 'O'rite.'

A conversation was then struck up about seeing each other at England games, home and away. (The lad was actually mistaken, but it seemed to smooth things over.) While they'd been chatting, I'd been on the blower to the minibus and they'd just arrived in Stafford, a usual stop-off place for a beer on our away days. I didn't fancy crossing swords with the Stoke boys as we'd started getting dirty looks off some. It was time to leave before we outstayed our welcome, and the train was pulling into Stafford. I'd sorted a lift out while on the mobile for Pia and me as I wasn't a happy chappy with the day's events.

After coming out of the station, we entered a pub opposite and it was bursting at the seams; full of big grippers celebrating something. They were Stafford Rangers fans whose team had also gained promotion out of whatever league they were in.

The mates off the minibus were in and the party mood soon took a turn for the worse. I don't think they liked supping alongside Preston, taking the shine off what they'd achieved. We were treading on their toes at 'their' promotion party. The boozer split into two with battle lines drawn. Once more that day, we were well outnumbered with the odds stacked against us. It was time to go and the landlord was on the phone to the local constabulary, saying he wanted us to be removed. Pia remembers, 'It started to get on top in a pub in Stafford so I mentioned to the minibus driver to get the bus near the doors ready for the off. These were nasty-looking lads and I would rather call it a tactical retreat.'

We slowly moved backwards, not turning away, with the odd punch and glass thrown off both sides. We made our way out of the doors and the driver of the van was waiting, revving the engine. He didn't want any attention off the police, due to being overloaded, so he left the scene rapidly and headed home.

I was physically and mentally drained, mulling over some of the Preston's lads' actions that day. I was truly disheartened, along with other Preston lads' non-participation. Lying back in my seat while squashed between two old mates, I was thinking, 'Enough's enough.'

It was a short drive back to Preston, but it seemed to take ages, with me doubled up like it used to be in the early Eighties. Such is life... or is it? I was getting too old and I was starting to like my middle-aged comforts. I thought to myself, 'This has to be my retirement from the scene!'

13

INDIAN SUMMER

I still meet up with 'certain' lads and have a pint or two with them on Saturdays, but there has got to be more to life than watching a bag of wind being kicked around a field for 90 minutes or punching the wind out of someone... hasn't there?

It was a way of life, with football camaraderie and lasting friendships made. You can't just cut yourself off from the lifestyle – or, at least, I personally couldn't. I'd bleed to death.

The lads still come into town (now a city) for a few bevvies and a chat on Saturdays, even if they're not going to the match. They still turn out in their combat gear. The football culture lives and breathes between similar, like-minded lads with mutual respect given out. Those who've never been involved will never fully understand.

While stood in the pub, you will get the all-too-familiar wink and nod or handshake and an 'O'right, mate' exchanged. This can be followed by a brief word, short chat or a full-blown conversation. This could be with lads whom you've known for over 30 years or just that season. Lads with whom you've travelled the length and breadth of the country, even over land and sea. With some, you know their middle names and date of birth; others, you haven't got the foggiest what their real names are, just knowing them by their nickname. You might know some lads' daily business and their place of work; others, you haven't got a clue what they do 9–5 – they could even be Old Bill!

They're a football tribe, not yet extinct, social lepers and mindless thugs to the courts, the media and Joe Public. They're also family, best mates and friends for ever to like-minded lads.

Solicitors, teachers, top chefs and artists, to name just a few, are in this book. So put that in your pipe and smoke it.

As I walk off into the sunset, here's a few more short stories off the lads. Mine will reflect what I'm about nowadays!

And while the times have changed for me, so, too, have Preston's fortunes on the pitch. For the 2000/01 season, could it really get any better? Yes, it could! It started to get a bit boring, all this winning lark. Preston fans had nothing more to moan about in the pubs after the match. Fans also seemed to start appearing from everywhere, gracing the new stands with the Bill Shankly Kop newly opened.

Preston finished fourth and the two-legged play-off against the Blues of Birmingham awaited us. But before meeting that particular set of Blues, we had a score to settle with some others – Portsmouth. It had taken a good few years for the lads to get their act together for a return to Fratton Park. An 80-seater coach was booked, setting off early one Saturday morning with many on board having a bone to pick.

J1:

Even though I wasn't living in Preston when the 6:57 had rolled into town in the early Eighties, the lads had filled me in with all the gory details. So much was spoken about the coming season with Portsmouth now in the same division as Preston. It was a date for the lads to mark off on their calendar and fixture list. For the younger ones amongst the ranks, it would be a new adventure going to the home of the famous 6:57 crew.

The New Year had come and gone with myself and a mate making arrangements to book a coach to the south coast. It was time to lick and also reopen some old wounds. We'll fly the flag. The lads who would be travelling weren't born yesterday, having come a long way since the Seventies. These had been times when the older lads went to Fratton Park in the mid-Seventies and some are touching 50 today. On one occasion, they'd been run all over the ground having to make an escape via the pitch.

When the early Eighties arrived, the 6:57 had a big reputation and most didn't fancy their chances in Hampshire. A long trip with the regulation good hiding wasn't fancied, so no decent-sized firm had travelled up until today. This game was one that a lot of the lads were going to be well up for.

We soon realised we'd have to book two coaches or a big modern one. After phoning round, a decision was made to charter a big, plush double-decker.

There were a few problems in the lead-up to the game. The Friday before we were to travel, the Big Fella received a phone call off the coach firm asking for the full amount of £1,100 up front. Fair play to the big man, he'd pulled it off and, on Saturday at 6am, a new, pristine double-decker bus pulled up outside the Crest Hotel in Preston. Looking round, there was a fair turnout of lads – a good mixture of young blood and big guns. I would also say all were like-minded, with many on the same wavelength.

Settling in on the long journey to the south coast with a large beer consumption en route, the tales began flowing of previous adventures and trips. And things are never dull when you have Pia onboard.

We arrived in Portsmouth for opening time and the coach pulled up alongside Fratton Park. We all spilled into the first pub we'd seen which was just around the corner from the Milton Arms, allegedly the home of Portsmouth's lads.

After a couple of hours' drinking, we're joined by Scotty and his Maidstone mates. This is when a decision is made to make a move, sending a lad ahead as a scout. He'd entered the Milton to test the water with others ringing him about numbers, chomping at the bit. As we're on the move, we've attracted the attention of the local Old Bill who quite quickly throw a small bubble around us. They then proceed to escort us in the direction of the Milton Arms. I can't understand what possessed them to do this. We then start psyching each other up, not knowing who, or what, would greet us, or what our fate would be.

As we approached the pub, a lad from another boozer across the road sneaked up from behind, clumping one of ours who went down, knocked out cold. While a Preston lad looked after him, Pompey's boys came out of the Milton to confront us. Then all hell broke loose. They let go with glasses and anything else they could throw. Once they'd no ammunition left, skirmishes started to occur all around with more and more police starting to arrive as their associates had radioed for back-up in numbers.

The 6:57 crew soon took safe haven back in their pub. Portsmouth now knew Preston were in town looking generally shocked and surprised to see a mob our size which had travelled all the way down from Lancashire.

Eventually, the Old Bill managed to move us up towards Fratton Park with Pompey having regrouped, trying to get at us with little joy. We were taken straight to the turnstiles and put on the ground, under heavy protest. When the game kicked off, Pompey's lads were situated to our left, giving it the big come-on.

So at half-time, a few of our lot made a move to go out and join Portsmouth outside. Only two Preston managed this before the Old Bill twigged and closed the gate. Once outside, Portsmouth confronted them but didn't seem to want to get too close. There were 12 Pompey and 2 Preston, and they just didn't fancy it. One of the two lads was that wound up he was doing drop-kicks on wing mirrors on a police van. The silly lad ended up getting nicked.

The rest of the game passed with little incident and North End ran out winners thanks to a David Healy goal.

We all grouped up for the walk back to the coach and, on leaving, Pompey were everywhere. There were quite a few little scraps as lads broke out from behind police lines but we kept getting moved on. One Gamull lad who was with us knocked out the sneak who took the cheap shot at one of ours earlier that day – poetic justice.

We all rallied, grouping up on a grass banking near the bus for one last go at Portsmouth. Then one lad started running towards them shouting, 'Come on, Pompey, it's party time.' He ran straight into a concrete bollard that caught him straight in the bollocks. Lads from both sides *were now howling with laughter. He staggered off back to the coach holding himself mumbling, 'I'm done for the day... I know when I'm beat.'*

The Old Bill finally managed to push us on to the coach and informed us that we could get one of our lads out of hospital that'd been knocked out. The others, who'd been nicked, would be released shortly.

We were then escorted to a pub on the outskirts of Portsmouth where they let us wait for the rest of the lads to rejoin our bus. It was a family eatery and one hungry lad raided the kitchen for his tea. He then started walking round the pub with cooked joints of meat handing them out to all the hyenas and vultures amongst the party. Within seconds, the bones were tossed to one side. So, when the police arrived back an hour later with the released ones, the landlord wanted us out quickly and the police soon sent us on our way home. I make no bones about it, Portsmouth knew that we'd been that day.

Travelling back we decided to give the driver a big tip for all he'd been through and we managed to get him to stop off at Stafford for a drink.

Once we'd reached our destination around 10.30pm, we thirstily hit the bars and pubs. It also wasn't long before we'd attracted the attention of a group of Stoke lads on a stag do. Yes, you've guessed it; it went off again, with one Preston lad being glassed. Apart from all the other injuries, a most amazing thing happened. The same Portsmouth casualty, who got sparked out, only gets knocked out again! You know you've had a bad day when that happens.

After running the locals, and the Stoke lads, the cops finally rounded us up and put us back on to the coach for the final leg of our long journey back to Preston. What a top day out with two top footy mobs that day having learned a bit about Preston's lads. Plus Preston had taken three points.

Some time later, the 6:57 put together a book and mentioned the day. They seemed to have seen the events a bit differently. At least they mentioned that Preston turned up! The day also appeared on the National Crime squad web page mentioning both the Portsmouth and Stafford incidents.

It may have taken 20 years for days in the late Seventies and early Eighties to be levelled up a little, but most of the lads thought that they'd evened a score. It was a bitter pill for the 6:57 to swallow, but every dog has its day.

And so to the Battle of Saint Andrew's, which saw Preston, after the final whistle, leave Birmingham with a 1–0 defeat and bags of pressure for the second leg. It had been a tough game with plenty of yellow cards being shown.

Back at fortress Deepdale, Moysie had to field a team of walking wounded with Birmingham really fancying their chances, thinking they'd already got one foot in the Premiership.

The game kicked off with Healy missing early on from just over ten yards. Healy then made amends with a thundering volley in the 24th minute. Preston went 1–0 up and the rest of the half saw David Lucas in goal for Preston under the cosh, making save after save.

The second half got under way and Birmingham carried on from where they had left off, attacking. Geoff Horsfield soon levelled the scores.

Then, with ten minutes to go, Preston won a corner. The ball was floated in and a Birmingham player handled it. Penalty! Mr

Reliable himself, Graham Alexander, stepped up – he hardly ever missed.

SMASH. He slammed the ball on to the bar and away it bounced. If Preston ever needed the big man upstairs looking down on them, it was tonight of all nights.

Then up went the electronic scoreboard in the fourth official's hands and the announcer over the Tannoy announced, 'There will be four added minutes.'

'*Come on!*'

With one minute left on the clock, Preston were on the attack and every Preston fan in the ground was stood on tip-toes screaming North End on. Jon Macken laid the ball on to Healy only for his shot to be parried. Then a kind of Graham Taylor quote sprang to mind: 'What the fuck is he doing up there?' If there was anyone you wouldn't want the ball to fall to it was Mark 'Shabba' Rankine! In what seemed like slow motion... he tapped the ball in.

'GOAL!'

I went fucking mental, pushing J1 over the seats. I was jumping up and down that much I ended up taking all the skin off my shins as they rubbed on the seats in front of me and I had scars for months.

The ref then blew for the end of play.

Extra time brought no further goals and the place in the play-off final would have to be decided by a penalty shoot-out.

It had been decided before the kick-off that the penalties would be taken towards the Kop end of the ground where the Preston fans were situated. Mr Sulky Chops, Trevor Francis, twice walked his players off the field with an 'I'm taking my ball home' scenario. A great player in his time, but never management quality.

Finally, the penalty kicks got under way, with the time touching 11pm.

Preston went first and, after his once-in-a-lifetime miss earlier, Grezza puts us one up.

David Lucas then saves their spot kick. It remains 1–0.

David Healy sends the keeper the wrong way; 2–0.

The Birmingham penalty-taker then smashes the next one against the bar. It's got to be our night.

The big skipper himself, Sean 'The Governor' Gregan, then puts the ball on the spot... and scores; 3–0.

Brum score; 3–1.

Rob Edwards then misses for Preston – is he taking the piss or what? I just can't take any more.

Then they score again; 3–2.

It's all resting on the shoulders of the 'Wee-Man' Paul McKenna. Cool as you like, he places the ball, retreats, then runs up, strikes it sweetly... GOAL!

Scenes of joy and jubilation erupted with 40 years of hurt wiped out at that moment. Preston were now only 90 minutes away from top-flight football.

I seemed to lose myself in the moment, as the significance of the event hits home. I was as high as a kite from a game you call football. Add to this after the game more than ten pints of cider in Legends nightclub next to the ground, and I staggered into my home after three in the morning. And I believe I was chanting, 'Wembley, Wembley, here we come.'

On waking the following morning, after a few hours' kip, I was informed by the wife of the state I was in the previous night and how she struggled to get me to bed. I then started to remember singing, 'Wembley...' songs at the top of my voice – what a thick twat I was. Wembley Stadium was being knocked down at the time which meant a visit to Cardiff, South Wales and the Millennium Stadium. The opponents that day were our near neighbours Bolton Wanderers, the Trotters.

I'd been to Bolton's new Reebok Stadium twice; once drinking round Bolton town centre and the other time in Horwich and Chorley with over 5,000 Preston travelling on one of these occasions. I personally hadn't witnessed any sign of any trouble whatsoever. Most new grounds are on the outskirts of town in an industrial estate or a generally shite location for the lads' pursuits and for a decent drink.

But this is it – the big one. We met Bolton Wanderers in the play-off finals on Monday, 28 May 2001 at the Millennium Stadium in Cardiff. It was a dream come true and PNE could be in the Premiership come tea-time.

The missus woke me up early and I was still half-cut from a good drink on the Sunday. The mates were waiting outside to give us a lift up to town to board an 80-seater, top-of-the-range coach that was booked in another mate's name. We set off at six in the morning with what I thought to be 80 top boys on board the bus. Watch out, Wales, here we come.

I should have known it wasn't all going to run smoothly from the moment we stopped at the first service station. Some of the lads hadn't been to bed, they'd already had a huge amount of alcohol from both cans and spirits aboard the bus, and there had been a smattering of drugs... and they made use of their cigarette lighters by setting fire to Bolton flags and scarves hanging out of parked-up cars. We'd also met up with some of the mates who were travelling down in style – in limos. We then decided to give them a call once we'd arrived in Cardiff to meet up for a drink before the match. In hindsight, I wish I'd booked a limousine when I think back over the events that happened that day.

When we boarded the bus to continue our adventure through the lovely country of Wales, the atmosphere got more and more charged.

After arriving early in Cardiff, we had a wait for the pubs to open. One lad got arrested straight away for being drunk. What a good start! We then had to resort to McDonald's and KFC for brekkie while waiting for the boozers to open their doors. Other mates started turning up from all around the country and we settled in the part of the city that was designated for us. The boozers eventually opened and we made our way across town taking in untold pubs.

Then the old songs were struck up: 'Hello, hello, we are the Preston boys... Hello, hello, we are the Preston boys... And if you are a Bolton fan, surrender or you'll die, we all follow the North End...' Such songs echoed down streets and bounced back off tall buildings with everyone in full party mood for the forthcoming match.

Preston did have the inevitable bit of bovver in the form of a run-in with a few mouthy Bolton. However, the game was more important that day and priorities were very quickly sorted! A Premiership prize awaited the winners of the game with dreams becoming reality or totally shattered.

Well, Preston's were destroyed like a trio of Bolton bulls in a china shop. There was to be no fairytale ending for Preston North End fans, once again.

Preston had the first chance in the game after five minutes and it looked like they hadn't woken up. Then it was first blood in the 17th minute. A bad clearance fell to Bolton player Gareth Farrelly, and his shot took a deflection, ending up in the net; we were 1–0 down. Bolton then stepped up a gear, taking it to North End. Preston managed to go in at half-time still only one down, so there was still hope.

The second half got under way and PNE trapped early, finally putting the Trotters on the back foot. To and fro the game ebbed, until five minutes before the ninety were up. Michael Ricketts rounded the 'keeper and Preston were two down. Then, with only seconds to go, Ricardo Gardener scored a third to rub salt in Preston's wounds; 3–0… game over.

Preston North End that day took 32,000 fans to Cardiff; where had they all appeared from? They must have been in hibernation since our trip to Wembley in '94. The fair-weather, so-called Preston fans had jumped on the bandwagon once more. I bet the directors wish they would start attending Deepdale, putting money through the turnstiles on a regular basis. I personally have put a decent lump of dosh into the club over the years and I've as much right to be there as anyone else. That day, I witnessed grown men crying, having been let down at the final hurdle once more by Preston North End – the 'Football Club'.

We left the stadium disheartened, and entered a bar up a flight of stairs, wanting to numb the dull pain of losing and drown our sorrows. We heard other Preston in the bar had asked the doormen if the Soul Crew fancied meeting for a drink only to be told that they were banned from entering the city centre on days like today. Also it didn't take 30 minutes or so to drown years of failure and, by the time we'd regrouped to board the coach, it was a good few hours later. Our coach was the last one to leave Cardiff and, considering it was the first to park up, it made it a very long day.

When we finally set off, we were a few lads down who'd

been locked up for various offences and facing various charges. By now, we'd outstayed our welcome in the valleys.

The first piss-stop after we'd driven over the Severn Bridge was Ross-on-Wye, even though we'd a toilet on board. Some of the lads were well choked about losing but others had seen it all before, got the T-shirt, and alcohol was needed. Ross-on-Wye wasn't expecting 80 lads, some of whom had turned into cartoon characters, all looking a bit loony-tuned. One pub wasn't best prepared with the landlord going down into the cellar to change a barrel. While down there, ugly events started to unfold. The only thing the Big Fella and I borrowed was ice from the ice bucket to some strange looks off the lads.

The coach drivers, both of whom had been sound all day, started to get agitated because certain people started taking liberties, really taking the piss. I had to inform everyone to get back on the bus as we were going to set off and then I nipped into the off-licence for two bottles of Bailey's. But when I went into the shop, most of the shelves were empty! It was only meant to have been a 20-minute stopover. Finally, we got moving an hour-and-a-half later. Then it started to go pear-shaped big time.

Unbeknown to me and others, one so-called 'lad' was acting up, whacking the coach driver with a bamboo stick saying, 'Faster... faster, Ali... Ali, faster...' That sort of behaviour wasn't on at all. What he didn't realise in his fucked-up state was how good the drivers had been. I was then informed that they needed to pick up a third driver in Stafford, the drivers having both overrun on their tachographs. While all this was going on, we'd picked up a hitch-hiker and he'd fallen asleep in the aisle upstairs. A lad then proceeded to put rolled-up newspaper under his arms and set him alight. Another was using an air-freshener aerosol can as a flame-thrower and other things were happening. Honestly, me and the mates downstairs were totally oblivious to the events as we were sipping our Bailey's and ice.

In Preston, we left the bus none the wiser to what so-called certain mates and lads had done.

Next day, I rose with a raging hangover, about to set off for work, when the mate who'd booked the coach rang me. Remember – myself and the mate between us had laid out £1,100 for the trip up front. This we got back in dribs and drabs and never made a penny. The mate then informed me what went on the previous day and the fact that the coach firm had to pull the bus off the road, as it was not fit to take some old-age pensioners on a day out. The coach firm wanted compensation and the third driver's wages. In my drunken haze, I replied, 'Right then...'

Talk about burning your own bridges!

The mate was banned from hiring another coach from them for life and they'd informed all the other hire companies of his name in the surrounding area.

I personally thought I'd been to Cardiff with lads I could trust. Was I wrong! Phone calls were then made telling people to pass the word on that certain individuals had been well out of order with events that day.

When the next season kicked off, I started bumping into lads at the match, asking exactly who'd done what.

'I don't know who...'; 'I didn't see owt...'; 'It wasn't me.'

I began to put two and two together and certain names were going into the little black book for a rainy day.

A few weeks passed and a rumour got back to me that me, and the mate, had grassed people up on the coach that day – really! Why then had the coach firm not been in touch with certain individuals? And why hadn't the police been round to certain addresses? Why not? Because I now knew exactly what some people were about and I'd let time run its course. The saying 'there's no smoke without fire' was completely unfounded this time. The reason they'd got ideas like we'd 'grassed' was because their brains were like mush because of white-powder paranoia setting in; also numerous other drugs and alcohol had taken their toll on certain individuals. These sorts of substances were not good for those of a less stable disposition on board that day. They should have known that someone with the number of skeletons I had in my closet would never do something like grass on certain people of his acquaintance. Dream on!

Then, I bumped into one or two of the aforementioned empty-heads with apologies forthcoming from them. Others I had to front, and they have never been seen at football again. Needs must when the devil drives. They should have known me better. I even fell out with one mate who I'd knocked around with for over 25 years.

These events led me to have an even tighter circle of football mates, ones who I could thoroughly rely on through thick and thin, with no looking over my shoulder.

* * *

The first three points Preston picked up in the 2001/02 season were at home against Millwall after five games into the season without a win. This was watched at Deepdale by a third of the fans who'd attended Cardiff. Then an 11-match unbeaten run during the season, with other good results, saw North End finish eighth. No chance of the play-offs this year. We did have a bit of a result at Deepdale though – Preston's third new stand was unveiled, the Allan Kelly Town End Stand.

And talking of results, we didn't have high hopes when we drew Chelsea in the FA Cup. But it would have been rude not to go, wouldn't it? A coach was booked with a town-centre pick-up arranged outside a hotel next to Preston bus station, which was once the biggest in Europe, but is now more infamous for its suicide rate with more deaths than lovers' leap.

With Sky having hijacked the game, and with no chance of a train to London and back in a day, it was a minimum of four hours on a jammed-up, bumper-to-bumper, gridlocked, full-of-Sunday-drivers motorway to put up with. To add to the hassle, Pia was being his usual 'pain in the arse'.

When we finally arrived in London, a decision was made to catch a train to where we would meet up with Scotty and the cockney Whites, then maybe the famous Headhunters – only kidding.

On entering a boozer, we were greeted with smiling faces and handshakes off familiar boys. The lads wanted their Sunday dinner in liquid form. We then got bedded in for a couple of hours catching up on tales.

Scotty was with a dozen or so exiled Lancaster and Morecambe lads, playing cards. They were blokes who'd moved down to cream off the south. They'd found work earning big bucks – 'Shut your mouth and look at my wad.' The streets and areas in and around London were well and truly paved with gold for these boys. They were sat round a table, cards in hand, and I was looking at them intently. Now I'm not saying I'm the most handsome bloke on this beautiful planet but these fellas' looks were something else – scars, bite marks, broken noses, an ear missing and not one of them with a full set of railings. What a motley crew. I was later informed that one of them, when drunk, pisses himself, and they'd had a bet at the start of the day which leg the smelly, yellow stuff will run down. Most have been brought up on one of the lovely council estates in north Lancashire – they were a right bunch of 'rum 'uns', to put it politely. Both Lancaster and Morecambe are downwind of Sellafield nuclear power plant, so it might not all have been down to genetics or what they got up to at weekends. God bless this nice-looking bunch of boys.

The Preston lads were going for it big time. The liver is evil and it must be punished. Someone said, 'Come on, it's about time we made a move.' Pints were emptied with everyone fuelled up for the game and a short Tube journey was undertaken to Fulham Broadway. Up the escalators and out into Chelsea's manor we went. Great, we had a welcoming committee; not Chelsea's lions, but our intelligence officers with a large contingent of Met bobbies. We were then escorted to Stamford Bridge, passing pubs with faces pressed against windows. Cockneys popped out of other boozers to take a look at our impressive 100 or so. It kicked off briefly with a couple of scuffles and a few Preston lads were lifted.

It hadn't half changed around the ground since the last time Preston had played there nearly 20 years earlier, which was my last visit.

The North End were also shown how to play football that day. The gulf between a team from the Premiership and PNE was very obvious to see by the end of 90 minutes, even though Preston went 1–0 up, and then missed a sitter. I can only think that Chelsea must have been toying with the North End. They pulled three back with ease and we exited the FA Cup.

As we funnelled out of the stand at the end of the match, the gobby cockney wide-boys to our right started to give us grief. Once we were outside, they all seemed to have disappeared. We then went walkies trying to find the coach as we'd sent it up to the ground empty. Some Preston lads were rounded up after getting collared trying to enter one of Chelsea's pubs. They were then marched back and put on their bus, others to their cars and the Tube station. The only thing to look forward to now was possibly making last orders in Preston, that's if we got out of London, as it was more congested than the motorway on the way down.

Willy G:

It's the first time we've played Coventry in the league for many a year and a coach is booked with all the top boys informed. There's even a couple on board that night still fresh out of jail after being naughty. We'd a contact number after bumping into Coventry one evening in Preston after they'd played Blackburn with us having entertained the Dingles at home. Stories about England away trips and numbers had been swapped for further reference. Also, Coventry were on a downward spiral and got relegated to the Championship at the end of the season.

It's a night game at the Highfield Stadium and the coach driver informs us that he will have to radio in to the police ten miles from Coventry as it's the law. Out comes the AA road map with a little village found, just out of bounds and we arrive in time for tea.

A couple of pints later – 'and the beer tasted just like piss' – the London lads arrive. With a fleet of taxis booked, we're off to meet the Legion. The coach driver is advised to make his way to the ground and we will contact him later. I would have liked to have seen the Old Bill's faces when the coach pulled up empty, then the driver having to explain where his occupants had gone. We'd arranged to meet for a bevvy with a good Coventry lad who I've met several times at punk gigs and England games. He'd informed us that most of the old Coventry lads are cheesed off with what is going on at club level and doubt if many will show. If any would, it would be the younger element that would probably turn out.

On entering a pub, we see there's one geezer in and he's a right throwback to the good old days. He's about my age, and he's got a suedehead, Harrington jacket with two-tone badges pinned on, Sta-Prest trousers and Doc Martens. He's stood at the bar flicking his two front false gnashers with his tongue. Tones of the Seventies and Eighties rang out.

We then visit a few more lushers, on the same street, more or less next door to each other like Preston's very own Meadow Street. Coventry then start arriving but most soon do one. We heard on the grapevine sometime later (allegedly) that our intelligence officer had been in consultation with Coventry's local force, informing them that we weren't making a show that day, while enjoying a cup of tea. Then word came back to the station that Preston had arrived en masse in taxis. It's not the first time we'd outfoxed our IO but he was getting wiser with every game.

We leave the boozer 20 minutes before kick-off with the lads up front spotting unknown waiting faces near the ground, which are soon moved with little or no resistance. There's four of us bringing up the rear a couple of 100 yards behind, when 30-plus Coventry come charging up the road launching a few bottles and bricks. Turning, we see two

'Specials' [special coppers] walking up with Coventry scarfers, all of whom start taking cover.

Without a word spoken, we set off to meet the throwers and they're on their toes, only trainer soles and jeans' labels to be seen. We stop after 25 yards knowing they're not a willing party. Someone in the crowd making their way to the ground shouts something like, 'They'd have deserved it if you'd caught up with them but behave yourself and get on up to the ground,' as the special coppers get on their radios for back-up.

The not-so-willing 30 get brave again and come bouncing back up the road when they realise there's only our gang of four. This is only to be moved once more.

Finally, we make it on to the game and into a stand more befitting of a Third Division club. Most of the lads have had a pull with the usual stop and search. Then it's old Seventies and Eighties football songs trying to be sung by all the tanked-up old boys. We start getting strange looks from our own fans, never mind the Coventry sections, and looks of disgust from the now cheesed-off Old Bill. We've spoiled their afternoon cuppa.

Eventually, the police start lifting the lads and try to cuff Yatee – who's crackers. He would only give them one hand at a time and kept lifting the other one constantly above his head to loud cheers. It took three coppers to get him down, shackled and away.

With the match over, Preston are out roaming twice round the ground with the song 'Ghost Town' befitting of Coventry that night. The police finally round us up and we're put on to the coach and sent packing out of town.

We manage to talk the coach driver into stopping for

last orders on the outskirts of Coventry with phone calls made to the police station. They start releasing the lads who've been lifted after watching CCTV coverage and finding nothing to charge them with. Taxis are caught to the pub and the last lad arrives as we wait on the hard shoulder just after midnight. What a gent the driver was.

Also, what a nice little reunion it had been, even though Coventry hadn't turned out. No disrespect to them, I suppose you can't rise to every team that comes to your manor. By now, most of Preston's old boys grace us with their presence every now and then, coming out to play for the day. The teams in and around Lancashire don't give Preston enough respect where respect is due. They've short memories, local firms, and most live in cloud cuckoo land.

Anonymous:

It was a Sunday afternoon and the last game of the season, a day we usually drown our sorrows. And also there had been no reported incidents before the match with the Nottingham Forest Executive Crew or Nasty Squad. I'd gone into a local watering-hole to sample a few ales after watching PNE win 2–1 and just fail to get into the play-off places after an up-and-down season. While in the pub, I struck up conversations with different sets of people who I knew, then someone suggested we make a move towards town for another drink. Not a bad idea I thought, so I joined them. It would be rude not to.

Lads started to drift out in dribs and drabs, ambling up St George's Road, and I was one of the last ones, noticing a Preston lad, having what I thought to be banter with an Asian youth. The youth was stood on the opposite side of the road mumbling something as I chatted away with a couple of lads while walking along. Then the youth began chanting, 'Osama Bin Laden... Osama Bin Laden,' bouncing up and down on the pavement, his arm raised, fist clenched.

Feelings among the general public were still raw with what was happening around the world at that particular time and I personally thought it was well out of order.

One lad in the party that day starts to advance across the road towards the preacher. The lad in question is a good sort and well respected among Preston's boys. 'Can I have a word with you, mate?' he says to the Asian while crossing the road.

The youth replies, 'What do you want, man?' and spits on the flagstones. How disgusting.

They're now face-to-face with the youth still chanting, 'Osama Bin Laden... Osama Bin Laden.'

Then he tries to launch several blows to the body of the Preston lad who bobs and weaves like a seasoned boxer returning jabs back. The youth then bolts like Road Runner, still chanting, as the Preston lad shouts to him, 'Here... I still want a word with you,' hot on his heels in pursuit.

There's a small crowd gathered up ahead at a chicane in the road. There's been an accident with both parties involved not wanting to take the blame and the police are in attendance, sorting the matter out. The lads who've been in the Deepdale pub are also jogging up for a butcher's. I then witness, just before the lone Preston lad arrives, that the crowd, previously stood around the cars, have turned their attention towards him. Then ten Asians attack the Preston lad, fists and boots flying in.

Luckily, within 30 seconds, he's got back up, but the situation is worsening. Then one of the officers in attendance pepper-sprays all the Preston fans. The situation suddenly changes with lads being temporarily blinded and there's a lot of confusion about the reason why the policeman did this. One woman present asks the policeman why he's just sprayed a few of the brawlers, and not the youths who've attacked one man on his own. He replies, 'It's their area.'

The politically minded types have also disappeared in all the commotion. Then someone else asks, 'What do you mean it's their area?'

'I did what I thought was right in the situation,' replies the Old Bill.

Then I notice the lads who've been victims of the spray phoning people, and others are helping their mates who couldn't see. They then head up to the Charnock pub to get their eyes washed and sort themselves out. A few stop at the crash scene, not happy about what has just gone on.

In the next few hours, Preston lads started turning up in their droves in the Deepdale area of town after finding out about the events that had gone on. I also witnessed a group of 50 lads turn up who I believed were from Coventry, having attended a match at Burnley. They were heading towards the Meadow Street area of town. I don't know whether it was for just a drink but they were met by a large presence of police cars and riot vans.

Later on, reports were coming back of fighting in the Deepdale area with vigilante groups roaming the streets. Also, cars from other parts of Lancashire and surrounding areas were reportedly coming into Preston. I'd left the area and was now drinking in town where rumours were rife of widespread disorder taking place. When I retired home for the night in a taxi, I didn't witness or catch a glimpse of any incidents myself.

On rising to the clock radio the following day for work, with yesterday's stale ale taste in my mouth, I was suddenly shocked sober. The alcohol soon left my system after hearing a news bulletin on a local radio station of race riots in Preston the previous night. After listening intently, I switched the television on while having a coffee and every channel I flicked to there was either a reporter in Preston or a newsreader relaying last night's events. I was shocked to say the least.

Over the following weeks, I spoke to lads who were out that day, and, with what I witnessed, this was not, I repeat not, a 'race riot'. Whatever their nationality or the colour of their skin, the people involved that day were not motivated by race. It started with two males having opinions, then disagreements, followed by blows. One of them was chanting a name which touched a raw nerve as people were losing their lives in war zones, with families having to bury their loved ones. Allegedly, the name being chanted was one of the main perpetrators. The chanter had launched an unprovoked attack on the questioning male. Like I said earlier, I knew him by sight and I've personally seen him drinking, and in conversation, with whites, blacks and Asians. So I personally don't think the man in question is a racist and I never heard any racist comments or words used in any way or form that day.

Preston lads ended up in court for incidents that happened that night which led to fines and men losing their jobs. One lad ended up being banned from attending matches at Deepdale for life.

The last comments on the subject of the so-called race riot are: Why did a police officer call it an Asian area? The Deepdale district is a British multi-cultural area, a place where all should be safe to walk the streets. This is Preston, in Lancashire, in England, in Great Britain! I myself personally am not a racist. I think I'm more a realist!

Oh no... for fuck's sake! They only went and appointed Craig Brown as manager of North End! Yeah, the one who managed Scotland – enough said.

Preston didn't win 'til the fourth game of the 2002/03 season, a 4–3 thriller against Stoke at home. Wins were hard to come by and we finished mid-table. North End's big shout that season was beating Burnley at home 3–1. I also had serious doubts over Brown, and I wasn't the only one. As Brown himself pointed out, 'I went to a supporters' night and half of them were cheering and half were booing. The problem was that the half that were cheering were cheering the half that were booing.'

Billy:

We'd a night game in the League Cup against Aston Villa and we head to the Midlands on Tom's Tours. A minibus is our transport with as much beer as you could sup for an all-in price of £15.

We arrive early tea-time and phone calls are made to the other lads in vans and cars to meet up in a pub near the ground. A good 80 lads turn up with other Preston followers filling the boozer. Spotters are then sent out telling any likely-looking Villains where Preston were drinking and asking them if they fancied coming down for a drink. It must have been the £2 entry fee into the public house that put them off.

Eventually, we leave the pub to look for the Villa, and there's none to be found. They probably aren't bothered about turning out for so-called little clubs like us, fellow founder members.

Preston that night get smashed all over the pitch losing 5–0 and minor skirmishes erupt inside the ground. Our minibus-load leaves with nearly 20 minutes to go to set up camp inside Villa's pub. The well-oiled 15 on Tom's Tours are going nowhere until they've had another drink!

However, our intelligence officer with plenty of Brum police in tow turns up. A request from them for us to leave was met with blank expressions. So we're asked (told) again or we might be heading somewhere other than home. We presumed they meant in a different mode of transport from the one in which we'd arrived. The landlord has also been advised to shut the bar and the lads begin to be escorted out one by one.

One funny thing about that night was when we parked up we noticed an Asian barber's with about 50 heads waiting to be sheared. Then, on returning to the bus after the game, there's another 50 bonces still waiting to be scalped. Should have got an Aussie sheep-shearer over on price, he'd have made a mint!

We decided on heading to another new ground, hopefully with a good drink before the tea-time kick-off. Forty of us trapped early, knowing we'd have to leave some time in the second half to catch the last train back to Birmingham for our connection onwards.

We'd arrived in Leicester at twelve-ish and the police were on to us like a rash straight away – we were only there for a good drink and to watch the match. After a couple of beers, we made our way into the city centre and, unbeknown to us, we took up residence in Leicester's main pub. Eventually, the police came in and moved us up the road to another boozer. If the local, baby-faced boys weren't too happy that we were in there, they should have said. Later on, we were escorted up to the ground and a few brave baby-faces gave it the big one. Some Preston managed to break out from the escort and easily move them.

Halfway through the second half, we left again under a heavy escort and were taken to the train station. The police were really doing their job, ready to lift anyone who stepped out of line. We just about managed to catch the train with the full set of lads who'd arrived in the morning and we had the chance for a few quick bevvies in Birmingham before catching our connection from New Street to Preston – which we did.

The train pulled out of New Street Station still with a small presence of police on board when the younger element started to sing a few songs like, 'Harry Potter is our friend...' and other favourites.

Then when the train pulled into Wolverhampton Station, and finally stopped, on steamed plain-clothes police, pulling on their baseball caps complete with badges. Let the lifting begin. Lads were dragged off and nicked for singing songs. What next? Possibly for farting too loudly, or if you've enjoyed yourself too much?

I got off the train of my own accord for some information on the situation. I was informed that it wasn't worth waiting around in Wolverhampton as the lads weren't getting released until Sunday at the earliest. With only a train left to Crewe, which I caught, a good friend – Arkie (RIP) – picked me up from there at four in the morning to get me home.

Nowadays, you seem to get into as much trouble for singing songs as you do for fighting. The arrested received fines and three-year bans from attending football. What about bringing back flogging?

Rick:

I was meeting some of our lads in the Lamb & Packet for a few pints; we met there because the pub was due to close down for a while so the beer was a pound a pint. North End were playing Bradford that day, but we didn't expect any to turn up.

There were about ten of us in the pub when two lads we knew came in; they told us there were some Bradford in the Old Black Bull, just up the road, so we drank up and went to have a gander.

When we got to the Black Bull, we saw four Bradford lads stood outside, and one of them said to us, 'There's only four of us... you can't do us, that'd be out of order.'

I said to him, 'No, mate, we've just come up here for a beer and a chat.' They were shitting themselves.

Anyway, later we left them and went back to the Lamb & Packet for our cheap ale. One of our lot asked the four Bradford if they wanted to come with us to the Lamb, and they did.

After about an hour of chit-chat and name swapping, one of their lads, an older lad, showed me a tattoo on his arm – 'Ointment' – the name of their firm. He was never off his phone, always texting. One of our lads said to me that he thought he was setting us up.

The Bradford lads decided to leave and, on their way out, the older lad said to me that he'd told the Bradford firm where we were and that there were 30 of us when really there was only 10. Why? The mate was right; he was stitching us up, good and proper! Twat!

About half-an-hour after the Bradford lads had gone, having forgotten about them, I was on my phone outside when Mutch came out and said, 'Look up the road, Rick.' I looked up and saw about 30–40 Bradford bouncing down the road towards us. Mutch went into the pub, and then the pub door was shut, leaving me outside on my own. The landlord had bolted the fucking door! I wasn't going to stand there on my own, so off I went round the back of the pub, with about five of the Bradford lads after me. I stopped, turned to face them and they stopped. Then one of them, a fat lad, came towards me with his arms out saying, 'Come on, Preston, have a go!'

I shouted back, 'There's five of you, you fat twat.'

After a bit of shouting at each other, they just turned and went back round the front of the pub. I could see the Bradford lads looking through the windows into the pub, but the landlord wasn't going to open the door. After a few minutes, the Bradford lads decided to leave; they went across the road to another pub called the Sun Inn.

I'm back outside the front of the pub; the doors open and Mutch came outside. The Bradford lads saw us and came bouncing down towards the pub again. About four of our lads came out to see what was happening so that meant there were six of us.

The Bradford lads got right up to us, only one or two at first, and they stopped dead in their tracks when they saw we weren't for moving. That's when it went off; glasses, bottles and one of our lads was down, getting booted all over. Then a few more of ours came out – Tids, Fillium, Mattie. There was more Bradford upon us now and I could see tattoo boy up the street, he was just stood there watching. We started to back off when the police turned up; Bradford went one way, and we went the other. Nobody got nicked; what a result! Or so we thought.

About eight months after that day, we were playing Burnley at home and we all met up early doors in Strettles Bar, near the university. There was about 40–50 of us in the pub, when the police came in and arrested me, Mutch and Tids for the incident just mentioned, eight months earlier! I couldn't fucking believe it. All of us are lifted because I think a certain person wanted to look good in front of the cameras. (Granada TV was following the police around that day for one of those Street Crime UK or whatever documentaries.) And, as far as I'm concerned, we were the puppets for the cameras.

We were all charged with violent disorder which was all captured on CCTV. They tried to ban us from football matches for five years – none of us got a ban. I don't know whether that was a good or bad thing!

The highlights of the 2003/04 season were Preston smashing Burnley 5–3 at home just before Christmas with Ricardo Fuller running the show and scoring a hat-trick. And away at Upton Park, Preston footballed West Ham to death, running out 2–1 winners.

Another mid-table finish and I was also getting sick of the same old crap off Craig Brown. His final notes read that season: 'Having failed to achieve this season, please stick with us and I'm sure we won't let you down.' Really?

To take my mind off the relentless under-achievement, I had another away fixture to look forward to – and this time, it was on the other side of the world. One of my mates had finally decided to make an honest woman of his girlfriend, and the place where he'd put the ring on her finger would be Australia. A few of us decided to witness the event, even though it was a few thousand miles away. Our route was to take in Thailand, Bangkok – sleaze and all. I love it. What you can't find or get in Bangkok isn't worth asking for. We'd booked flights with Kirky – 'I'm a lover, not a fighter' – who was also making the trip and who was obsessed with his clothes.

Setting out on our travels, he informed me that his mission was to find an original Penguin. Penguin is by Munsingwear, which was a big favourite in the fashion stakes with Northern Casuals in the early to mid-Eighties. Old American crooners and golfers would be seen wearing such items on television. Around 2005, it made a big comeback after Justin Timberlake wore a top in one of his videos.

During our time in Bangkok, a pair of socks were found in a department store and purchased, plus an old bloke was noticed on the monorail wearing a yellow V-neck jumper. I thought Kirky was going to mug him for it.

In the mornings and afternoons, we would do the tourist bit, going sightseeing, taking in the likes of the Grand Palace and different temples. One such temple housed the biggest leaning golden Buddha in the world and, before entering, you had to remove your footwear outside as a mark of respect. While removing our sandals and flip-flops, Kirky only spotted a pair of Adidas Stan Smith's, the ones with his name embossed on the back, a much sought-after trainer for collectors. The next thing, he picked the pair of Stan's up, giving them the once over and a closer inspection for quality and their size. 'They're a size seven... just a size too small for me... damn,' he said.

Some poor Japanese bloke would have found his prized pumps gone if they'd been an eight! A classic photo taken at that moment shows the rest of us staring inquisitively at the Buddha, with Kirky looking back over his shoulder thinking about squeezing into the Stan Smith's. Sadly, the photo was lost.

Drinking round Bangkok brought us into contact with a few undesirables – 'Septic Tanks', Yanks. They thought it was very clever and big saying snidey comments between each other when we entered a bar, such as, 'Here come the ice-cream sellers.'

The slimy cunts were monkey-suited up with a Thai girl on each arm, smoking Cuban cigars. We turned the other cheek, not fancying a night or two in the Bangkok Hilton. Either that, or I was getting too old for any fisticuffs. We supped up and headed towards another bar before it turned nasty.

This had a big sign above the bar on entering that read: 'PLEASE HAND YOUR GUNS IN AT THE BAR' – what a right dodgy gaff. But when in Rome – sorry, Bangkok – we still ordered up a bevvy and had the banter with the bar staff who were transvestites and lady boys.

There were also some very interesting 'performances' in certain establishments, such as Ping-Pong Banana! I wonder when that's going to be entered into the Olympics – now that would be well worth a watch.

On arrival in Sydney, Australia, we were off bridge climbing and visiting the zoo just to ensure that we caught a glimpse of Australia's native species – kangaroos, koala bears and crocodiles. We even saw a Tasmanian Devil which was a real ugly little fucker, that reminded me a little of J1. Kirky was then off to find his precious Penguin with, up to then, only a rip-off version found.

We then travelled on down to Wollongong, a place about an hour away from Sydney. A mate lives there who I've mentioned in earlier stories, namely Chris P. He has lived in Oz for over 15 years and done really well, every credit to him. We also got introduced to some locals and resident Poms one Friday night and decided to go to a local match, Wollongong Wolves v South Melbourne. A local derby if there is such a thing down under.

After paying a few dollars' entrance fee, we went and stood on the banking which was a grassed area to one side of the pitch where you could drink beer or have a picnic. This was in near sub-zero temperatures and I thought it was meant to be hot in Oz all year round – well, not that night. The game was a pretty shit event as well with Wolves getting dicked 2–0. And with ten minutes to go, we decided to make a move for warmer conditions in the clubhouse. The game had attracted a crowd in the region of 2,500, including the away fans, who numbered around 10. I don't blame others for not travelling, it being a plane journey away. The South Melbourne Greeks that had attended I reckon lived somewhere rather closer.

There were six of us leaving the ground, including the bride's 60-year-old father, walking past the away fans when one Greek turned round and proceeded to bark towards the groom something about Wolves fans. Then they started squaring up. 'Fuck me, we're halfway round the world and it might go off.' The Greeks were still giving it large when an announcement came over the Tannoy: 'Security, security, over to the bank quickly.'

The situation turned a bit iffy.

While this was happening, the ball had gone out of play and we had 22 players and the rest of the crowd staring our way; talk about being under the spotlight. No one was for backing down, when the Greeks spun back round, turning towards the playing surface, not wanting all the attention they'd drawn to themselves. We stood there for a few moments while our mate explained to them we weren't even from Wollongong and asked what their problem was. Then, with the security homing in, we started walking off, not wanting any more grief or attention.

A short time later, in the clubhouse while having a scoop, the father-in-law-to-be said, 'What was all that about at the match?'

We shrugged our shoulders. 'You should've stuck one on the Greek... that would have shut him up.'

And with that we all burst out laughing, breaking the ice.

Like anywhere, you always get loudmouths, no matter what part of the world you're in. I suppose they were lucky that they weren't taught a lesson in manners – wrong time, wrong place, once again.

Kirky carried on his search while in that part of Oz, then it was off to Melbourne and on to Singapore on the return journey home. No rock-hoppers were to be found.

A few months later, I was opening a birthday present and it was only an original Munsingwear Penguin, the missus having found a shop in Preston who'd just started to stock it. A round-the-world trip undertaken and it was only on the doorstep! I let Kirky know and he was down the shop as quick as a flash buying a polo shirt.

The next time we met up for a bevvy in the Angel boozer in

town, he only walked in with the exact same stripy top that I'd got on. Talk about great minds thinking alike! We both then had to stand at opposite ends of the pub with the mates taking the piss.

Back in the UK, we eagerly awaited the fixture list for the 2003/04 season, and the first game offered a tasty treat – a home tie against the Hammers. West Ham had been relegated and a larger-than-normal Preston firm had been mobilised down Plungington Road in many drinking establishments behind closed doors. Sky had also hijacked the game and it was an early kick-off. Boozers were bursting at the seams by official opening time, as anticipation escalated. It turned out to be a non-event as reports came back to the lads (of which I was no part) that any ICF that had travelled were pinned in the railway station until an escort was arranged. A couple of West Ham-following mates, and an 'Iron' who we knew, came up the night before and many a tale was swapped between the old heads that were present. Take it from me that these lads were out to quench a thirst on the hottest day of the year. Lads were literally dripping with sweat and ice-cold lager wasn't touching the sides as it was gulped down.

After the match, many a beer garden was hit and eventually lads melted away as darkness drew in after a heated, all-day session.

Tom's Tours minibus was booked for the away fixture for our tidy little firm of drinkers, together with a couple of coaches and the train for the rest of the Preston lads. It was just into the New Year when we set off under a moonlit sky with only the stars for guidance. Our driver didn't have a clue on the direction to London, having never driven there, who we were or what plans we had that day. He'd been told to drop us at Watford Station and that was the only instruction he'd been given. We managed to convince him that he'd heard wrong and that Kilburn, north London, was our drop-off point. It sounds similar, doesn't it!

Ale cans were open by the time we'd passed the Tickled Trout Hotel, joining the first stretch of motorway. The early-morning drinking was a regular occurrence to us, but amazed the driver. I myself was on the 'wagon', which was an age-old tradition after the New Year's Day fixture. This was not for health reasons but to test my will power, having drunk enough in the previous year to sink a ship. It's funny when you're on the ale as you can relate to all the nonsense spoken and laugh at all the unfunny jokes. My tipple for the day was Lucozade and cans of Red Bull. Normally when on the lash, Guinness is the only solid I consume!

We had a piss-stop on the motorway services, where J1 devoured a credit card-priced, Desperate Dan, dustbin lid-sized breakfast with four slices of toast and he nearly wiped the pattern off the plate. And he was ill?

The minibus arrived in Kilburn, the home to many an Irish pub and also the home of the Blockheads. Not fancying tales from the Emerald Green Isle and how great Potato Land is (I'm married to a spud picker), we jumped straight on the Tube to meet Scotty and a few cockney Whites.

Standing on the Tube station, we finally sorted out which coloured line we needed for our meeting place. It was a pub opposite the Flying Scotsman, which was another regular haunt on our London jollies. Al, Eddie, Tony and a couple of Millwall who we knew were already in and we ordered drinks while waiting for Scotty. As usual, he was late and I was on the Rola

Cola. There were 30 'Boro in the boozer en route to Highbury when the predictable Met Old Bill strolled in doing their rounds. There was the usual 'we're your pals' act going on while they asked where we were heading as Scotty turned up. We then headed over to Plaistow for a quiet drink until about two-ish and then jumped back on the Tube to Upton Park.

As we came out of the Tube station, Preston's 10 was waiting with the Met and followed our 20 up the road as we made our way to the Boleyn Ground. Everyone in our party then watched Preston play a superb game of football, winning 2–1. We were chatting to other Preston lads who'd been in a pub near Upton Park before the game, and they told us they'd had a right old cockney rhyming-slang row with some West Ham boys. The Preston lads had been giving the 'Ammers the right hump and they'd bottled it.

It was a good job that the old ICF boys who were out and about after the match hadn't been in that particular boozer, or else you never know what might have happened. This rumour was confirmed by a good mate, Ray K, who'd been in the said pub and it was full to the brim of skins and seasoned heads going to watch Cockney Rejects later that night. This was at West Ham's Working Men's Club. I've since read in Jeff 'Stinky' Turner's book, *Cockney Reject*, that 550 attended the gig. The club only had a capacity of 250 and allegedly the likes of Bunter, Hodges, Skully and Cass Pennant were in attendance – enough said.

We'd only just stepped out of the North Stand after the match and the Old Bill were on to our 20 like a ton of bricks. They then enlightened us that, if we so much as stepped out of line on the quarter-mile walk to Upton Park Tube station, we would all be nicked. Under protest from many in our ranks, nearly double our number of Metropolitan Police wrapped the 20 of us, most of whom were touching 40 years old, or over, in a tight bubble. Then a senior copper got the right hump reading the lads the riot act. Out of a 28,777 attendance and 1,806 travelling Preston, they escorted our 20.

Then we were forcibly made to make our way to the Tube station. And then we were treated like royalty. The police moved a barrier from in front of hundreds of Londoners waiting for the Tube, advancing us through the temporary fencing and on to the train. They escorted us on our journey for at least half-a-dozen stops, out of their district and out of their manor.

Isn't life a bowl of cherries!

* * *

Craig Brown was finally relieved of his post for the 2004/05 season (thank fuck), and his assistant Billy Davies took over during the first half of the season. Preston then went on a winning streak after beating West Ham at Deepdale in December, with North End beaten only once in the next 20 games. This took Preston to the dizzy heights of fourth in the league.

It was Derby County in the play-offs, with PNE winning 2–0 at home and getting the result they needed at Pride Park with a 0–0 draw – Carlo Nash saving a penalty, to boot.

'Cardiff, Cardiff, here we come...' again against West Ham. It pains me to write that Preston got beat 1–0 in the final; they were never at the races that day – rabbits trapped in headlights. It wasn't to be once more. I nearly even shed a tear! Will Preston ever make the Promised Land? Never mind the local derbies, we're going to be the 'big boys' in Lancashire very soon!

And talking of big boys – or, they used to be, at least – bring on the mighty Leeds! It had been 20 years since we met in the FA Cup and we'd never had the pleasure of meeting them in the league until now. Just a few years before, they'd reached the semi-finals of the Champions League and then they'd gone and shot themselves in the foot.

With the last petals falling off the rose bushes, we set off on a chilly autumn day aboard an early train. There was no love lost between Lancashire and Yorkshire and we knew the trip would not be a bed of roses. This hatred spills over into the cricket season when lads enjoy hours of drinking in the current bun and old rivalries begin re-emerging.

Two of us got off the train on to a packed Leeds Station and it was shoulder to shoulder with blokes the size of rhinos – Leeds rugby fans. They were on their way to some sort of final to chase an egg-shaped ball round Old Trafford. With a piss and a pint needed, we nipped into a bar adjoining the station. Forty other Preston who'd been on the train also entered the bar. And, as is 'the norm' nowadays, 'I am only here for the beer' along with big Dave.

Ale ordered after a wait, I scanned an eye around – old habits die hard. Mingling in between bull-necked drinkers – the sort who had eaten too many Yorkshire puds – I clocked a dozen normal-sized humans in military-style Stone Island gear on their mobiles.

Two quick flyers later, Dave and I made a move. A pub was found and a phone call was made to the mate to come up to Beckett's Bank when he arrived. Nattering away, I once more noticed three or four lads who had expensive tastes in clobber. Coincidence or what? And their mobiles were also glued to their ears. Fancying a change of scenery, we once more made a move and made a phone call to the mate once again.

While mine and Dave's Tetley bitter was settling in the next pub, a major interruption had arisen and it was clear an incident had occurred, as we could also hear numerous sirens in the vicinity.

BH:

16 October 2004 was the much-awaited match of Leeds United away. Preston planned to meet on the train station around nine o'clock for the train to Yorkshire. Everybody was dressed clobbered up to the nines, the usual suspects in Stone Island, Aquascutum, collars up and caps down. You get the picture!

Lads walked on to the platform to wait for the rest of the boys and, before long, there were about 40 of them ready for the trip to Yorkshire. The train to Leeds pulled in and on they piled. Leeds here they come!

Everyone was supping cans on the train, swapping tales on how Leeds were meant to be one of the best. Off they got at Leeds Station with no Old Bill to be seen, which was good. They got a beer in the station bar which was full of rugby fans but fuck knows who was playing. They didn't care. Two pints later, they got on their way into Leeds centre, walked out of the station and did a left into the city, deciding to go into a pub called Beckett's Bank. They walked in like a small army.

After being in the pub for about 20 minutes, a few of the lads noticed a couple of Leeds hovering about, taking a look. It looks like they now knew North End were here. One lad in particular with a black CP jacket on was looking over and getting on the phone. A few of Preston decided that they should move on and see if Leeds followed. They all drank up and made their way to the door on the left of the pub. As North End came out, they heard a shout of 'Come on, Preston.'

Preston looked to their right and there was a mob of about 30 Leeds. That was it. 'Come on!'

Preston started bouncing towards them, adrenalin pumping with a massive roar in the air. Two sets of lads were about to clash. A few bottles started flying from behind, and then the lads fought with fist and feet flying in. Preston were bang at it. They were now in the middle of the road, cars were stopping and shoppers watching in horror. Preston were a lot more game and Leeds started backing off, running round the corner. The few brave Leeds who stood took a bit of a pasting. The other Leeds who'd been in the pub then came out and a few North End went towards them and they moved back in sharpish. The job was done!

Preston then started walking away as they felt that the Old Bill wouldn't be far away. From round the corner, a massive roar went up from another mob of about 50 Leeds. They had caught them walking off, putting them on the back foot. Was it a set-up? When a few start to get on their toes, nine out of ten times everybody does.

Preston retreated, going past the pub to the corner, and slowed down and turned. Most of the Leeds had stopped but a few game lads were still coming. North End had gone about 10 metres to a café on the corner to arm themselves with chairs for some more action. Saturday shoppers were having a drink outside the café while lads were helping themselves to other items. About ten Leeds had come to have another go and had chairs thrown towards them for their troubles. Then they were ready for a second charge but, the next thing, the Old Bill turned up on horses. The chant went up, 'Oh yes, oh yes, we are the PPS!'

The Leeds mob was ushered away by the police and Preston got moved down the road by the horses. Preston had just had it with Leeds in their city centre and got the majority of a result.

A Leeds lad later shouted over, 'Fair fuck to Preston!'

As I wasn't party to any of these antics, I can't comment on the events that day. But I can certainly comment on the size of the crowd – Preston took over 4,000 to Elland Road in a crowd of 30,000. I wish Preston could muster half of that at home... but that's another story!

I tried to get off as soon as the final whistle went to meet up with Dave who was in a different section of the ground. Not a chance. I had a copper sticking a camcorder under my nose, saying, 'You're going nowhere 'til a bus arrives to take you lot to the train station...' I wonder what he meant by 'you lot'. Anyway, I got off before the bus arrived.

Walking back, there was a good turnout of Leeds stood outside a pub overlooking a dual carriageway. Might have been because they took a bit of a spanking before the match, which I did know at the time!

Six Preston lads were arrested some time later, five of them fined and banned from attending matches for the next five years.

Preston only had three weeks to wait for Leeds to cross the border. There had allegedly been threats on the Internet, phone calls... blah, blah, blah.

I'd arranged to meet a few mates in the Old Black Bull in town at eleven-ish for a liquid lunch. Unbeknown to us, Leeds were escorted from the train station to the Assembly pub. This was no more than 100 metres away from where I was drinking with the mates – we found this out later on in the day. The Assembly pub was cordoned off by a heavy police presence.

A dozen or so of us set off to the Sun Hotel pub an hour later, on a route that takes you up to Deepdale. It's a trip that takes in plenty of stop-off points where you can quench a thirst. Not more than 50 paces into our hike, a fuzz car pulled over. Out got the same cameraman from a few weeks before and a Yorkie cop. Stephen Spielberg's sidekick asked, 'Where have you been and where are you going? Wait there.'

We just carried on walking, and I was thinking, 'Was he talking to us, as we've done sweet FA?' The lads I drink with sup like fish, so every second counts. However, before I had a chance in the Sun alehouse to say, 'Four pints of your best, landlord,' the copper had followed us in. A mate had also asked the Yorkshire copper outside the pub a few questions.

'What's your problem? I'm only doing my job,' said the boy in blue to us.

'What's *our* problem?'

We then explained we were out for a drink, that's all!

He left.

Five minutes passed and Preston's main IO entered, and once more we explained a few things; he understood and left. We moved on.

The ref signalled the end of the match ten minutes after I'd left. I was already halfway through my first pint in the Charnock, after having had enough of watching Preston get smashed all over the pitch. It ended up 4–2 to Leeds. The Charnock pub is a little hidden boozer down a side street not far from the Deepdale stadium. If you get 50 in there, there's no room to fart, let alone get a beer, and by now it was rammed! Someone then started to inform everyone, above all the noise, that Leeds were on the way. I was trapped between the devil and the deep blue sea. The devil came second and I did one.

Turning left, and then left again, within a minute I'd bumped into two Woollybacks roaming away from their flock, both gobbing it off. They were soon away cartoon-style into the evening's cold, dark mist. Talk about wanting to avoid certain situations. I then bumped into two more sheep and these two started bleating on. I'd rather let sleeping dogs lie these days, only I'm on the horns of a dilemma. Fuck it, I might as well be hanged for a sheep as for a lamb as they bounced towards me. 'This will separate the sheep from the billy goats.' If our new-found friend in blue turned up, it would have confirmed to him that I was a black sheep just like he'd thought. Beware of the fury from a patient man.

BANG! We locked horns. One of them was a cross-breed; nearly twice the size of his counterpart and it was getting hard work, with me being a bit ring-rusty and having love-handles the size of John Wayne's saddlebags. During the to'ing and fro'ing, a little council bus pulled up alongside the ruck and the passengers had free ringside seats to the event. BASTARD! One of them caught me in the eye and I could feel the old 'Panda One' is going to make an appearance in the pub later.

It was getting to be a case of horses for courses when reinforcements arrived in the form of a mate, Cuey, just as I was enjoying being a lone wolf, and was ready to shear them. Now it was equal numbers they just didn't fancy it. I think they wanted to rejoin their flock and they were off faster than 'sheep on 'roids'. I still had a bone to pick with them, so I followed the white curly Yeti into a nearby petrol station. He only bounded over to the petrol pump and proceeded to pull out the hose while lifting a cigarette lighter out of his pocket. There are three things he might attempt: (1) squirt four-star in my direction like a flame-thrower; (2) douse himself to become a wannabe stuntman; (3) fill his mode of transport, this being his Adidas Kick trainers.

The thick Yorkshire pud didn't realise that a petrol pump won't dispense fuel until the CCTV or staff have clocked a registration plate, his being 'NOB H3AD'. I just burst out laughing and stood well enough away, not wanting to get on film myself. Anyway, I didn't fancy my meat and two veg getting flame-grilled. I do hope old farmer McDonald rounded these two up, taking them back over the Pennines into the Yorkshire Dales with pastures green and plentiful.

I walked across the road and went into the Moor Park pub for a pint and asked the barmaid for some ice-cubes wrapped in cling film to put on my now rising eye. Why did I stoop to those two sheep-shaggers?

I was stood mulling over my thoughts after thanking the mate for coming to my rescue when in walked the rest of the lads. J1 burst out laughing. 'What the...?' as I'm shaking my head.

Greenie:

Preston received a phone call saying, 'Leeds are on the move.' They were leaving the ground and giving abuse to everyone, even children. A girl who was on crutches at the time even got pushed to the floor. Well done, Leeds! The word was passed round the Charnock that Leeds were en route via Moor Park Avenue. A few lads went straight there but Leeds had cut down St Paul's Road, ending up on St George's Road. Preston spilled out of the pub and a lad at the front of the Leeds firm, who'd also fronted it in their city centre nearly a month ago, shouted, 'Let's have it for real this time!'

BANG! The first punch was thrown, it hit him, and Preston went straight in. Quite a few Leeds did one, as glasses and bottles rained in. Fair play to their main man as he was well up for it along with another big geezer who ended up on a car bonnet with a Preston lad! The police turned up pronto, spraying pepper everywhere. That was it, day over.

All in all, if Leeds are honest, they should admit they twice underestimated Preston, finding out numbers and age don't matter if you're up for it. Preston had once more flexed their muscles! Leeds were keen as mustard but just couldn't cut it. The once-feared gave a bad account of themselves, dragging their already-fading reputation through the mud once more.

He's a good 'un, that Billy Davies. A jittery start to 2005/06, then a 25-game league and Cup unbeaten run, taking Preston up the table. Then the jitters came back. I hoped Preston wouldn't fuck it all up with seven to go. No, they didn't. Six wins and a draw out of the remaining games saw North End facing Leeds in the play-offs.

Wil:

A coach was booked on an alleged pretext that 50 lads were having a day out at Beverley races! The coach driver, who was known by sight, liked a flutter himself and didn't even twig that there was no meeting that day. A good tip was placed into his pocket and he dropped them into the centre of Beverley, where he was informed that everyone would be back between seven and eight. The driver was spotted later on disappearing into a bookie's and I bet he did the lot in.

A few beers were had in the lovely Yorkshire market town and then there was a short train trip to Hull. They left behind a few of the lads who were banned.

On coming out of the station, some lads get collared having not paid and Preston's Intelligence Officer is waiting. The day's gone tits up. The lads then wander off, then double back, but all to no avail. They're still being followed so the majority go into a pub with others going into the one over the road. They're informed by the police that they could stay in there until two o'clock when they would be moved up to the ground. The pub door was booted shut and the brass bolt was slid into position – if your name's not down, you're not coming in.

Quarter-past-two and the Old Bill are pulling at the locked door, and having to contact the landlord to open up. The lads are now all revved up and ready to go. Once outside, they're bundled on to a waiting double-decker bus by no-nonsense police.

On arrival at the ground, the police have shut all but one turnstile, and lads trying to get on have telescopic batons brandished at them, even though they've got tickets and have done nothing wrong. The reason that they wouldn't let them on was that they wanted to shut the bars down inside, not allowing them a drink.

About turn and they march off, getting past the barrier only to be halted at the next one, followed by police hot on their heels. Only one lad managed to get through. 'If you carry on walking, you will all get arrested for breach of the peace,' an officer bellows out. About turn again, quick march and it's back to the turnstiles that have finally opened, letting them in.

The one who got away rang up, informing the lads where he was. And just after half-time, lads start exiting in ones and twos. The coppers eventually sussed this after about 20 got out, standing by the exit doors knocking the rest back; the free ones joined their mate in a nearby boozer.

The lads are having a quiet drink with some locals, with one bloke explaining about the city's two rugby teams and why different areas follow which club. All is calm, when in comes Preston's Intelligence Officer with his buddies. A few gobby Hull follow in behind them, eating fish and chips and one gets pulled off a Preston lad. 'Oi, you, big mouth, you think you know it all giving it the big one.'

'Yeah.'

'Well, what fucking fish are you eating?'

Everyone's laughing at him and he's totally bamboozled.

The Preston lads are then escorted back to the ground, meeting up with the rest and pushed back on to a bus. They're then escorted on and off the train with the coach in Beverley backed right up to the train station's door. And the coach driver's wondering, 'What the fuck is going on?'

The bus leaves town with a cop car out in front and two others and a minibus full of police behind with blue lights flashing all the way out of Yorkshire.

No sooner had the police peeled off when another lump was stuffed into the driver's pocket with him pulling off at the next exit to find a pub. The only entertainment had that day was a game of killer pool. 'You can't help but try,' one of the lads says. And I don't think that anyone even had a bet that day!

It was 101 per cent North End's season and Preston feared no one, not even in the play-off against Leeds. It was the away leg first at Elland Road and PNE ground out a 1–1 draw. Then it was back to Fortress Deepdale and surely it was only a formality in the second leg.

Well, the dirtiness did return to Leeds United's game and their plan worked; they kicked lumps out of the Preston players. Their tactics were spot on, with Leeds winning 2–1. I suppose you use whatever measures you have at your disposal to win in a fight – just ask Mike Tyson!

To drown my sorrows after the match, I sank ale like it was going out of fashion. Then just before last orders in the Moor Park pub, I was having to be held back as the head went. A traveller with his clan came out with a saying that only a woman can get away with to me. In his smarmy accent, he went, 'Never mind, laddie, it's only a game.' The cheeky cunt wanted a reaction while nudging his mates and smirking.

Never mind – there's always next season, and I had to remind myself just how far PNE had progressed.

And when the next season came round, Billy Davies left for Derby County and Paul Simpson came in as the new manager. We'd heard before the appointment but couldn't get a bet on it – we're in the know, you know!

Preston got off to a bad start, but soon pulled it round. At one stage, we topped the league, our highest position in many a lifetime. It's definitely got to be PNE's time, surely? It's been far too long!

Preston North End once more fell at the final hurdle; we finished just outside the play-offs.

To get a real sense of the highs and lows of following North End, there's no one better than Richie H to put things in perspective – he's been following the club for over 35 years.

Richie H:

Following Preston North End over the years hasn't been the most pleasurable experience and some wouldn't wish it on their worst enemies. From North End falling to the depths of the old Fourth Division, and having to apply for re-election, to travelling to non-league clubs grounds, I've witnessed my beloved team get beat on so many occasions. From going to Wembley and the Millennium Stadium twice, winning titles and even seeing them reach their highest position in over 50 years, I've been there! For good or bad, through thick and thin, for richer or poorer and in sickness and in health – it sounds like I'm married to PNE, doesn't it? In a way I am! You can choose your partner in life and also choose a team to support, but there's only one you can part company with! Or is that just me? Passion isn't just a fashion, it's for life!

While watching Preston, I've been involved in trouble, right or wrong. I've been kicked from pillar to post, ending up in hospital numerous times. I've also been up in front of many a judge having to explain my actions and exactly why I did it. Why? I loved it and all the trimmings that went with it – the camaraderie, the bonding, the craic, the travelling, the clothes, the lifestyle, just being with the lads. I was 100 per cent committed to the cause, full stop.

The 2006/07 season saw the Preston lads travel up to Sunderland, home to the Seaburn Casuals, and right down to Plymouth to see if the Central Element were still active.

Preston also arrived in Birmingham at 10am for a Saturday afternoon game 50-strong, on a coach. They then proceeded to drink in Brum's manor while making tracks towards Saint Andrew's, unopposed. Eventually, they got collared off the police while on the move and settled into a public house with two vans of police and Preston's IO parked outside. Then four Brummie lads, maybe Zulus, came in and informed Preston that they were the first firm to show in nearly three years mob-handed.

Later on, Birmingham start to gain entry into the pub and suddenly it goes off. Tables, chairs, glasses, all the lot go and the Birmingham who've gained entry are backed off. Within seconds, the riot police charge in with telescopic metal batons drawn, dishing out whacks. Finally, the police regain order with several Preston lads getting arrested and others taken outside, given a Section 60, filmed and details taken.

They were then marched up to the ground surrounded by a heavy police escort with a helicopter hovering overhead.

When the police left, some of the lads entered the away end but others in the car park hid behind coaches. And when the coast was clear, they headed back into town. It goes off again under a barrage of glasses in a boozer in the centre with some Villa.

Arrangements had been made to meet back up at 7pm where they'd been dropped off that morning. In the city centre, the lads' phones started ringing about 5.45pm from the others who'd been on the game; the coach was now going at 6pm on police advice and they had to make their way back to the bus.

On arrival at the pick-up point, the coach is nowhere to be seen. A motorcycle cop then turns up followed shortly by ten riot police for four of the lads. They're then led to the coach with the Midlands Police well miffed about the day's events.

On boarding, the rest of the lads inform them that 70–80 Zulus have followed Preston back into the city centre with police in between. The coach then sets off with riot police aboard stood in the central walkway fully kitted out – shields and batons drawn. The Old Bill travelled with the coach for the next 30 minutes with police riot vans to the front and back.

Arriving back in Preston, the lads have a welcoming committee. There's over 30 police present with dogs, arresting more of the lads and firing a warning shot across the bows that they would be watching their every move that night.

A few weeks later, I was talking to a Goosnargh PNE White who'd made the journey with his mates to Birmingham. They'd jumped in a taxi outside New Street Station asking to be taken to a quiet pub near the ground. And just as they were pulling up at the pub, a stool came through the window! They then told the driver to carry on as they passed lads running in every direction.

More recently, a mob of Wolves got run down Deepdale Road one Saturday. And Preston Youth, or whatever name they go by, have been turning out tidy firms with numbers varying for different games. By all accounts, they are well active.

Besides Burnley, let's not forget Preston's present rivals, Leeds, who won't admit that they've been turned over twice in recent years off Preston. That's true, they have, no lies.

A firm of Leeds wasn't seen at Deepdale this season for a night match. The away fixture was brought forward to Friday night and saw a minibus load of Preston leave at 2pm. They'd been in Leeds city centre a couple of times, so they decided to pull off at the turning after Elland Road into an industrial estate. First port of call was a scruffy pub full of Swedes, Danes and other Leeds followers. They then moved on from pub to pub getting nearer and nearer to Elland Road, pint after pint.

One of the lads present had brought along his flag for a photo and it's unveiled outside a boozer with more Preston joining up. It's a 20ft-square Union Jack, the bollocks. This prompts the locals to present arms – not for long.

Preston then retire back inside the boozer for some more fine Yorkshire ale. While relaxing back inside, the door bursts open, only for the Leeds to turn and run again. Then the inevitable happens. Leeds' silly games have attracted the attention of the law and Preston's 10, and it's day over and they're escorted to the ground an hour before kick-off.

Give Birmingham their due, as they turned up in Preston en masse for the last game of the season. Also, reports were coming in that the Zulus had arrived on Saturday night in Preston. And over 200 of them were in Blackpool for the weekend, allegedly teaming up with some Hearts boys. Preston were also informed on Sunday morning, when the police finally traced them in the Lime Kiln pub, that the Zulus were just about everywhere. Preston knew they couldn't have lived with them that day with the numbers they'd turned out. However, every dog has its day and Preston had had theirs a few times during the season.

Preston don't reckon they've got the biggest and best, or hardest firm at all, but bump into them on their day and it may be at your peril – as many a so-called 'big' firm have found out. All good things come in small packages. (So the Missus tells me.)

Preston fell out of the traps in the league at the start of 2007/08, and an early-season League Cup game at Deepdale saw North End get routed 2–1 by our near neighbours Morecambe.

After getting beat 3–0 off Hull City, and with the team hovering just above the relegation zone, Simpson went a few days later. Then Alan Irvine, Moysie's side-kick from Everton, got the nod for the vacant manager's job, even though he had never managed before. He pulled North End away from what looked like certain relegation at one stage to a final position of 15th in the Championship, of which the main highlight was a 4–1 drubbing of Derby at Pride Park.

Of course, there were always old rivalries – and old wounds – to pick over and enjoy. Preston lads antagonised Blackpool fans by leaving messages hanging from bridges on the M55 for the Seasiders to read returning home from the Wembley play-off final – which they won. There were fears now that, because both teams were back in the same league, old rivalries might re-emerge. If it meant moving kick-off times to stop trouble, then so be it. But do they really believe moving kick-off times would ever stop trouble? No, it didn't!

On Saturday, 8 December, Blackpool were to visit Deepdale and, on police advice, the kick-off time was moved to an earlier slot in the day.

Preston lads turned out bright and early as well, drinking in many an establishment behind closed doors. The game itself was a major let-down with North End on the wrong end of a single goal. And there's nothing more annoying than your local rivals having bragging rights about a derby-day win, especially on your turf.

I heard on good authority later that, after the match, nearly 200 Preston made their way to the Stone Cottage public house, a little hidden boozer in between the ground and the town centre. And when they made a move to leave the pub, the police surrounded the exits with horses, dogs, riot vans and a large foot presence – no way were they letting the lads decamp and slope off.

An hour or so later, the lads did manage to set out from the alehouse in small groups, the majority heading for another pint in the Black-a-Moor Head. And come sunset, the police thought fit to leave the lads to drown their sorrows. It is also alleged that, not long after this, several taxi and minibuses were ordered to take upwards of 70 of them over to Blackpool.

On arrival in the seaside town, the first taxi-load entered the Hop Inn watering-hole only to be confronted by locals with pool cues, glasses and an assortment of weapons. The locals, who well outnumbered the Preston, backed them out of the premises. Just as they were doing so, the remainder of the party from Preston pulled to a halt outside. The pub was then put under siege. Within minutes, the police had appeared and arrests were made.

Later on, 30 lads received Section 60s on Blackpool Station because the other 40 of them had disappeared into thin air!

That season, Preston had a new IO and he'd informed lads, old and new, that the Preston police force had received extra funding to combat potential troublemakers connected to football. That meant that banning orders would be served by the courts to anyone suspected of being involved in disorder or trying to organise such happenings. And they were.

There was also trouble that season at the Ricoh Arena when over 100 Coventry attacked coaches of Preston fans at a non-policed match. And there were also reports that the youth movement, the PFP, were active and causing havoc. I'd heard about Everton at home on Deepdale Road after a pre-season friendly; Hull in Beverley; and numerous other incidents arranged well away from the match.

The following season, 2008/09, Preston were up to their old ways yo-yoing up and down the Championship like a game of snakes and ladders. North End finished in sixth spot on goal difference.

Along the way, Preston came away from Blackpool's Bloomfield Road with all three points for the first time since 1992. And in the play-offs, PNE drew with Sheffield United at home 1–1. At Bramall Lane, it wasn't to be once again, with North End going down 1–0. Eight times Preston North End have tried to gain promotion through the play-off system, and eight times they've failed.

In the FA Cup, after a near 40-year wait, we had the pleasure of the mighty Reds, Liverpool FC, at Deepdale. In front of over 23,000 fans of both teams, Preston had three penalty shouts turned down and a goal disallowed. Liverpool scored two cracking goals and North End were dumped out of the Cup as per usual. In the season of 2009/10, all seemed to be quiet on the violence front, or maybe I'm just not 'in the know' any more.

* * *

I never wanted to glorify, advocate or promote violence in this book, merely document events that have happened and bring some closure to them. And having distanced myself from goings-on off the pitch, the football on the playing field is the be-all and end-all for me once again. Saying that, activities behind the scenes at club level, and ever-increasing politics associated with football in general, have driven many a fan away from the once beautiful game.

With the introduction of all-seater stadiums, and the non-existence of terracing and standing at the match, it seems to have led to a somewhat sterile atmosphere, especially at Deepdale. Overzealous stewarding and frowned-upon chanting at the opposition have also taken the 'fun' out of attending a game. Add to this the price you have to pay to watch 90 minutes of so-called football – and this can sometimes be twice a week – it doesn't take a mathematical genius to work out why attendances have started to dwindle.

Bill Shankly once said, 'Some people believe football is a matter of life and death; I am disappointed with that attitude. I can assure you it is much, much more important than that.'

Really?

So what does the future hold for Preston North End on and off the pitch?

On: we're still waiting for glory! Surely, very soon our dreams must come true and the comatose giant will awake.

Off: with films like *Awaydays*, and the remake of the Eighties' classic *The Firm* gracing the big screen, will a new breed of 'hooligan' be spawned after watching such flicks? Also, the Eighties clobber is back with a bang and many an original item is exchanging hands for mega bucks on eBay. And with many a fiftieth birthday reunion due, only time will tell what the future holds! Peaceful times, I hope – but there's no guarantees in life, that's for sure.

Part IV

A BIG SHOUT OUT

14

THE LADS' STORIES – JACKANORY TIME

A Veteran:

Where do you start? Where it all began for you personally, one particular era or try and sum up everything?

I bet we've all read the previous books written on the subject of hooliganism and, granted, the first few were probably read avidly cover to cover. Nothing had been written about it before and here was someone talking the language you understood, what made you tick, your weekend. After a few of these books, however, didn't you get a little bored with the 'we ran them, though well outnumbered' scenarios? Let's be honest, that's not what it was all about. It was the 'buzz', the camaraderie with your mates, the laugh and the brilliant days out, weekends away and turning out in some hell-hole in some far-flung corner of the country knowing it's a token gesture. The point is you turned up, you were with your mates and you might have been done, but sit round a table with a pint and your mates and you can talk for hours: 'Do you remember going to X?

Do you remember so-and-so doing whatever?' It can be the most ridiculous of things, but it is all part of being a football fan and it will be a part of you forever. I'm sure you've read already about particular great away days where everyone turned out and mega battles ensued, so I'll try and write a résumé to give a flavour of different eras.

Personally, I've been through most of the hooligan eras from the late 1960s to the present day: pre-skinhead, skinhead and suedehead, the punk era, Eighties Casuals and right up to the modern day and more organised mobs with their mobile phones. Makes you wonder how anybody found someone to fight with in those far-off days!

The first real football violence I ever witnessed was when I travelled to Aston Villa on one of my earliest away days unaccompanied by an adult. At Villa Park in November 1968, it was still the early days of 'end-taking'. The PNE fans filed straight on to the Holte End. If you've never been there, it was an unbelievable size and probably the biggest end I've ever been on. If you wanted to try and take an end back then, you had to turn up a lot earlier in those days so it would have been about two o'clock.

The PNE fans made their way straight up to the back, probably about a 30-minute climb remembering the size of it! I remember a mob of Villa up there beating a drum and the chant of 'Villa!' – BOOM... BOOM... BOOM – 'Villa!' It echoed out under the roof and I was impressed to fuck when, all of a sudden, a scuffle broke out and a PNE fan stuck his foot right through the drum. If I remember rightly, PNE won the game 1–0 but the match itself is all a bit of a blur to me now, though unsurprisingly events off the pitch are still quite vivid, even after all these years.

Later, on the coach park, a mob of Villa turned up. Everyone was stood outside the coaches and I'll always remember the Old Bill encouraging everyone to set off after the Villa fans (probably saving them a job). Imagine that happening nowadays! As the older lot set off through the car park, I set off behind them. I don't know what I'd have done if I'd actually caught up with a Villa fan. (Maybe he'd have fallen on the floor laughing and I could have taken the opportunity to do him then!) This was my first experience of that 'roar' of charging mobs. I was hooked. You'll know the feeling yourself, and I bet even now, if you hear that roar in the distance, the hairs on the back of your neck stand up and you want to be wherever it is as the adrenalin starts to pump.

Aaah, the adrenalin! I'm stood on the Kop at Deepdale with a few mates – 11 October 1969, PNE v Leicester City. There are no signs of any away fans on there as we wander about weighing things up. Word then goes round that they're outside and, all of a sudden, they're on the Kop. We stand there mesmerised as a mob of about 70 come up the steps on one side of the Kop and walk in formation along the alleyway that separates the covered part of the Kop from the open terrace. Fuck me! I'm fucking speechless; I'd never seen anything like it! The first mob of skinheads I've ever laid eyes on – half-mast jeans, cherry-red Docs, Ben Shermans and braces, and the obligatory shaven head. It's hard to describe nowadays the impact that the sight of this mob made. Remember, it was all long hair and flares in those days.

They made their way to the back of the Kop and, for the rest of the game, all I can remember is staring at them and thinking, 'Fuck me, they look the business, fucking awesome!'

From that day on, every game you went on somebody else you knew had taken the plunge and appeared with a shaven head. You had to look twice to make sure it was someone you knew; everybody looked that different. The Leyland lads went for it in a big way and, in my mind, were always a step ahead in the fashion stakes for a mob in those days.

The skinhead/suedehead era is a book in itself and I could tell a thousand tales from the time. Sta-Prest, reggae, Harrington jackets, Royals, red socks, Tuxan red polish, checked Ben Shermans, loafers, Crombies, Northern Soul, half-mast jeans, two-tone suits, 15in vents, sewn-in creases, parallels... the list is endless.

The fighting and violence was much more disorganised in those days. Saying that, you'd just turn up and you were more or less guaranteed an 'off', home or away. Mobs didn't have names, though there would be little mobs from Leyland, Chorley, Bamber Bridge and Preston who all joined together as one. Colours were also still worn – a scarf looped around the neck, looped through braces and later around the wrist.

It was a lot more dangerous travelling away in those days as most places had a mob of some sort and if you were caught in the wrong place and separated from your mates you were usually in for a kicking. When the gates opened with 20 minutes left, you would see the fans start to stream out from the home end to come round and wait for the fun to begin. Bloody hell, the feeling when there were only a couple of dozen of you gathered in the away end at some godforsaken place and hundreds start to stream round. What do we do? Stand? Split up? Or fuck off? If you've only been on in the days of situations, I can tell you it could be fucking scary or fucking brilliant. You never knew. What you did know is that you would get some sort of ruck everywhere you went.

Alan Ball had taken over as manager in 1970 and he was a fans' manager, the first I had ever heard mention the fans. He actually christened the PNE fans the 'Gentry' in an article in the local paper and from that time on the name was taken up by the younger element, which most of the travelling away support was made up of in those days. Not like today's family-orientated game with plastic seats and plastic fans. For years, when following PNE you actually knew everyone's face; they were all young lads and almost all were up for a good ruck if it did happen to go off. It was just a fact of life following a football team in those days. 'The Gentry' couldn't have been a more fitting name in the days of the Crombie overcoats with a red hanky in your top pocket, blazers, polished shoes, tailored trousers, Prince of Wales check and umbrellas, which were not carried to keep the rain off your head! A lot of The Gentry even took to wearing bowler hats and it became a bit of a badge of honour pre-Clockwork Orange.

PNE had a good away following in 1970/71, especially as it was the year they won the old Third Division Championship and their first ever season outside the top two divisions. Travelling away could take any form in those days: trains, coaches or alternatively a tranny van, which never seemed to have seats in the back but, fuck me, you could get some numbers in there. PNE had their own famed mode of transport – a large Sunblest bread van that travelled the length and breadth of the country. What a fucking beautiful sight when you were already in some grim town with a few of you contemplating a good kicking and the locals are already mooching around and the old Sunblest van pulled into the car park. The locals were bemused when the back doors rolled back and out would pour a motley crew of skinheads. I still don't know how they used to get so many in there at times and why it has never made the Guinness Book of Records is still a mystery! I personally travelled to every game home and away that season and the 'aggro', as it was known, in those days was guaranteed wherever you went.

The regular meeting place for all the lads was the Black Cat Café on Butler Street, outside the railway station for home and away games. In fact, it was one of the skinhead headquarters in Preston for quite a while. I don't know what any old dears used to think when calling in for a cuppa and the darkened area at the back of the café was packed out with lads planning the day's action.

I was at the Bristol Rovers away match in 1970 (mentioned in the book Bovver by Chris Brown) and it was exactly like Chris Brown tells it. A top day out and we're on their end, singing as he calls it, a strange chant of 'We Are Superior' until numbers proved that we weren't as superior as we first thought.

The day we first went top of the league was away at Barnsley and again we were all on the Barnsley end with fighting going off all over the place. And there's the biggest skinhead I'd ever seen in the middle of the Barnsley lot wearing a white butcher's coat and white, half-mast baker's pants (another little sartorial gem from the early skinhead days).

I remember PNE quickly arranging a friendly fixture as they'd been knocked out of the Cup and had a free Saturday, an away game at Grimsby (which was pretty rough in those days). My mate and I decided to go as we'd not missed a game. And as no other form of transport was available, our only option was the train. Not our wisest ever decision as there was only a train one way and none returning after the game until the day after. A minor problem when you're young and mental. The only other lad I remember going (sadly no longer with us – RIP) decided to brave the trip on his red Vespa scooter like Pole to Pole with Michael Palin in pre-motorway days. He actually followed the team coach over the Pennines and spent hours driving in the spray off the back of it. My mate and I were also having a torrid time in sunny Cleethorpes with a few of the local welcoming committee sussing out someone had actually turned up.

We did manage to make the safety of the players' entrance where we met up with our scooter mate and managed to blag three tickets off the players (not much of a feat as there was nobody else there who wanted them). We then went inside the ground and our scooter mate had removed his helmet and goggles by this time and we nearly fell on the floor laughing. Fuck me, he looked like a giant panda with white eyes and a completely streaked, black face – this was pre-CP goggle jackets. Perhaps he started the trend. Even the welcoming committee inside the ground had to laugh.

We made our way into the stand, as did a mob of lads

from Grimsby who immediately took up position a few rows behind us and then proceeded to throw things at us for the rest of the game until they got bored with it. We headed straight to the player's entrance after the game and, thanks to Alan Ball, the British Rail two were allowed a lift back on the team bus – result! We saved ourselves a kicking and got a trip straight home apart from a stop in Doncaster where the team had a meal booked. A director gave us ten bob each (50p!) and told us to make ourselves scarce.

While walking round we came across a shop with a window packed with checked Ben Shermans and were sorely tempted to do a smash and grab. Visions of the News of the World headlines of 'Team Bus in Shirt Heist' stopped us.

The final away game that season was at Fulham and the league title was there for the taking – it was nearly ours. We travelled down the night before on the train to Euston, a regular thing to do in those days – no hotels like today – just doss about all night on Euston Station (I like my bed too much for that nowadays).

We then made our way to Victoria Coach Station and dossed around there all morning and I'd never seen as many PNE coaches turning up – they seemed to be everywhere. The rest is history. A 1–0 win, and the chance to be champions thanks to a diving header from Ricky Heppolette. Joyous celebrations and angry home fans made it a top day out. As you might know, the title was finally sealed in midweek with a 3–0 home win over Rotherham in front of over 30,000 fans.

There were loads of places that were classed as rough in those days – Bradford, Barnsley and Chesterfield all had their own skinhead mobs ready and waiting for you.

August 1972, and we're drawn away to Barrow in the first round of the League Cup. Everyone met in the Black Cat as usual prior to the train journey up there for the Tuesday-night game. There were about 80 of us and it was pretty uneventful when we came out of Barrow Station and as we made our way to the ground. Unlike nowadays, the events first unfolded on the ground itself where a few skirmishes broke out with the locals.

We made our way to the covered terrace behind one of the goals and camped in the middle. You could walk around three parts of the ground, something not unusual in those pre-segregation days. A mob of locals quickly built up on the side and, all of a sudden, prior to the kick-off, they charged en masse towards the PNE mob.

Suddenly, we were heavily outnumbered and most of the PNE ended up in the top corner of the terrace. I think I would have been there myself expect I was with one of our better-known lads – Arky – who was always up for a fight and was wearing a denim jacket without a shirt.

As the mob quickly approached, throwing missiles, he pulled the said jacket off and said, 'Hold this.' He then proceeded to stand there, facing the onrushing mob, completely bare-chested with me like a pillock stood at the side of him holding his jacket and casting envious glances at the retreating PNE lads. Somehow this persuaded a few others to return and, all of a sudden, the battle was on, and the day was saved.

What a top lad Arky was and sadly another no longer with us. In another unfortunate incident, a lad who was with us got hit in the face with a stone and lost his sight in one eye. Like I say, even the small towns could be rough in those days.

The Barrow mob were all over the place after the match – which PNE won 2–0 – looking to avenge the scoreline. Somehow, en route back to the station, we ended up making our way straight through some allotments that ran alongside the railway lines and emerged further along Holker Street. Armed with a variety of weird and wonderful weapons, we kept the baying mob clear until we reached the station. Well, would you go near a mob of adolescents armed with garden rakes, plant pots... and I'm sure I can remember someone pushing a wheelbarrow! But, then again, the mind does sometimes play strange tricks!

Moving on to the mid-Seventies, the first real organised mob appeared: the 'Spotty Dogs' had arrived. This was the era of private-hire coaches, with amenable drivers who would drop you and pick you up wherever you wanted as long as you had a whip round. Up to 70 of us on a 50-seater and a bucket for pissing in – all mod cons in those days! We would turn up pissed out of our heads and nine times out of ten straight in the home end.

One that sticks in the mind is after a mega drinking session in Winchester we turned up at Portsmouth. As usual, we were going on their end, straight in, no messing – and then along the side of the ground where Pompey used to congregate. I don't know why, beer perhaps had taken over us, but we actually did the conga single file straight into the middle of them. For a minute I thought, 'Fucking hell, we've got a result here, we've taken it!' It was always rough at Portsmouth, so this was defo a result! They were probably rubbing their eyes in disbelief at our entrance but, once they collected their wits, they steamed straight into us. Rucks are going off all over the place and we're now getting a kicking and all split up. Someone gets on the pitch and we eventually all end up over there apart from two. They're still well known today, so shall remain nameless. However, they were, and still are, top lads, giving it their all in Pompey's end, and actually giving a fucking good account, it has to be said. The teams are now out as we cross the pitch and suddenly it's funny to do the dying fly in the centre circle. Ah, Tiswas!

We stopped in Birmingham for another piss-up on the way home. And we must have had a conga fixation because I remember 70 lads doing it round a roundabout at chucking-out time. This was until about six police vans turned up and we were politely shown our way on to the coach and the way back to the M6.

Next up was the Eighties' Casual era – Lacoste, Fila, Pringle, wedge haircuts and train travel, courtesy of Persil. FA Cup third round at Leeds. Believe it or not, a big draw in those days – how the mighty fall!

After a fun-filled afternoon imbibing the local brews, our Lostock Hall/Leyland coach turned up at Elland Road at the same time as a coach packed with lads from the Lane Ends pub in Preston. Their coach always left late in those days. It was about 2.45pm when we parked up away from the ground. En route we met a small mob of Leeds under a subway who were duly dispatched. Then we paraded outside their end and generally took the piss, probably due to being pissed. I always remember being very disappointed in Leeds, who then, as now, had a big reputation but, personally, I've always thought it's just a numbers thing with them.

The coach returned home minus a few bodies due to the

over-zealous constabulary and over-consumption of beer on the way back. Again, hundreds of tales to tell from this era could go on forever.

Jumping forwards to the late Eighties and early Nineties, and we're in the minibus private-hire era. No colours, no scarves and it can be just a few of you or a convoy. We used to have a loose-knit mob of a couple of dozen Leyland, Eccleston and Preston lads, so you could usually rely on at least a vanful for almost anywhere.

On one memorable trip to Hartlepool, we'd planned to stop in Sedgefield for the obligatory pre-match session. On the way into the village, we saw a car full of PNE who were driving away. I can't remember how, but somehow we had a word with them and they advised us to find somewhere else to drink, as Sedgefield was full of Burnley on their way to Sunderland. 'Fuck me. Go somewhere else? No chance. It's like winning the lottery. Sedgefield, here we come!'

We pulled into the centre of the village and there must have been five or six coaches of Burnley there. 'Oh joy! The Dingles are in town!' Give them credit, they've always had a mob but their reputation is pretty low in Preston as they are well known for attacking anyone – scarfers, women, a bus full of kids... we've seen it all. For fuck's sake, they even smashed up their own town and caused £250,000 of repairs after a defeat by their local enemy, Blackburn Rovers! That's the mentality I'm talking about here. Definitely no class.

So we pull up next to the village green, outside a pub, one that is particularly packed with Dingles, inside and out. Word must have gone in and, all of a sudden, you can see faces peering out of the windows. Fucking hell, we're all buzzing in the van and 14 of us are straight out and march straight inside giving it the large one. It's packed with them and the adrenalin is pumping round and we're straight to the bar. We're asking for it and I can see them thinking, 'Who the fuck are this lot?' They must be thinking we're mental because they just didn't want to know.

On returning to the bar for another beer, I'm stood behind two lads and I hear one of them say to the other, 'If they [meaning us] start, we've all got to stick together.' I nearly piss myself laughing.

A football card then goes round the pub and someone sticks PNE in a square. And yes, believe it or not, it won! Bloody hell, it's the first thing PNE have won for years.

We stay in the boozer until they leave and seriously expect it to go off big time. But they get on their buses and leave with our laughter ringing in their ears. We took the piss big time and there must be someone from Burnley who remembers this. Suicide Squad? You're having a laugh.

Same era, another van, where the exact opposite happened to us, big style! We've been in Albion's pub before the game and we take a few liberties. When we come out of the pub, a few of their lads have taken exception and give it the old 'come on, have a go' stance until someone gives the one at the front a right slap.

After the game, it's decided to have a few more beers. We drive down a road for about a mile towards Smethwick and spot a little pub on the corner of a cul-de-sac, The Prince of Wales. It looked a nice, quiet, local pub, so we park the van down the side road facing a dead end, then head into the side entrance of the pub. Fucking hell, it's packed and we march in in single file. There's a disco on in the back and it's surprisingly big inside. It's also full of lads of every ethnic persuasion and it is buzzing.

The alarm bells begin to ring in the head but it's too late now. We order our beers and then someone says, 'There's the lad who got slapped outside their pub!' Shit! Some of our lads have supped so much they don't seem to spot what's going on. Even some of the locals chat all friendly like and we stay in there quite a while, long enough to get through another five pints and I'm still alert. Adrenalin is the best way to stop you getting pissed!

The atmosphere is beginning to get more antagonistic. One of our lads ends up going for a slash and as he's one of our more pissed-up members me and another lad decide to follow him to make sure he's OK. He's not in there, so we take a look outside and he's up against a wall down a back alley, head against the wall and slashing.

Two lads then appear out of a back gate and give him a right slap and – BANG – he goes straight down, blood pouring out of his head. 'Fucking hell, here we go!'

We shoot down the alley and they're back off through the gate and into the pub. So we drag the mate, who's a fucking dead weight, back up to the side road. Next thing, the locals all steam out of the side door and there's two of us there holding the mate up and they're in front of us on the balls of their feet. Most of the rest of our lot come out of the front door behind them and – BANG – it goes off as two of ours jump on them from behind. We've had to drop our injured comrade, who's now lying in the gutter with blood seeping out of his head.

It is going off all over but they are turning up out of the pub in numbers and we finally end up getting run or we'll get fucking murdered! The problem is, where do you run? We shoot off in all directions and three of us head to the van. Don't ask why. The driver opens it but then disappears so we jump in and sit at the open door while a few of them say, 'Come out, you soft bastards.'

Soft bastards! For fuck's sake! They don't come in, though, and, after a bit of argy bargy, they go back up the road and we sit there thinking, 'What the fuck do we do now?'

It seems to have calmed down up the road, so, hearts pumping, we decide we've got to go back for our injured party. They're still all there but someone says, 'Leave 'em, they've had enough.'

Enough! Fuck me, that's an understatement, a good hiding and a half. Then a couple of younger element start circling us again with bottles in their hands saying, 'Let's do 'em... they'd do us.'

Here we go again. And I don't mind admitting it, I was shitting myself but thought, 'Fuck it, I'm not going anywhere again.'

Then the cavalry arrive in the form of a couple of police cars and a riot van. Why they took so long I don't know; they never seem that slow when it's the other way round. An ambulance also arrives for our mate, who we think is half-dead by this time. But as he's lifted up on a stretcher, he sings the immortal lines, 'Nobby Stiles' super white Army...' We fell about.

One of the coppers says, 'You couldn't have picked a worse pub, lads.'

'You don't fucking say! Thanks for that.'

They won't go in the pub themselves. What made it even funnier is that there was a mosque on the other corner and they are all stood on the steps watching like it was a late-afternoon show.

We had to follow the ambulance to the local hospital in a convoy with the police. A few lads were patched up and then we were convoyed back past the pub and on to the M5. One famous Leyland voice who was imbibing a bottle of wine shouted, 'Stop! Let's do the bastards!' He didn't even know we were in an escort he was that pissed.

Another little tale from that day is that a well-known Chelsea fan from Leyland, who only ever went to the odd PNE game, has never been seen on one again. He never returned home with us. And folklore has it that he set off down West Bromwich High Street, jumped out in front of a bus and hijacked it to anywhere he was going. Nobody to this day knows where he went or how he got home!

And so to the present day – the days of all-seater stadia, segregation, CCTV, no swearing and no smoking. And most of the fans you wouldn't know if you fell over them in a ruck. Families, women, stewards who think they are somebody for two hours every other Saturday, dry coaches and trains. No tackling on the pitch, players on tens of thousands a week, extortionate ticket prices, Football Liaison Officers, evidence gatherers, political correctness gone mad, parachute payments, all-ticket games, half-time entertainment and canned music drowning out the chants. Is this progress?

Somehow, despite all this, you can sometimes still manage the odd decent away day!

Happy days!

Dave:

Growing up just outside Chorley, 12 miles south of Preston, I could have had my choice of teams to support, but, with my old man being a North End fan, I didn't really have a choice at all.

I remember my dad taking me on to the North End in the late Sixties; only my first recollections of fighting were when watching Preston v Manchester United in 1972. I stood on the Kop down near the front with all the other kids and with one eye on the back of the stand as rival fans fought for virtually the whole of the match.

However, my first real experience came not at Deepdale, but at Bolton. One of my mates from school was a Bolton fan and used to go to the home games on a coach from Chorley, and I joined in for a gander! In the late Seventies and early Eighties, coach firms in Chorley used to run to local Lancashire clubs such as Preston, Bolton and Blackburn. And for those with an unhealthy interest in donkeys, a minibus went to Blackpool.

Around 1976, North End were languishing in the old Third Division with Bolton riding high vying for promotion to the top flight. Their opposition were the likes of Forest and Chelsea who brought big followings and, with that, trouble.

By 1978, Preston finally started to awake from a coma under the astute guidance of Nobby Stiles and it looked like we might achieve promotion. That season, I hardly missed a home game and started to get more involved with the trouble. This also was the year I left school and I was your typical gangling teenager – over 6ft tall but built like Peter Crouch. Some of the older and 'cooler' lads had started to gather on the Town End at Deepdale, so some of the mates and I started to congregate alongside them.

I'm not going to mention any names, only nicknames. I think most lads that were involved would prefer it that way but one lad I will mention is sadly no longer with us and that was Crookie. I already knew him as we went to the same school; he was a couple of years above me. At the time, quite a few lads from Leyland had started to go on the match and a mob formed with him as the natural leader.

In those days, gangs of football lads were just that; no fancy names, you were just associated with the area you came from, hence the Leyland crew.

In 1978, not many teams brought much of a following to Preston – with the exception of Sheffield Wednesday and Bradford. It was against Bradford that I got involved with my best battle to date. As the game was coming to a conclusion, the stewards used to open the gates and that was the signal for us to mob up. The Town End was divided from the away fans by a double fence. That particular day, as the game ended, the police moved outside the ground expecting trouble might kick off. But inside the ground, we had running battles with Bradford on the stretch of waste ground between the back of the Town End Stand and the perimeter wall. It seemed like the fighting went on for ages: as one set of fans charged, the other backed off and vice versa. Finally, with more lads coming in from other parts of the ground, North End got on top. I remember two North Enders holding a Yorkie down as their mate ran in and drop-kicked him, splitting his top lip and nose wide open.

Eventually, we did get promotion back to the old Second Division and, in my opinion, the early Eighties became the halcyon days for football violence – until Thatcher poked her big nose in after serious incidents at Luton v Millwall, Heysel and Hillsborough.

That first season back in the 'semi-big time', bigger clubs came to Deepdale with bigger crowds on the match. We started to organise ourselves a little better, usually meeting in the Bull & Royal pub before making our way towards the train station to hassle the away fans and all the way up to the ground.

However, most trouble occurred after the games along the edge of Moor Park as the Old Bill tried to escort the away fans. If the away following wanted it, they usually managed to get away from the bizzies and pitched battles would ensue.

One such battle that sticks in the memory was against Newcastle on Bank Holiday Monday. The traditional fair was on the park and, after the game, pitched battles were going off all over the place and even the fairground lads got involved. A mob of Geordies (with shaved heads, painted black-and-white, and wearing kilts) were steaming down Deepdale Road. One North Ender dressed in white jeans and white top piled right into them and got his nose spread all over his face with blood turning his outfit red.

That year, I was training as an apprentice joiner and, for my day release, had to go to the Library Street annexe of Wigan Tech. Wigan 'Pathetic' had just been voted into the league and that January were drawn away to Blackpool in the FA Cup. Preston hadn't played Wigan and, owing to a postponement away to Stoke, some North End decided to travel to the Wigan v Portsmouth game before the match.

Crookie was at the game as he, too, did day release at

Wigan and knew quite a few Wiganers. We stood alongside Wigan on the covered terrace that ran the length of the pitch separated from Pompey by a wall of Old Bill; the superb stadium that was Springfield Park didn't have any segregation. Friendships were made that day, with some of the Wiganers later on coming to Preston for the occasional game. Two lads I remember from those days were called Moose and Cammy. After the match, there were some running battles in the side streets with North Enders right in the thick of it.

For the Blackpool game, I was persuaded to attend by the lads I went to Tech with. We caught an early train out of Wigan and arrived in Blackpool about eleven o'clock. The Wiganers steamed out of the station and into town. They'd quite a good turnout with some handy-looking lads.

The first Blackpool they encountered was a lad on his own who gave them the big come on. He was wearing a white, knitted, roll-neck jumper (the type Captain Birdseye used to wear) tucked into his jeans and he had on a pair of gloves with brown leather on the palms and that beige lattice stitching on the back (like my granddad wore driving his Ford Anglia). As Wigan bore down on him, he ran into the nearest shop which happened to be selling women's lingerie and hid behind the knicker counter. The Wigan left him alone and headed for the seafront.

On the way, we passed an Asian stall with racks of V-neck sweaters which were fashionable at the time. Loads of Wigan lifted the jumpers but some of the more mentally challenged started wearing them.

As we then walked down the prom, a paddywagon passed with the Asian in the front pointing out his jumpers.

The bizzies got busy making arrests. The rest of the Wiganers were herded on to the beach and a police sergeant proclaimed that we would be escorted to the ground and left inside there after the game. I said to the lads, 'There's no fuckin' way I'm going on the ground with three hours to kick-off,' and I sloped off to the back of the escort and made my getaway. I ran down a side street and the first pub I came to had Crookie stood in the window with a pint in his hand. Inside the pub, I found about 20 Leyland lads who decided that Wigan away at Blackpool was a better option than North End at home to the mighty Orient.

Also in the pub were the same number of Bolton, who, at the time, had nothing against Wigan but really hated Blackpool due to a stabbing incident a few years earlier. We had a few run-ins with the locals on the way to Bloomfield but the best was after the game.

It was freezing cold with a bitter wind – typical July weather in Blackpool – only it was January and twice as bad! On the way back to the railway station, the Leyland lads stuck together and, at one stage, got in front of the escort managing to get down a side street and into the Donkey Lashers. That was the first time I encountered Benny, Blackpool's main face. At the station, the Old Bill put the Wiganers on the train then asked us, 'What you lot waiting for?'

'The Manchester train,' was the reply, and with that the police left the station.

We waited ten minutes for the Old Bill to clear the area and then, along with the lads from Bolton, made our way back into town. Passing behind the bus station we found a group milling around outside a chippy. We steamed right into them, only, the funny thing was, Nipper, a lad from Leyland, was supposed to be a Seasider, and he led the way.

A few years later, I went to Wigan in less friendly circumstances as North End drew them in the League Cup. It was a night match early in the season and we took a good number of lads. Springfield Park still had no fences on the home end and you could walk from one end to the other. We paid on to the home end and gathered just inside the turnstiles, then made our way along the length of the pitch on the covered side right into the Wiganers massed near the away end.

Leading the way that night was Taz and, before they knew it, we were straight into them scattering most of them down and on to the perimeter track. They regrouped but we now held the higher ground and easily repelled their advances. Eventually, the police got control and we were escorted over the wall and into the away end.

At that time, Wigan had started to climb the league ladder and, inevitably, North End dropped, so encounters between the two clubs became more frequent.

Another occasion was a Saturday league fixture at Wigan, when we parked in vans and cars on the car park opposite Wigan Casino. We made our way on to Market Street and found a firm of Wigan in a pub opposite the John Bull. And when we tried to enter the boozer, they locked the doors and wouldn't come out.

After the game, about 80 North End came out of the away end and, instead of heading down the street, we all cut down a grass embankment towards Woodhouse Lane, heading into town. We'd almost got under the radar when one copper passed in a van and spun the van round to follow us. We legged it up a side street and came out opposite the old bus station next to the covered market.

Up ahead of us were Wigan being pushed up the street by plod on horses and, when they saw us, they turned to face us – but we were already on our way. Wigan spread out across the street and fighting broke out all the way up as far as the Bricklayer's Arms. We ended up being railroaded by the plod into Makinson's Arcade, where they blocked both exits and eventually escorted us back to the car park.

Yet again another night match at theirs; we had gathered in the Market Tavern pub with a couple of spotters on the side door. Sure enough, Wigan turned up and when the shout went up we piled out of the pub. Wigan came down the street from the market end and launched a hail of milk bottles but, as we dodged the glass, we charged. They retreated back up the street before we could get near. This happened again before the sound of sirens and the inevitable police presence arrived.

Back in the Eighties, and early Nineties, Wigan never made much of an effort at Preston but over the next decade they have become a well-respected crew.

Over the years, my best memories have probably been some of the derby games against our Lancashire rivals. Blackburn has always been a good day out, although finding them was sometimes a bit of a problem.

In this era, every pre-season North End would play our local rivals Blackburn in a mini-tournament. One such game at Ewood Park was a really boring affair. A mate and I left the Darwen End early, bumping into Crookie outside and made our way up Nutall Street. On the corner outside their end, a group of skinheads had gathered. Crookie marched right up to the biggest and asked if he and his mates wanted a go, meaning us three against their six or seven. The reply was 'No.' He then told them that skinheads were supposed to be hard and they were the worst excuse for skinheads he had ever seen. The skinheads left with their tails between their legs.

As the home fans started to leave the ground, we stood in the middle of the street as Crookie offered them out and called them soft as shit – we got no takers. Even the three of us stood outside their end, against overpowering odds, we still couldn't get a ruck with Blackburn.

Burnley was the 'land that time forgot'. What a depressing place it is, and also full of in-breds and numbskulls. I first went to Burnley in 1979, just after the town had been wrecked by Celtic in the Anglo-Scottish Cup. It looked like the aftermath of the St Patrick's Day parade in New York, green and white paint everywhere.

A couple of seasons later, I went on the train with a dozen or so from Leyland. We made our way into town and found a big stone pub – I think it was the Falcon Hotel, or something similar. The pub was packed with North End, drinking and having a laugh. Looking out of the window, a lad who worked in the Clobber clothes shop in Preston was being chased up and down the street outside by around 15 hillbillies – only everyone just carried on drinking. He must have passed the front of the pub about three times before eventually some of the lads inside took pity on him and ran out to chase the Dingles off.

Tiswas was a popular Saturday-morning programme on TV at the time and little Gaz from Preston was stood on a table doing his best impression of the guy who sang 'Mule Train' while banging a beer tray on his head. As time got nearer to kick-off, the crowd in the pub got rowdier and the landlord had had enough when the lads started to throw bottles at his knick-knacks lined up on the shelves behind the bar. He phoned the Old Bill but, by the time they arrived, we were well and truly gone.

At the ground, we tried to gain entry to the home end but, due to the number of black lads with us that day, the police were having none of it. After the game, we held back and, as the escort to the station set off, we headed into town. Outside the Cat's Whiskers nightclub opposite the bus station, divided by a dual carriageway and fencing, we spotted the hillbillies on the other side. They started chanting, 'We only want your niggers...'

Little did they know that Taz and some of the other black lads had doubled back and then steamed into them from behind. They didn't know which way to run as we vaulted the fence and charged from the front.

A few years later, I was working on a building site in Burnley when I met a so-called Burnley face on a banning order who was supposed to be in their 'main' firm. He remembered the incident and told me a black lad had given him a good fucking leathering that day – result!

In 1982, we again travelled to Burnley towards the end of the season for a night match. Burnley won 2–0 with Billy Hamilton scoring both to secure them promotion back to the old Second Division. After the game, we made our way into town, and around 40 of us were in vans and cars. The plod soon sussed us out and we ended being escorted back to the motorway. When we reached the motorway, the Old

Bill decided their job was done and left. Some of the lads thought driving into Padiham was a good idea, so we carried straight on and ended up in a pub.

One pint later, we travelled back into Burnley expecting the pubs to be full of celebrating Dingles. We parked up and went looking but we only found one pub full of them. And as soon as we arrived, the Dingles fled through the fire exits at the rear. In another pub, some of the lads decided it was a gay bar and the lads pulled their trousers down around their ankles, flashing their arses to the locals! Leaving the pub, we were again rounded up by the police and asked, 'What are you up to?'

Dave, a very smart and funny black lad with us, said, 'We're looking for the beach.'

The coppers weren't amused and, for the second time we were escorted out of town, and this time they followed us on to the motorway and home.

We only clashed with Blackpool a few times during the Eighties and Nineties as, for the most part, we were in different divisions. A game I do remember was in 1982. Before the match, I couldn't find any of our main lads as I'd travelled to the game on my own. These were the days when the only person with a handheld communication device was Captain Kirk; there were no such things as mobile phones.

Walking up Deepdale Road, I could see a group of Blackpool about 100 yards in front. And on the opposite side of the road, there were two black lads from Preston offering the Donkey Lashers a 'go.' Every time Blackpool went to cross the road, the black lads stepped up the pace and moved away.

Finally, the Lashers stopped on the car park in front of the Old West Stand. And as I got closer, I could see that Blackpool were dressed in tracksuits with expensive trainers and looked the part. There were about ten of them and they looked like they were waiting to meet up with more lads or pick off some Preston. As they stood talking, I decided I was going to have a go so I walked straight into the middle and smacked a big fucker with dark, curly hair. I know it was foolish, but I was young and had no fear.

The next thing, it felt like I'd been hit with a sledgehammer as they piled into me, only I didn't go down. Then, all of a sudden, my arm was being hoisted up my back and a copper was shouting, 'You're nicked!'

'What for?' I asked.

'What do you think for?' he replied.

By this time, two coppers had hold of me and started to drag me away.

'I was only trying to get past them when they jumped on me,' I said.

'Get past?' the copper said, 'They're the only people on the car park.' And with that he started laughing. 'What you going to do now?' he asked.

'What do you mean?' I replied.

'You're going to go home and listen to the match on the radio, aren't you?'

'Yeah, I am,' I said.

'And if I see you again today, you will be properly nicked. Now do one.'

I can't imagine that happening in today's world of policing methods. That day, I was wearing a blue fisherman-style coat which was yellow on the inside and reversible, so I turned the coat inside-out and went on the match. I stood in the West Stand Paddock with my bright-yellow coat looking like a Fleetwood fisherman!

It kicked off big time after the game on Deepdale Road and Moor Park, only the Old Bill were out in force that day and prevented any major incidents that lasted any length of time.

Bolton, for me – above all the Lancashire clubs – deserve respect. They have never failed to show and always put up a good account, including when I visited Burnden Park with Chelsea once.

I remember a night match when a good-sized mob turned out for Preston which was complemented with some proper lads from Chorley and Leyland. The Bolton lads knew Nipper and were calling him through the fencing all night.

At the end of the game, we waited for the escort to move off then we crossed the road and slowly moved up Manchester Road towards town. Bolton had stopped on the corner of Manchester Road, near a road that takes you over a railway bridge. As we got closer, Nipper and Crookie, who were at the front, broke into a jog and the low murmur of the 'Ooh! Ooh!' chant started. Just about where the two roads joined, we bowled over and backed Bolton's firm up the road. They were on the back foot for 50 yards until the lads at the front rallied the lesser ones and they stood toe-to-toe. All in all, it only lasted a few minutes before plod got in between. At least we showed face and gave it a go at theirs; not many would.

A few seasons later, we got it on with Bolton at the bottom of Deepdale Road near the County Arms pub, with a good old-fashioned fight, when no side gave an inch. Much respect to Bolton over the years.

Looking back, that's why lads like Crookie, who would stand right to the end, were invaluable in maintaining morale in Preston's crew of lads.

The lads I grew up with have moved on now, and different lads have picked up the baton forming new allegiances. I still go to the games and hang round with the 'old men.' We still meet up and have a drink and, if the occasion arises... I'd better leave it there!

For me, it was never just about the battles but the camaraderie, the craic and having a good time. The one thing that bonded us is still in our hearts. That was – and always will be – Preston North End Football Club.

Kirky:

I'm a lover, not a fighter!

As a 17-year-old in 1981, the only things that we lived for were music, drink, football and our clothes. Our lives were built around bands such as The Clash, The Jam, The Specials and also classic Northern Soul. In our eyes, the perfect band was The Jam because of their aggressive style of music and their 'Mod' style of dressing.

Way back in 1981, The Jam appeared at Preston Guild Hall, and a mob of Scousers turned up with the lads and girls all wearing Slazenger jumpers, bleached jeans and classic Stan Smith trainers. They'd also turned up for the gig with no tickets but managed to get in by rushing the doormen and pushing them out of their way. It was a case of every man – and girl – for themselves. Going to Morecambe Pier for Northern Soul nights was a great experience with the Wigan old heads still dressed in their Seventies gear, while us young Eighties youth dressed in Fila BJ shorts and danced to modern soul in the small room. You could be there dancing next to other football lads with no trouble, you were just there for the music.

In the early Eighties, times were a-changing from the boot-boy era, and sportswear was the order of the day. New clothes labels were being introduced from around Europe, such as Lacoste, Fila and Sergio Tacchini. These clothes were worn, and introduced to us, by lads from other cities such as Manchester or Liverpool. The ones to follow were the Scousers, clobbered up to the nines and their classic hairstyle, the 'wedge' or 'flickhead' to us.

Dressing to the letter wasn't cheap though! Going to Manchester on a Saturday morning to buy a tennis shirt you would have to ask the lad in Hurley's with his 10ft pole to lift it down so you could part with your hard-earned cash. Then you'd trot off to Top Shop to buy a pair of classic Adidas shoes.

Being a Casual in Preston was like being in an elite group; later, we would become known as 'The Slick 50'. I got to know lads from all corners of Preston just because of the clothes they were wearing. Some of these lads supported different football teams such as Man United, Liverpool, Man City or Everton and this is where they got their latest fashion ideas from.

Match days were the best; other teams' lads sat quietly in the corners of pubs because they knew they were foreigners in our town. We'd chase them out of the boozer and proceed to batter them and some lads would even pinch their clothes. In the early Eighties, we caused mayhem on the terraces while wearing expensive Pringle and Lyle & Scott diamond jumpers. It was up there with, and I likened it to, being a Mod running riot on Brighton beach in 1964.

These clothes are still fashionable to the youth of today; I wore those clothes then and still look fucking good in them nowadays!

Elli:

One incident that made me start to think 'Is it all worth it?' was a game against West Ham at home. We'd miscalculated, thinking that they would try and take the Kop. The ten or so that tried got a slap for their troubles. It had also gone off in the West Stand seats, so we knew that West Ham had travelled.

At the end of the match, we set off jogging down Lowthorpe Road, turning right on to St Stephen's, then throwing a sharp right back on to Deepdale Road to be met head on by the oncoming ICF. We were now fanned out right across the road and it was too late for thinking or even backing off. We went bang at it within seconds. To my right, I witnessed one Preston lad slashing away at them. I was up for a good old ruck with boots and fists but knives had never been my scene and never will be. When lads started going into Woolworth's DIY department on Saturday, in the centre of Preston (how conveniently it was situated) to get 'tooled up', I started to question myself as to what the fuck was going on.

It was well on top after London's finest put on a forceful show.

And talking of the finest, many a name could fall into the 'legend' category at PNE: Crookie, Paz, Dave H, Big Jacko (RIP), Joey and Johnny F, Franky R, Illy, the Twinies, Joe K and even a certain Joe 90. There was another, though, who, there is no doubt, could punch above his weight. Pound-for-pound, Wiggy was one of the most game lads I have ever seen in action, fearing no one, except, perhaps, his wife Bev.

The first time I saw Wiggy up close and in combat was after a game at home in the FA Cup against Bristol Rovers, season 1980/81. In horrendous conditions, with the wind cutting across the pitch from one goalmouth to the other, Preston were 4–0 down at half-time. Why I never left at this stage I have no idea! Maybe because I was young and foolish, thinking Preston could pull the scoreline back in their favour. They nearly did!

Preston came out in the second half with the wind up their arses and gummy bite marks off Nobby Stiles on them. They proceeded to score three quick goals with shot after shot being saved, hitting the woodwork or just wide of the nets. An equaliser never materialised and we were out of the Cup for another season in the third round.

On exiting the paddock, my attention was drawn to the two coaches parked tightly against the Town End gates which had most of the travelling Rovers fans already on board them. Joining their ranks and dishing out plenty of 'fists in style' was Wiggy and his mate. It was like a scene out of the programme *Worzel Gummidge*. Heads were literally being knocked off with straw and cider-flavoured blood flying everywhere. I don't think Wiggy was after their scrumpy – he would later be put off the stuff for life.

I'd seen him round and about Gamull Lane and Brookfield as we both grew up in the same part of Preston, and also later drinking in the same local as him. He wore the tightest, knotted silk scarf I'd ever laid my eyes on; it looked more like some laces a teddy boy would wear. And at the match, you were more likely to hear him before you'd see him, he was always having a heated discussion with someone. Beside this, I'd heard many a rumour from lads who'd attended the same school as him about his temper and combat qualities – many thinking, to their regret, that his size might be a disadvantage. A lad playing cricket on the school fields once found this out resulting in the sound of willow hitting skin and bone.

And any opposing fans that would land a fist on target sometimes, knocking out one of his now numerous missing teeth (he has a story for each and everyone one of them), would usually end up drinking through a straw.

So off I went to interview him before a North End game in his local club. It's just gone six o'clock and in he walks with his lovely missus, also taking charge of the Sky remote – who's arguing? The man can tell a story, though it's usually short and sweet with an all-too-familiar ending, often a brawl. I had to filter through the tape trying to make a lengthy story of his match-day antics and cut out numerous four-letter words.

So, without further ado, ladies and gentlemen...

Wiggy:

Man United in the FA Cup at home is my first recollection as a kid of going on to a Preston North End game. Tickets were purchased to go and watch the greats of the time and, once on, and me being that small, I couldn't see the match. So I was passed aloft by spectators on the Spion Kop down the stand and over the wall to sit on the cinder path behind the goals. Alan Gowling scored two for United with Preston losing, but I got the footy bug. I was soon watching Preston home and away; this led to me eating more porridge for the Whites' cause than the curly, golden-haired one and her three hairy mates.

My brother – who, by the way, hates football nowadays – had the thankless task of taking me to the games or he couldn't go. So I blame him for over 40 years of hurt – only kidding, kidder.

Mid-Seventies, Carlisle at home was my first time I got sent down. I was with lads of a similar age who were more intent on giving 'V' signs or abuse than getting stuck in. Not me; I waded right into the Carlisle, only to get nicked and carted off to Lawson Street Station. On my appearance in court (after numerous other arrests mainly off dog-handler Barry), the judge handed me a three-month stretch in Buckley Hall.

I'm back out in time for a pre-season 'not-so-friendly' against Bradford City. A short coach trip is undertaken full of the faces of the time with plenty of pale and brown ale sneaked on board and drunk on the way. In these days, a fight was more usually to take place, and be had, on the ground, so that's where we headed. Preston that day only took just over 100 with half being on our bus.

On the away stand, there seemed more Bradford than Preston, meaning it was a dead cert to kick off and it did. The Bradford lads who were mainly wearing donkey jackets looked menacingly our way with one of them flashing a blade all the time. This happened all through the first half until, at half-time, I heard a cockney voice say, 'Fack it, let's have 'em!' This was from Cockney Rebel, God rest his soul, leading a charge into the Bradford.

I was still only young and wary. Standing at the front of the Yorkies was a 6ft-plus skinhead wearing a sheepskin. Preston's finest proceed to slug it out toe-to-toe, sorting the boys from the men. By the end of the match, which had only a handful of police in attendance, most of the donkey-wearing crew had disappeared.

Later, boarding the coach for our journey home, what sight greets me? The lads are only holding up the sheepy coat as a prized possession. They'd only sheared it off the skinhead in the mêlée and, anyway, why was he wearing it at that time of the year?

Just into the season that year, I went on the same coach with the same lads to a night match at Hull and that was a rough place to visit with us getting it from every angle.

Another good story a few years later involving Cockney Rebel was at Wrexham's Racecourse Ground. We were on a big end that was split into two with the refreshment bar being on their half. Five of us managed to make it over to it undetected, or so we thought. We'd ordered our cups of tea and pies when I noticed Wrexham's boys heading in our direction. I tapped Rebel on the shoulder, informing him about the situation. He spins round, launching two cups of boiling tea over the first of the Welshmen shouting, 'Who wants some?' I'm now thinking, 'There's no way out of this one.' True to form, Rebel only then grabs the full tea urn, throwing its entire contents on the advancing Taffs – scattering the lot of them. This gave us a chance to get back to the Preston lads for a hero's welcome, Rebel giving it, 'It's fackin better than London, this is!' while laughing his head off. He was a right character was Rebel.

During an incident at another match while we were

fighting on the terracing, he shouted, 'Stop!' He managed to get both sets of lads to stop fighting with Preston lads searching for his false teeth which had been knocked out before carrying on the scrap.

There are hundreds of stories to tell. Going to Burnley through the years and at home wasn't as bad as they make it out to be, although I have never rated them. Blackburn never seemed to turn out either at theirs or at ours. Chester and Wrexham away, we've had a few good tear-ups.

Blackpool was the one! It wasn't looked forward to in the Seventies home or away. At theirs, we had many a torrid time once we'd left the train station. They'd be at us walking to the ground, throwing all sorts at us while on Bloomfield and then all the way back to the station. Blackpool was rough as fuck in the Seventies but the tide turned.

The next time I got potted was against Carlisle again at Deepdale; it was a Tuesday night match. I'm fighting away behind the Town End and who nicks me? Dog-handler Barry again! Six months at Stoke Heath this time.

Stoke was rough at theirs. You'd be in a pub with only ten or so, and I'm sure the landlord would ring up another boozer because within five minutes there would be 50-plus Stoke lads baying for your blood. Even after games at Port Vale, they'd be waiting at the train station to have a go.

Birmingham at St Andrews was hairy. You always seemed to get attacked from a side street just before you arrived at the ground.

Once I was up early one Saturday morning and I was just nipping to the local paper shop for some fags when a car pulls up with three lads who I knew. 'Do you fancy coming?' one asks.

'Where?' I reply.

'Exeter for the day. Are you coming or what?'

'Go on then.' I jumped in and off we went.

It was a time when Preston were in the basement league and not a lot made the trip; less than 100. Preston got beat as usual and I decided to drive back because I'd not had a drink – probably the only time I haven't.

I'm doing a steady pace and the lads fancy a flagon of cider each which were for sale at farms along the way for £1. Scrumpy purchased, and I get my foot back on the gas, the only trouble being half-an-hour later they need to stop for a piss.

I pulled up at a pub in a place called Bridgewater and, while they were in there, they decided on having a couple of pints. The lads started to get a bit giddy and having verbals with the locals. Sensing it might go off at any second, I decided to go and get the car from down the road and bring it up to the pub for a quick getaway. By the time it took me to walk back to the car and drive back up, the fighting had begun.

So I opened the boot which had an assortment of tools inside it and steamed right into them. After running battles, one lad was sparko and the rest of them were on their toes, so we jumped back into the car and set off home once again. I informed the lads the next stop would be Preston or motorway services just for the toilets. The only trouble being I couldn't see a sign for the motorway, so we pulled over to ask someone the directions when one of the lads informs them, 'We've to do one quick because we've just been involved in a mass battle.'

I'm now on the motorway and I thought the headlights

on the car had stuck on full beam. No they weren't! It was a helicopter overhead and, all of a sudden, patrol cars are alongside us with blue flashing lights forcing us on to the hard shoulder. We were all nicked.

On our final Crown Court appearance for the incident some time later, two of the lads get a walk out with a 'not guilty'. The third, six months – and me... nine months! That day, I wasn't even meant to go, didn't have a drink, caused the least trouble but got banged up the longest! That really did my head in!

Before a 6–0 hiding at Wolves, we'd a right good kick-off with loads of arrests on both sides outside the ground. We were all banged up in holding cells under the stands then shipped out to different stations in and around Birmingham, there were that many of us.

Trips to London were often eventful when visiting the likes of QPR and West Ham. The Hammers even turned up at Orient once for a go! I've been to Millwall twice on coaches and we've come back with the majority of the windows put through. Crystal Palace you'd get escorted back to the train station then left. Just round the corner, all the Palace would be waiting with it kicking off like mad.

Even further down south, at Plymouth, it went off one year with us well outnumbered but we soon had them running for cover. I was whipping them like mad with my belt.

Probably the most frightening one was after a game at Kidderminster in the FA Cup; we'd stopped off on the outskirts of Wolves on the way back for a few beers in a pub. A vanload of us were having a drink, winding the locals up, when one of them didn't take too kindly to the banter and left. The psycho only returns with a gun, I kid you not.

Just as he pulls it out, one of the lads whacks him right over the head with a pool cue, shouting, 'Run!' He didn't need to tell us twice; we were out of the door and back in the van before the loony could get back up. That one was a close call.

The last time I was in court for football was for an incident that happened in Wigan in the 1993/94 season. I'm with half-a-dozen of the mates and the missus in the Bricklayer's pub in Wigan's town centre. It's quite full of their lads who weren't taking much notice of us as we chatted away amongst ourselves. I also knew Preston were round the corner in another pub drinking, so if it went off there would be no problem. Anyway, I get off with five of the mates to go for a drink with the Preston lads before catching the train, leaving the missus with another mate to finish up their pints.

The next minute, the missus comes running in with a gash to her head screaming and the mate had his face smashed in. Well, all the Preston lads heard the commotion and, within seconds, the pub emptied with everyone steaming back round to the Bricklayer's. The few brave Wigan that did come out didn't last long and the pub got totalled. Even the window frames were hanging out, never mind the glass.

By the time the police turned up, lads started scattering everywhere with the unlucky ones – me, the missus, CV, Nobby and four others – getting lifted. When the boys in blue finally managed to calm me down, one of them mentioned, 'We've been trying for two years to get the Bricklayer's shut down and you lot have managed it in two minutes.'

The case ended up in Crown Court and, on the first day, me and another lad got a 'not guilty'. The next day the other lads got it thrown out, and on the third day the missus got found 'guilty'. Her punishment that day was to be bound over for the sum of £1 after hearing exactly what had gone on.

I don't bother nowadays with any trouble as you know that if you're not lifted on the day you will get a knock on the door a week or so later – guaranteed. The Seventies and the Eighties were my time. The police didn't have a clue.

Not all the contributors to this book were free to write whatever they wanted – one in particular, currently residing at Her Majesty's Pleasure, had to jump through a few hoops to get his recollections over to me. But he's a game lad, and he managed it. Here's his letter.

O'rite, Billy lad,

I've just received your latest letter and it looks like you haven't received my last one. I first wrote four pages about three months ago but the screws read it before it was sent out and stopped it. I had to go in front of one of the Governors and explain it all. Apparently, they didn't like the level of violence that was being written about! They said that I was not addressing my offending behaviour. So I explained to them that I wasn't in here this time for any violence – football or otherwise. Then they explained back to me that they didn't like the bit that I wrote about prison, especially this one. Anyway, they said they were not allowing it to be sent and that was that. They then told me that, if I was going to write about things like what I wrote about, I would have to 'water it down a bit'. What a load of fucking bollocks!

Anyway, about six weeks ago I wrote to you again and basically watered it all right down. I presumed you got that one but, looking at your letter, you obviously didn't. I will try again with this one and, if this one doesn't make it to you, I will probably have to wait until I get out.

My first experiences with football violence was when I was a young lad growing up around the Deepdale area. Every other Saturday there were bits of scraps going on before and after most football matches at PNE's football ground. So, from an early age, I had the 'buzz' for it.

When I was about 16, I started getting into football violence myself and I remember in the early Nineties going to Wigan and having a good laugh at Preston smashing their main pub up – the Bricklayer's Arms. I knew the Wigan lads were going to turn up at Preston the next time we played them and they did. About 40 of them came by train but they were escorted up to the ground more or less as soon as they got off. We managed to get word to them to swerve the police after the game and make their way up to the Stevie's pub at the bottom of Deepdale Road.

At around five o'clock, I managed to get to the pub and noticed that there were 30 of Preston's finest in, although most of them were a bit pissed as they'd not been on the game because of various banning orders. A lot of the lads didn't think the Wigan boys would turn up but I was confident that they would because of what Preston had done to their main pub.

After about ten minutes, I walked out of the pub and

across Deepdale Road to see if any of the Wigan lads were anywhere near. Sure enough, they were – about 40 of the ugliest, pie-munching freaks you've ever seen. I walked back to the pub and called the lads outside and it emptied in seconds, making our way back to Deepdale Road.

As we got there, we could see the Wigan lads were up for it and it didn't take long for the Wigan lads to charge straight at us. We were slightly outnumbered but not one of the Preston lads moved back an inch. Fists and feet started flying in everywhere and it also didn't take long for the police to come wading in, splitting it up. They pushed the Preston lads back towards the pub and rounded the Wigan lads up so they could escort them back to the train station. A few of us got together and decided to have another go at them while they were being escorted but the police were having none of it. They got the Wigan lads back to the station and on to the train for the short ride back to Wigan. The Preston lads who I was with thought that would be the last we would see of the Wigan boys for that particular day and went off to their local pubs, and some even went home.

About ten of us decided to go up town for a few beers and just a general good night out. At about 8.30pm we went into a small pub on Church Street called the Old Dog Inn. The pub was busy with the usual Saturday-night crowd and, as I was stood at the bar, I noticed the pub filled up very quickly with young men. I didn't take much notice at first, just picking up my drink and turning away from the bar.

It was at this point that I realised that the young men who'd now filled one side of the pub were the Wigan lads who we'd had a battle with early on that day. They must have decided to come back and have another go. We were well outnumbered, down to about 10 of us, and there were about 25–30 of them. Also, you could tell that they were going to go for it there and then.

I knew for a fact that the lads who I was with would not be running anywhere, so it gave me a bit of confidence. One of our lads had the bright idea to empty the pool table for a bit of ammunition. This was a good idea because no sooner had the balls come out, we heard a shout going up from the room where the Wigan lads were. They'd started smashing glasses and throwing chairs and tables around, and one lad was even trying to rob the till from behind the bar. The usual Saturday-night crowd emptied the pub straight away, leaving the Wigan lads in one room and us Preston lads in the other. We got ourselves together and steamed straight into the room where it was all going off.

As I got there, it looked like a bomb had hit it and the Wigan lads didn't hesitate in getting stuck straight in to us. There was the usual fists and feet flying in from both sides, plus bottles, chairs, tables and glasses coming our way. One of them had even managed to rip down the chandelier light from the ceiling. The fighting continued for a couple of minutes until one of the Wigan lads let off a can of CS gas.

The pub quickly filled with the gas and we left sharpish to continue our battle on the street, where the Wigan lads got the upper hand. It was only when we all regrouped and charged at them that they started to get on their toes. We ended up scattering the Wigan lads all across Church Street. And once they were split up, they stood no chance. Preston chased Wigan all the way up Church Street and all the way back down to the train station. A few of them tried stopping and having a go but it was a waste of time really. With the amount of Preston lads who'd rallied, and we're now after them, they stood no chance.

Looking back on the day, the Wigan lads really came and did what they wanted to do but I don't think they were expecting the response they got. As I've said earlier in this letter, I've had to water this lot down a bit. I could have written twice as much, but you can fill in the blanks.

Another game that sticks in my mind was from about 1996/97, Preston being away at Burnley one Saturday afternoon. We all met up around eleven o'clock and there were about 50 of us who were all looking forward to the trip to Burnley. This was because we knew they could turn a decent mob out on their day. I was working that night at Yates's Wine Lodge in Blackburn so I decided to wear my doorman's uniform and shoved my Stone Island jumper over the top!

At around midday, we boarded the train for Burnley thinking we might stop off at Blackburn first for a few beers but a decision was made to go straight to Burnley's Manchester Road Station. This station is a bit of a walk from the football ground so there were plenty of pubs on the way. A girlfriend of mine at the time was a landlady in one of these pubs, so we decided to go and see her. She informed me that the local police had told her that they were expecting trouble today and that she should close the pub during the hours of 1–3pm, and 5–7pm.

Before the game, it was fairly quiet and the Preston lads enjoyed a good few beers and a bit of a laugh. As we headed up towards the ground, the mood changed as we were expecting to be met by Burnley's famous Suicide

Squad, but they never showed. Just a few little scuffles here and there but nothing really to get a hard-on over.

During the game, there was the usual banter between the fans, nothing out of the ordinary. It wasn't until North End scored that things started to liven up. One or two of the Burnley lads started to throw coins and half-eaten pies. They even tried getting into our end of the ground but were soon stopped by the police and stewards.

The game ended with Preston winning 1–0 and we all knew that the Burnley boys would be waiting outside even though they never showed before the match.

As the away stand started to empty, about 40 of Preston's hard core hung back a bit to let the fans and families get out and on their way. This turned out to be a very good move because the police escorted them back to their coaches and cars. This left us to walk out of the ground at the back of the crowd.

Turning right on to the main road we could see that there were three or four pubs on both sides further up. One of these pubs was the Brickmaker's Arms and we could see about 15 lads outside, waiting. As they spotted us coming up the road, a couple of them shouted for the rest of their lads inside to come out. At this point, the pub emptied and the numbers were now more or less equal.

As we approached, walking in the middle of the road, they were still on the footpath and a huge roar went up from both mobs. We clashed with punches flying in from both sides. At first, it was more or less evens but, as the Preston lads surged forward, we started to get the upper hand with Burnley backing into the pub. At this point, the Preston lads knew that they were on to a winner and steamed in to finish off the Burnley lads who'd stood. The Burnley mob were now back inside and had no intentions of coming back out. A few of our lads started to chant, 'Where's your famous Suicide?'

As we made our way towards the town centre, we were expecting more fun and games with the Burnley boys; and we didn't have to wait long for them to reappear. A small mob had got together at a roundabout and tried a bit of a charge at us – it wasn't worth the effort really. The Preston lads just laughed it off and carried on towards the centre. As we approached Yates's Wine Lodge, you could see a couple of spotters on the corner, only we didn't take much notice at first. This was until one of our lads walked up to the corner and shouted back that a Burnley mob were here. I could tell by the way he shouted there must have been quite a few of them round the corner. We bunched up tight with me and one of my best mates right at the front. We then ran round the corner and I couldn't believe what I saw; there was about 80–100 Burnley lads coming straight at us. I could also see that a few of them looked well pissed off.

The clash took place straight away with punches and kicks flying in from all angles. This is what it is all about. The next few moments will stick with me for the rest of my life. The Burnley boys at the front started to take a bit of a pounding, backing away. The ones behind them also didn't fancy a go and, before you knew it, they were all on their toes. We then chased them right up Manchester Road with one or two of them getting picked off on the way. I couldn't believe it – we were outnumbered at least two to one, but managed to do a right number on the Burnley boys.

I've spoken to a few of the Burnley lads since and

they've admitted that they were run all over that particular day.

There is a hell of a lot more stuff I could write, but, like I'll say again, it would all have to be watered down. So for the time being, all the best, and hopefully I'll see you soon.

Daz

CV:

Growing up on the same council estate as Bill, we'd knocked round with each other on and off since being knee-high to grasshoppers. I was also into a bit of mischief myself as a young boy and always up to no good – a bit of this and a bit of that. I, myself, also got the football bug at an early age. Twice I'd watched the Jocks over the years smashing up Wembley snapping our (England's) goalposts and generally taking the piss. This made my mind up; I'd decided to dish out a bit of retribution.

The motorway that runs all the way up to Scotland and beyond Hadrian's Wall (if they want a price to rebuild it, I know a good brickie) runs past Preston, no more than a mile away from where we lived. So one Sunday morning, off I set with two mates for what when I think back now was a very, very dangerous revenge attack. But at our age you don't realise the seriousness of our devilish deeds. We filled our jumpers with stones and half-bricks and made our way to a bridge that crosses over the M6. It was a route we often took to school when jumping on the coal train to Courtaulds Cotton Mill.

It was a Sunday afternoon, but we thought that there

had got to be some tartan wearers who'd stayed in London for the evening. We then spotted a coachful, heading our way. We offload, as quick and hard as we can, all our ammo. Direct hit! We've struck gold; right through the windscreen one of the stones has gone with the coach swerving and having to pull up sharpish on to the hard shoulder.

Fifty mad Jocks are soon off of the bus scrambling up the banking towards us. I was still thin then and could run pretty sharpish and the chase was on. I managed to get home but it wasn't long before I got a knock on the door – a regular thing in those days. It was the police who'd been given a description of three lads and presumed one of them was me. As soon as I'd got in, I'd wet my hair and told my mum to say I'd been in all day and I'd just had a bath. I was glad that it was the Old Bill who'd got to me first and not the Bay City Roller Army. All three of us ended up in the cells and were interviewed – all denying the incident. One lad was already in care and the other looking at a Detention Centre, so I took the rap in the end.

After many court appearances, it ended up decision day and, luckily for me, all the evidence was either lost or had gone missing – case dismissed!

I did eventually run out of luck and a few stints at Her Majesty's Pleasure came my way. But walking out of court that day, I thought to myself, 'That evened the England–Scotland score up a bit.'

What an evil little twat I was!

My first recollection of being involved in football violence wasn't at a professional game, it was at school level. Me, Bill and a couple of others got on our bikes and made our way one Saturday morning to a school game at the other end of town, nearly five miles away. Bill had been banned from playing because of his usual messing about at school. But he, and us, would be there to give the team our vocal support. They also had a few down watching and the banter started between us both – name calling, which soon led to threats.

After the game, we'd just set off for home, only to be surrounded by the other lads with one giving it the big one. He, and the rest, got sorted and we carried on with our leisurely bike ride home, not thinking any more of it.

On Monday morning at school, the lads who'd attended the game got called to the headmaster's office. We were then told, 'There has been a report that you lot, out of school hours, assaulted a group of teenagers with one being hurt. You will have to report to the police station tonight with your parents.' They'd grassed us up!

Turning up that night at the station, with butter-wouldn't-melt-in-our-mouths looks, we were taken into a room one at a time with our parents. We then received a severe bollocking off the nick's sergeant, proper hairdryer treatment. So much so, we ended up with spit dribbling off our faces – we all received a caution.

On returning home, we all changed into our 'scally' outfits and met up on one of our street corners where we used to hang out on the estate. 'Was that it?' I said. 'What shall we do now?'

'Let's pay all the undesirables on the estate a visit,' one of the mates replied.

'Yeah, yeah, let's do it,' we all repeated.

We then set off doing the rounds, trashing windows of

all the people we didn't want on our manor. And just as we've finished the last one, having gone on our toes, a police patrol car pulls up at the side of us as we're drawing breath. Down rolls the window and the bobby goes, 'Have you been in the areas of...' He then reels off half-a-dozen or so addresses with us shaking our heads about every one that's mentioned. 'I thought not, lads, but let us know if you hear 'owt or see anything and you'd better make your way home, it's getting late.'

You would think we'd have learned a lesson earlier on in the night, wouldn't you? That is one of many, many incidents that happened when growing up on Gamull/Brookfield council estates.

One thing I do remember about the early days was when Bill came into school one Monday morning going on about a fight that had happened down Meadow Street on Saturday afternoon. A lad nicknamed Taz was having it with five big Leicester blokes on his own, when he shouted over for back-up off a couple of frightened school kids. I bet you can't guess who one of the young lads was? The lad in question, Taz, did them all nearly single-handedly until he got help off a couple of spotty kids. One of the poor Foxes ended up with a split to the head and his mates having to ask, 'Where's the nearest hospital?'

'100 yards up, turn left and you can't miss it,' said the cool-as-you-like Taz as he dusted himself down, strolling off into the afternoon – legend!

Tony R:

Many years ago, Preston had a home game one Saturday against Wigan and we'd taken a phone call off them, being informed, 'After the game, we are coming down to the Stevie's pub to smash it up and smash you up as well!'

Bring it on then, baby!

Just before the call had been received, 30 of us had all dropped a Mitsubishi (an 'E'), and it was just starting to work wonders. What Wigan hadn't banked on was that we were already in the boozer having not bothered with the footy.

Wigan usually do tricks like hanging back, picking off small splinter groups or lads on their own, so we're ready. Heads twitching, eyes bulging, feet tapping, the rush has kicked in, mixed with other things. The lads are now itching for the return call to say they're on their way, with others wanting to make a move. 'No, sit tight, they'll come.'

Everyone's well wired when a call comes in off a Preston lad that Wigan are making their way to the pub not too far away. That's it, our heads have gone... let's do it! We're out of the pub door, full steam ahead into battle, away from any cameras.

Turning right, 100 yards up ahead, we spot our targets and lock in with the enemy making an advance. We charge at them and, give them credit, they stood but they were no match for the turbo-charged loonies. They'd equal numbers that day but got taken to the cleaners. The ones that stood got wasted and the rest were chased up St Paul's Road towards Moor Park, taking a few casualties along the way. I'm glancing round and the Preston lads' eyes are popping out of their heads like a scene out of the film Return of the Zombies.

Then, all of a sudden, a car screeches up with four designer-wearing lads jumping out. We thought it was more Wigan – wrong. It was undercover coppers; they'd to resort to their telescopic batons to beat us back. I bet they were scared shitless of 30 loonies frothing at the mouth. 'Police... Police... Stop!' one of them shouted. At this stage, everyone did one at 100mph, only they didn't pursue us – I wonder why.

Who said 'the drugs don't work'?

D Ladd:

We played Blackpool away in the late Eighties with 20-odd of us going in a tranny van. The Old Bill had it well covered before and during the game. Anyway, after the match we all jumped back in the van, going for a drive down the promenade.

Then, all of a sudden, a tatty old, red transit van in front of us braked heavily – so did we. The back doors of the van in front swung open and out bounced a dozen or so of Blackpool's boys tooled up. Some of us got out of the back of the van knowing we didn't really stand a chance but we would give a show then dive back in the van, and do one. Only the driver panicked and put his foot down! This left a few of us behind, facing the lads, one of whom had a bike chain swinging above his head, one with a pair of nunchucks and others with baseball bats. Before any of them made connection, our van slowed down enough for everyone to get back in. Luckily, no one was seriously hurt.

You would think we were woodpeckers and liked a bit of wood!

H Butt:

We'd drawn West Ham in the League Cup in 1986, and the

Famous ICF were in town. On St George's Road after the match we had a tidy little firm including the Lancaster and Morecambe lads with us. Just as West Ham were being escorted up the road, near the traffic lights, we went straight into them and they stood with a good old toe-to-toe.

I got lifted with one of their lads and thrown into the back of a cop van. As I looked the cockney up and down in his Ellesse skiing jacket and Nike Wimbledon trainers, he was giving it large. Then when a copper jumped in the back for the drive to the station and informed us that we were probably in the cells for the night, the soft twat only started doing his nut. And I thought they were all meant to be tough from down there!

From West Ham to Blackburn for an FA Cup game as Preston were playing Chorley there. And after having had a good drink round Blackburn, we'd ended up in Yates's for a final one before the match. As we came out, the police on horses were keeping a watchful eye on us, and also one of the funniest things I'd ever witnessed happened. A police horse had deposited its stomach contents all over the pavement. One of the lads who was with us – MM – scooped some of it up and proceeded to rub it in his mate's face! What a picture.

Zek:

We weren't put off by our experience in Mansfield in 1980, so it was up hill and down dale once again; three vanloads of us. Only this time it was a no-show off Mansfield. Anyway, a decision was made to head over to Doncaster after the match which had been a twelve o'clock kick-off because Doncaster were at home to Gillingham – our rivals to the title.

On arrival, the gates to the ground's away end were already open and half of the lads went in while the others waited outside. Up went the chant, 'We are top of the league... say we are top of the league!' The Gills fans turned round to the lads at the back, saying, 'No we're not... we're second.'

To the reply sung back, 'Oh yes, oh yes, we are the PPS! Come on then!'

I'm outside with the lads and a Southerner flies past saying, 'Get fackin' off, lads, Preston are in there and there might be murders!' This was met by roars of laughter from us.

The rest of the Gillingham on the ground were scattered by the lads. Eventually, we were rounded up and escorted out of town.

At a home match against Wigan later in the season, about ten of us decided on a couple of beers rather than going on the match and went into the Fox & Grapes pub on Ribbleton Lane. We'd heard a rumour that Wigan's lads hadn't bothered going on the match either; finding out that 30 of them were in the Cemetery pub only 500 metres away, off the main drag. It was now a waiting game for us until the rest of the lads arrived after the match.

After an hour we fancied a change of scenery so we headed up to the Skevington pub, then the Derby Inn.

When approaching the Derby Inn, we noticed the pie-men were on the move and, not yet having numbers, we got in the pub sharpish. I think some Preston had arranged a meet with Wigan but were soon running past the boozer. As

Wigan passed the pub windows, they noticed us and came in. We retreated towards the toilets to hold our ground, knowing that we didn't stand much of a chance with the numbers weighed in their favour. In the onslaught, we were backed into the pub's yard, having to jump over the wall.

Later, we found out one of the lads had hid in the bottle bin!

J:

Over the years, North End have held their own with not much of a reputation but can clearly handle situations. I just wished I'd have experienced the Seventies and Eighties because that was when it was naughty. As the years rolled by, it started to get on top with police and cameras, so I've given it up. I still see all the lads at footy when I go, catching up and reminiscing about times gone by. There are too many incidents to mention; here are just a few which stick in my mind.

Sheffield Wednesday, early Nineties – we were all drinking in the Deepdale pub, about 70-strong, when a mob of no more than 30 Yorkies turned up, game as fuck. We all steamed out, adrenalin pumping, and got into them but they started to back off.

Next thing, about six of them at the back had crates of empty milk bottles, which they started to throw at us backing us up into the pub yard. When their ammo had run out – BANG – we went straight back into them again.

On the game, both sets of us were taking the piss out of each other and we had it again after the match. I ended up getting lifted for my troubles.

The Donkey Lashers, a night game at Deepdale – every

credit to the Scum, they turned up with no escort, about 70 boys. Six others and me had just left the Hyde Park boozer with all our boys still left inside it and we spotted the Lashers. I told one of the lads to go back and tell our lads as we kept an eye on the Scum. About 50 of our top lads turned up and fronted them and a few fireworks began to get thrown. I was at the front when the surge from the back came and this was it; toe-to-toe in the middle of Meadow Street with no police in sight having it with our most hated rivals. It doesn't get much better than that!

I was throwing digs in and was receiving them. They didn't hurt as I was charged to the max. Leyland, Avenham, Ribbleton, Larches boys... all in a football war with Blackpool. But every rumble comes to an end and I must say that they held their own, maybe because they had more numbers. Well done, Scum!

Blackpool again, at home – there was no trouble before or after the match so 100 of us got on the train and went to 'Scumland'. After leaving the station, we bowled round their streets and pubs looking for them. Not a sniff. Eventually, we got rounded up by the police, being put on the train home. Preston took the piss that day with no opposition.

Bolton away, the last game of the season, the one that sent us down – we took a massive following and most didn't get on the game. There were little skirmishes all day but nothing major. Then, after the match, the riot squad steamed a pub we were in, batoning anyone in their way, which I thought was a major over-reaction. I got lifted with six others, resulting in a ban.

More recently, Leeds away – it went off big time with a few bans being dished out.

Leeds at home – they got it once again outside the Charnock pub. Later, six of us were walking to town when we bumped into about ten Leeds who quite clearly wanted it. No questions asked, straight into them we went. They were quite a bit older than us but we just kept at them and they were soon on their toes.

Burnley away in 2006 – Preston took a decent mob, with a good turnout from the young 'uns. Preston Foot Patrol must have been touching around 50.

These are just a few memories of many. Happy days!

Greeny:

It was around 3.15pm and the seven or eight of us who'd decided not to go on the game had just left Legends nightclub next to the ground. As we started to walk away towards Meadow Street, four or five taxis pulled up on the other side of the road. 'They're here!' someone shouted, and the Wigan lads came bounding across the road.

A brawl started and, even though we were outnumbered, we were more than holding our own. They had one big fellow with them and he knew how to give a punch, as a couple of our lads could vouch for later! He came towards my mate (K) and swung one out but, at that moment, I gave him a right cracker. The mate heard a 'BANG' and thought the pie-man had hit him! While in a state of shock, he opened his eyes to see the pie-man wobbling in front of him, then drop! Luckily, for both of us.

The police then came round the corner, with a police horse first on the scene. Fights were still breaking out and, as the horse was changing direction, it suddenly went over on to the floor. That kind of ended it. Fair play to both groups for a good, honest, no-tools ruck.

This one was after the game at about six-ish. It started off when a couple of our lads clocked Wigan in the Market Tavern pub in town. We were drinking in Hartley's near the station. The two lads that informed us on their phones were actually still getting chased, so we were ready for the Wigan. One of our lads was stood near the KFC to give us the nod when they were nearly on the scene.

When he did, we ran round the corner and straight into them. It was around 25-a-side, but quite a few Wigan got straight off. Fair play to the ones who stood, they went for it full on. Roadwork signs got put over a few heads and a couple got a right kicking. We did them over, but credit where it's due to a couple of their main faces who stuck at it.

Another time it was late on, on a Saturday night and we thought they'd left town – but they hadn't. A small group of Preston went into the Old Dog Inn on Church Street and, as soon as a couple of us got in, all hell broke loose. There were flares, bottles, glasses and tables coming at us. The shock and the timing of it was too much and they got the result the attack deserved. Well done that time, boys. But eventually they got moved off; Saturday-night drinkers joined us in the battle with the pie-men.

15

THAT'S ALL, FOLKS!

You know when to call it a day – all around you starts closing in, and it's only a matter of time before your freedom is taken away... maybe for some considerable time! There have been periods in my life when I've been on a road that has no turning, no junctions. The best things in life are free; money can't buy love and friendships that mean the most to you. As they say: '*Amor Vincit Omnia*'.

There are people out there – and you should know who you all are – that have been there for me in times when I've been at my lowest ebb. I wish to thank you one and all.

I've lost family and friends, never having explained to them my thoughts and feelings. Never given out embraces and affection. Never said the words 'You are a true friend' or 'I love you'. Never even had or been able to hold down a conversation on a one-to-one basis with them. It rings true, to an extent, just what the psychiatrist said after my first assessment aged 15: 'He keeps his feelings deep inside and won't open up to anyone.' I suppose he was right and I wish I'd have taken him up on his advice of returning for more sessions. You never know how I might have turned out.

There I am, stripped down to the bare bones! Or am I? I might have just scratched the surface of a human being, a person, an individual or character I have been or who I am now. Only I will truly know.

What finally made me give it all up was the hurt I've caused to the people all around me – family and friends. Was it all worth it? Yes and no.

A home game against Millwall (no, I never got my seasonal kicking, nor did it go pear-shaped in a ruck) and I'd gone for a pint in the Old Black Bull pub in town on my Jack – Billy-No-Mates. While stood at the bar, I received a phone call from a mate who said he'd pick me up en route to Deepdale, and then stop off for a bevvy in the Charnock pub before the match.

While in the Old Black Bull, Preston's IO and his Met mate had been in having a nosey as I was watching the nags on TV. Then the phone went again and the mate's waiting outside the pub. I finished my pint, went outside, jumped into his motor and the banter began. We then drove up to the Charnock and were looking for a parking spot in a street parallel to the boozer when an unmarked car with three Old Bill in drove by. In it were the two from the Black Bull and another with daggers being thrown our way.

'What's up with them?' the mate asked.

'Don't know... it must be you.'

They passed us by.

On entering the Charnock, I was bursting for a piss so darted off to the bogs and I left the mate to get 'em in. (Not something he'd have been too happy about.) Knob out, the piss started to flow with the warm, sensual feeling of relief entering the groin.

I then heard the toilet's main door creak open. Then a couple of seconds later, a deep voice said, 'Bill?'

'Yes,' I replied cautiously.

'Routledge?'

I now decide to take a look at who wanted me to confirm my name, turning my head over my shoulder. I found a 6ft-6in copper in his bright-green, hi-vis jacket standing no more than a foot behind me.

'Why... who's asking?' I replied, not flinching.

'Well, is it?'

I ignored him and carried on slashing, eyes locked on the job in question. I'd turned back to the job in hand, all the enjoyment gone.

Then he says, 'Are you going on the game?'

'Can't you see I'm having a slash?' I wondered if it had suddenly become a crime.

His voice became a bit agitated. 'I'm asking you a question.'

'I might be, I might not be,' I said, shaking my cock. I was zipping up and about to turn round to face him properly to ask exactly what the problem was when the toilet door opened again and the mate walked in. This seemed to stop the copper from asking his next question. It was also starting to puzzle me why he was giving me the third degree. The mate went over to the trough and my interrogator left with me hot on his heels. I now wanted a few questions of my own answering.

The OB carried on walking, right out of the pub door with the other Met cop. My mind was racing with all sorts of thoughts bouncing about. They'd rapidly got back in the unmarked car and shot off.

'What the fuck was all that about?' the mate said, snapping me out of a trance as I walked back in the pub.

'Fuck knows.'

'I could hear the copper questioning you while walking into the khazi.'

'Yeah, he was.' My mind was still ticking over.

'The two of them came in and the big one went straight into the toilets and I'm guessing you're the only one in there? But I'm waiting for my change off the barmaid.'

'Yeah, I'm listening.'

'The other one comes and stands right next to me. And when I'm handed the change off the barmaid, I try to make a move past him.'

'And?'

'He goes to me, "Where you going?" To the lavs I say. "I'd like it if you didn't," he says. "What! I'm not at school now!" I said, and I brushed past him. That's when I heard the other one questioning you.'

'Yeah?'

'Yeah.'

I try to paper over the situation with the mate laughing at me for the rest of the day, taking the piss. My head's in overdrive, wondering what it was all about.

Yes, I did go on the game. No, there wasn't any trouble – hadn't been for years with Millwall at home apart from a cowardly slashing of a Stoke lad who'd come up to Preston to see one of his Spurs mates. I can't even remember the score that day.

So what actually was going on? Fact: there were two of us out having a quiet pint and we weren't out for trouble. Not unless someone provoked us beyond reason.

Fact: they knew who I was because he knew my name. So what exactly were all the questions for? Was he going to be

Preston's new IO? I don't think so, because it was the same one right up until the end of the 2006/07 season. He wasn't a bad sort. Was he putting a face to a name? I don't think so; he knew my face and he knew my name. Something just wasn't right. Was I the fairy on the station's Christmas tree that year or was I a card in a pack of Iraqi-style playing cards of Preston lads – I'm the joker – even though I'm not involved nowadays? So why all the questions? I can't begin to wonder why. Only the officer in question could answer that.

It's good this bitter. The second one's coming my way – froth running down the glass with a storm going on inside. On to the bar towel it's placed, still erupting.

'We love you Preston, we do... We love you Preston, we do... We love you Preston, we do... oh, Preston, we love you...' bellows out as I'm just picking my pint up.

Turning towards the window, I can see 30 or so Preston youths running past, aged between 15 and 18. A punter puts his beer down on the bar and heads towards the door for a closer inspection. On returning, he says, 'It's Preston lads running up the road with a few police in chase.'

I'm thinking, 'I wonder if they've have been up to a bit of naughtiness.'

'Yeah, they're playing Burnley tonight... should be a few in later to watch it on the box,' the landlord chirps up.

Back to the ale talk. I'm asking if he knows any of the real-ale drinkers from Preston that I know. Finishing up our conversation, and my pint, I thank the landlord for serving such a good pint and leave.

I hit the pavement, turning left. Out in front, I see that the coppers have rounded up the Preston youth and are escorting them. Where? I've no idea. The mind starts ticking again: 'I wonder what they've been up to.'

A couple of minutes later, I walk into a Wetherspoon's or a similar-type pub that has popped up on my left. I go in, dying for a piss, which I do before ordering.

As I'm waiting to be served, I read the sign above the bar: 'There is a football match on today, which is a Category A game and drinks will only be served in plastic glasses – thanks.'

'Yes, sir?'

'Just half a Guinness please, mate.' I hate plastic glasses; your drink always ends up tasting of it. I also clocked a few lads 'Stoney-upped' but all the badges were taken off. A lot of pub chains make you do this nowadays. It doesn't change the person wearing it, so why do it?

Downing the half in one, not that I'm jumpy, I want a proper drink. So into the town centre I head – the Swan. 'Yeah, I'll go into the Swan for old time's sake.' I'm talking to my little devil once again.

It's a bit livelier in here, an 'Olde Worlde' pub with nooks and crannies and sloping floors. You can tell a bloke stood next to me at the bar is a regular who's got his own spot and he's bending the bar lad's ear. The lad's half-listening while he's getting on with his job. An overweight girl has got her mobile out, sat on a stool. 'Send it me, send it me,' she says to a blonde girl on a stool next to her, trying to get served. Mobile phones! Can't live without them nowadays; texting, ringtones, downloads, the Internet, Bluetooth, emails, TV, video messages, photos, a computer in your hand – the art of conversation is nearly dead.

I'm stood back, soaking it all up.

Enter ten Burnley lads, you can just tell. Then a few more. Eye contact is made – no worries. Then cold, piercing stares begin to be thrown in my direction, I could just sense it. I then glance up noticing a couple of phones to ears. Finally, they're being used for what they were invented for! Fuck it, I go back to the bar and the 30 or so move on – nothing is said.

I finish up my ale; I'm feeling a bit peckish so decide that I will grab a pie or a sandwich when I pass a shop. With no food place in sight, I enter the next boozer hoping I can pick up a bap, barm, muffin, teacake or whatever you call a ham bun in Burnley.

Oh shit! I've entered a lion's den and the 30 Burnley have grown to 80. And with no time to think or about turn, I'm surrounded.

'Preston cunt...' ... 'Wanker...' ... 'Where's the rest?' ... 'Are your boys coming?'

Before I can draw breath, an older lad comes to the front of the baying mob. 'Leave it out, he's on his own.'

Other lads are still giving it the big one. 'I'll knock him out!' ... 'Fuck off now, or else!' ... 'You're a knobhead, for coming in 'ere.'

'Calm down, lads,' Burnley's voice of reason tells them.

'O'rite, mate?' the lad then says to me. He then starts informing me that he's clocked my face at most of the derby games over the years, while snide comments are still coming my way.

'You never turn up...'; 'You've never done us...'

I'm trying to give them explanations, and answers. Either they're not listening or it's not worth bothering.

'It's all right... leave it out...' my new best mate tells the rest of the lynch mob.

'I'll leave if they want me to?' I say.

'No, it's sound, mate.'

It starts to calm down.

Chatting away, I ask if Pot's in, the lad who wrote Burnley's book, *Suicide Squad*. The old head goes and gets him and I have a conversation with Pot about the ins and outs of writing a book. He informs me how much he makes and that he's going to do another one. No problems.

Burnley make a move. Salutations are said to some and looks that could kill off others back my way.

I then find myself talking to the doorman, a big, stocky lad in a duffle-coat, when two local Old Bill turn up – generally just being nosey but also asking him when his football ban is up!

I set out again on to the street, making my way to a pub nearer the ground, when up screeches a blue van and three Preston coppers pile out, pouncing on me like praying mantises.

'Where've you been?' ... 'Where you going?' ... 'What you up to?' ... 'This is a Section 60; we have the right to stop you,' I'm informed.

One copper pulls out Dave's handiwork from my inside pocket.

'It's for the forthcoming book,' I inform him.

I get a very weird look back and another check down my legs – they must have thought it was a Millwall brick!

'Right, on your way, and we're watching your every move.'

Under the bridge I head, going into the pub on the left. 'Fuckin' hell... plastic glasses again!' A quick flyer and the drink's starting to do its job. I then decide on a trip up to the Forrester's for a final pint.

On entering the Fozzie's, I realise that the Suicide Squad are in and I strike up a conversation once again with a couple of them. Most are on banning orders or even banned for life. They look after me for the next half-an-hour!

I leave just after the match kicks off. Walking round the corner to the ground, I go through the first line of coppers and up to the next blue line. You can hear the match through fans' moans and groans over the stands. It's end-to-end stuff. Preston are singing their usual favourites about Burnley: 'Your mum's your dad, your dad's your mum, you're inter-bred, you Burnley scum...'

A loud shout goes up – 'Penalty!'

It's turned down. How do I know? The chants start to question the referee's parentage and something about the fact that he masturbates.

I'm now confronted by the second string of Old Bill with a wide smirk on my rosy, red face. 'Sorry, Bill, you can't come on, you've had too much to drink.'

Another copper spouts up, 'Trot off home now, Bill.'

'OK, officers, I will. But I'll go back to the Fozzie's where my Burnley mates are for a last drink before I catch the train.' I turn and walk off into the dark, damp night.

I start wondering if they've been watching me that afternoon from a distance or was I really that drunk? I wasn't up to 'owt!

I did go back and have another pint before moving on to an alehouse nearer the train station. Eventually, I caught the train home and met up with the lads back in Preston. It had been a long, long day.

EPILOGUE

THANKS FOR THE MEMORIES

Save us from our memories! Memory loss, mental blanks, intoxicated and narcotic trances, with the worst of all – Alzheimer's. At some stage of our existence, we've all had one of the above, whether it be conveniently or inexplicably. Treasure your memories while you've got them, good or bad.

Memories are recollections of happenings and events in one's life. They are always rosier than reality maybe because we want to shut out realities, but not our memories. Is it better to forget than to remember and regret?

To cast one's mind back, reliving the moment, travelling back on a nostalgia trip, for me, brought many a smile, giggle and laugh on to my ageing face. Even though I'm one who looks to the future for new challenges and horizons, the mind is a wonderful place to visit. Always have an open mind – try to be at ease – never a closed one. Don't be driven out of one's mind. Sometimes, just speak your mind and give someone a piece of it. In my mind, a great portion of life is mind over matter. Every individual should broaden their mind and people will comment, 'That person knew his own mind.'

At first, when I decided to write the book, I ended up sceptical of my own self. Then there was encouragement and piss-taking, with others calling me a grass! This just made me more determined to carry on. Some of the people who made derogatory comments, others behind my back, are people with character and little else. When you know nothing, you should be silent. When you know it all, why speak?

I thought to myself in the early stages of writing that there are two sad words: 'if only'. So, the pen came out and I went to work on paper; the first blow is half the battle! Over 200 names who I would consider mates sprang to mind in the first hour. Then 200 more acquaintances came to mind during the course of the day. I bet there are over 1,000 lads who I've got to know through football, at least.

Twelve months down the line, I'd more than enough for a book. The majority took over 30 years in the making. Hopefully, it was worth it.

There is a saying: 'You should grow old gracefully'. My old age is an extension of childhood sometimes, and the wife says I'll never grow up. You're as old as you feel and act. That's my opinion, for what it's worth. *Carpe diem* – seize the moment; regret your actions later. The future is unknown. I personally never tire of life's pleasures, although sometimes being bored is the price for keeping out of trouble (the little devil's popped back up).

What exactly is reality? Is it an illusion; is there really life after death? God knows!

As the great man crooned: 'Regrets, I've had a few, but then again... too few to mention!' Think long, hard and deep and you will regret certain events. Then, eventually, after self-condemnation, re-approach your issues. They might be brought about by doubt, shame, grief, sorrow, misery, fury, love, hate, suffering and fear, or they might be the ones when you should have grabbed the bull by the horns and had the balls to go for it. We all have them, whether you admit it or not. Try to restore equilibrium in your life, because, if you ponder on your thoughts too much, your mind will not be at ease.

Time waits for no man. You can't turn the clock back, no matter how much money you have got – believe me, I've tried! Enjoy life, you're a long time dead. Today may be all graft; our yesterday's a fucking blast; but the tomorrows will soon be in the past... and do you really want to live there? Live for today. The art of life is knowing how far to push it and then... push it a little bit more!

So my final words: I've seen hundreds of situations. One-on-ones, fights, brawls, outnumbered beatings, mass battles and riots. These have been at football, on the streets, in pubs and clubs; all over Great Britain and abroad. These incidents have involved fists, boots, heads, lumps of wood, bats, glasses and bottles, an assortment of tools, blades and guns. Yes, guns! Injuries sustained have been black eyes, bust noses, split lips, cuts and gashes, broken bones... too many to mention.

Anyway, the guys in white coats are here to take me away for quite a while! Goodbye, for now.